GROUNDED THEORY IN PRACTICE

To our students

GROUNDED THEORY IN PRACTICE

ANSELM STRAUSS
JULIET CORBIN

EDITORS

SAGE Publications
International Educational and Professional Publisher
Thousand Oaks   London   New Delhi

For information address:

SAGE Publications, Inc.
2455 Teller Road
Thousand Oaks, California 91320
E-mail: order@sagepub.com

SAGE Publications Ltd.
6 Bonhill Street
London EC2A 4PU
United Kingdom

SAGE Publications India Pvt. Ltd.
M-32 Market
Greater Kailash I
New Delhi 110 048 India

Printed in the United States of America

Library of Congress Cataloging-in-Publication Data

Main entry under title:

Grounded theory in practice / editors,
    Anselm Strauss and Juliet M. Corbin.
        p.   cm.
    Includes bibliographical references (p.   ) and index.
    ISBN 0-7619-0747-5 (cloth: acid-free paper).—ISBN
0-7619-0748-3 (pbk.: acid-free paper)
    1. Social medicine   2. Medicine and psychology.   3. Grounded
theory.   I. Strauss, Anselm L.   II. Corbin, Juliet M., 1942-   .
RA418.G768   1997
306.4'61—dc21   96-45918

97 98 99 00 01 02 03 10 9 8 7 6 5 4 3 2 1

Acquiring Editor:	Peter Labella
Editorial Assistant:	Frances Borghi
Production Editor:	Astrid Virding
Production Assistant:	Denise Santoyo
Typesetter/Designer:	Yang-hee Syn Maresca
Cover Designer:	Candice Harman

Contents

Introduction

Grounded theory methodology and methods (procedures) are now among the most influential and widely used modes of carrying out qualitative research when generating theory is the researcher's principal aim. This mode of qualitative study has spread from its original use by sociologists to the other social sciences and to practitioner fields, including at least accounting, business management, education, nursing, public health, and social work. Its geographical spread is equally impressive. What this reflects is a great desire for theoretical explanations and, of course, the increasing use of qualitative materials and their analysis.

Most researchers who use this grounded theory style of social research learn its details from reading its specific methodological literature, including one or more of the following: *The Discovery of Grounded Theory* (Glaser & Strauss, 1967), *Theoretical Sensitivity* (Glaser, 1978), *Qualitative Analysis for Social Scientists* (Strauss, 1987), *Basics of Qualitative Research* (Strauss & Corbin, 1990), and *Handbook of Qualitative Research* (Denzin & Lincoln, 1994). Although many monographs and articles in the grounded theory mode are quite accessible, some are less so, and perhaps some people who use our approach do not seek out the substantive writing. From teaching research seminars, however, we know that students find invaluable, and probably essential, the study of substantive materials before they can become confident and skilled grounded theory researchers.

This book of readings is aimed at increasing the accessibility of such materials. The selection of published articles reproduced here is designed not so much to show the range of substantive topics or of the disciplines and practitioner fields in which grounded theory researches are written. The major principles of selection for these articles, aside from their generally high quality of research, is this: All of the authors (a) have studied directly with us, and all understand very well our vision of this style of research; (b) have used some of our methods, whether or not discussing explicitly the details of their use; and (c) have themselves chosen to emphasize different aspects of grounded theory methodology and methods, including (d) use in their presentation of materials and theory-formulated interpretations. After all, people always select from the overall menu of their learning. They take whatever items make most sense to them at the time, in terms of knowledge and skill. With regard to research methods, they certainly do choose with reference to their immediate work and aims. Grounded theory methods are no exception to this general proposition. Even the differential emphasis on various aspects of the general methodology obeys it. So it will not be surprising if you find one or more of these writings much more illuminating or useful than others. In general, however, they should be valuable in filling out with fuller coloration the more abstract discussions (despite all the illustrations in our method books). We shall present each chapter with an accompanying commentary. There are of course many kinds of statements that could be made about each, but we have opted for emphasizing specific points that might be particularly useful for readers of *Basics of Qualitative Research* or *Qualitative Analysis for Social Scientists.* Sometimes we point to the combining of sources—interview, field observations, and historical (Adele Clarke); sometimes to special emphasis on a major technique—the conditional matrix (Krzysztof Konecki); to unorthodox but effective styles of presentation (Leigh Star and Geoffrey Bowker); to the linking of theoretical concepts (Isabelle Baszanger, Joan Fujimura); or some differences between articles by very experienced grounded theorists (Kathy Charmaz, Carolyn Wiener) and those by less experienced ones who nevertheless have written excellent articles (Lora Lempert, Celia Orona). There is something, we believe, to be learned from each, whether in technique, presentation, and presentational considerations, or . . .

References

Denzin, N., & Lincoln, Y. S. (1994). *Handbook of qualitative research.* Thousand Oaks, CA: Sage.

Glaser, B. G. (1978). *Theoretical sensitivity.* Mill Valley, CA: Sociology Press.

Glaser, B. G., & Strauss, A. L. (1967). *The discovery of grounded theory.* Chicago: Aldine.

Strauss, A. (1987). *Qualitative analysis for social scientists.* New York: Cambridge University Press.

Strauss, A., & Corbin, J. (1990). *Basics of qualitative research.* Newbury Park, CA: Sage.

1

Deciphering Chronic Pain

ISABELLE BASZANGER

Commentary

This important chapter by Isabelle Baszanger, a French sociologist, illustrates three research modes, informed by grounded theory methodology and methods, that we call to your attention in this brief commentary. First, her chapter is a superb theoretical ordering of very complex descriptive materials unearthed through her extensive and skilled field work and documentary search. Second, the chapter systematically develops a substantive theory addressed to the concept of "operational knowledge" apropos to pain and its management. This concept pertains to "the problem of medical knowledge, of making it operational. The connection from operational knowledge to regimes of doctor-patient relations. . . ." Dr. Baszanger's chapter makes another important point: It points to a broader theory about operational knowledge in general.

To those ends, she has used several aspects of grounded theory—namely, constant comparative analysis, development of theoretical concepts and statements, and theoretical sampling, as well as the usual supporting techniques

An earlier version of this chapter appeared in *Sociology of Health & Illness, 14*, 181-215, and is used here by permission of the publisher. © 1992 by Blackwell Publishers Ltd/The Editorial Board.

of theoretical coding and memoing. She has woven in as necessary presentational elements much factual detail, both illustrative and persuasive, and a fair amount of quoted material. (Most of this we have deleted to save publication space. If you are interested in this material, please check the original publication.)

Isabelle Baszanger is one of the translators and the editor of a book of selected works by Anselm Strauss. She has also spent many hours talking with him during several visits to America, so her knowledge of grounded theory comes to her through this source as well as through reading its literature.

*   *   *

Introduction

Chronic pain is, above all, a problematic reality. Pain is a person's private experience, to which no one else has direct access. Others have only indirect access to it. It has to be communicated by the person subject to it. But there is another reason why chronic pain is problematic: Because it lasts, it is lasting proof of a failure that questions the validity of actions and explanations, both past and future, of all involved, whether lay persons or medical professionals. Because pain is a private sensation that cannot be reduced by objectification, it cannot, ultimately, be stabilised as an unquestionable fact that can serve as the basis of medical practice and thus organise relations between professional and lay persons.[1] This fragile factuality increases the work a physician has to do to decipher a patient's pain.

The aim of this paper is to examine how physicians specialising in pain medicine work at this deciphering. This work is all the harder for them because there is no unified doctrine on which they can unhesitatingly and unreservedly rely to characterise a patient's pain situation. As I have shown elsewhere (Baszanger, 1987, 1990), these physicians are constructing chronic pain as an original medical entity that opens up a new field of clinical practice, which, in turn, justifies this entity's existence. This ongoing work of construction sharply divides this professional group about how to define standards of practice. Crucial to this debate is the question of how to draw up an authoritative definition of chronic pain for delimiting the specialty and organising practices. At present, no consensus is in sight.

This speciality is taking shape around two very different poles. At the pole we might call "curing through techniques," the aim is to cure pain by means ranging from drugs and the simplest physical methods to ever more sophisticated neurosurgical techniques. Here, pain tends to be defined as a function of the technical possibilities for treating it. At the other pole, which we might call "healing through adaptation," the main objective is to control pain, which is defined as poorly adapted behaviour. To reach this objective, a global care must be provided that resorts to cognitive and behavioural techniques as well as drugs and physical therapy.

Two hospital centres specialising in treating chronic pain represent these two poles. Each of these centres has a heavy caseload, and is an entrepreneur. Their approaches have often set them at odds on important points, such as a pain centre's duties and educational role. By examining entrepreneurial activities and medical professionals' discourses in these two centres, I was able to reconstruct their very different conceptions of medical work on pain. These difficulties (the problematic factuality of pain and doctrinal debate) affect physicians' everyday practises and relations with patients. It forces them to work on the elusive information provided by patients so as to bring into being something called chronic pain. When doing this, they tap various, nearly incompatible, resources. In the case of chronic pain, they resort to strata of knowledge with which they are more or less familiar.

One is the widely accepted gate-control theory. This scientific theory is far from providing them with the means of regulating actual practices.[2] Although all pain physicians share this frame of reference, they are involved in an ongoing transformation of this theory as different maximalist and minimalist positions have been adopted. Actual practices are grounded in these contrasting options, as is the work of deciphering cases.

In addition to this theory, physicians also put to work knowledge of all sorts—about the environment, psychological behaviours, social factors, etc.[3] They also tap various scientific sources (biology, neurophysiology, anatomy, epidemiology, psychology, etc.) to forge practical knowledge for treating cases rather than explaining generalities.[4] The intellectual effort to "put odds and ends together" does not stop here. Another step is required: Medical work is performed on individuals, who are not "objective" data to be effortlessly read. People have their own ideas; they may change or resist change; they express emotions, fears and hopes. Each patient has a history. This has several consequences (cf. Strauss et al., 1982; and Wiener et al., 1980), one of which merits attention: During medical consultations, more is going on than just therapeutic and diagnostic activities in the narrow, usual senses. Indeed, many and different things are said ranging from body complaints to personal, family or work-related problems. Whether or not to listen to this information, understand and use it as data (and how to do so) are decisions requiring more than merely the application of theoretical knowledge. They may be related to a practitioner's personal approach or to a professional procedure (cf. Silverman, 1983; and Dodier, 1990).

Here, I shall study the way these multiple resources are put to use by physicians as they form judgements about cases. Beyond the problem of practical knowledge, I would like to look at the consequences for patients. The ways physicians put their varied resources to work can help us understand how they stabilise, at least for a while, the problematic reality of chronic pain as they try to hold on to it. By stabilising this reality in an interpretation, they can organise interventions on patients. By using as a field experiment two pain centres with opposite conceptions and practices, we shall be able to see how physicians in each centre determine patients' pain situations and formulate advice to them. I shall examine how the characteristics of this work involve physicians in specific systems of relations with patients, and how these systems are related to dimensions of this work: either to a justification of physicians' actions or else to a confirmation, or realignment, of the initial doctor-patient agreement.

Method

A grounded theory approach, as developed by Glaser and Strauss (1967), is adopted. The two pain centres were chosen after an initial phase of research, because I realised a comparison could serve to ground theoretical statements. Both centres are located in public teaching hospitals in Paris, France. They receive patients with similar pathologies, mainly pain in the skeletal system (low back pain, cervical pain, aftermath of back surgery), tension headache, migraine, neurological pain (phantom limb, postherpetic neuralgia, trigeminal neuralgia, . . .), in fact any pain which has lasted for more than six months and has been resistent to all regular treatments. However, although these two centres admitted similar patients, they do not have the same approach to pain. Centre I has a "curing through techniques" approach. Treatment is considered to be a phase in a total medical process. On average there are three consultations followed by referral back to the patient's usual physician once the treatment is adjusted. One neurosurgeon and two anaesthesiologists who have acquired the specific techniques to cure pain are the entrepreneurs of this centre. The multidisciplinary organisation of the centre takes shape around this "core of pain physicians." They are surrounded by consulting specialists to whom patients for whom specific treatments do not exist are referred upon arrival at the centre, whenever it is possible. It is different for the psychiatrist: After their treatments have been unsuccessful, "pain physicians" usually define the case as being beyond their jurisdiction and refer it to the psychiatrist. The second centre has a "healing through adaptation" approach which leads to the provision of extensive, integrated patient care. The average follow-up on a case usually lasts from eight to fourteen months. This follow-up necessitates team work and effective multidisciplinary organisation. The pivots of the team are those physicians, regardless of their specialties, who have adapted behavioural techniques for treating pain. Consulting specialists, including a psychiatrist, work with them in a perspective of total care; several doctors may simultaneously follow up a single case.[5]

I observed consultations with various physicians at these two centres for eight months. I was unable to alternate daily visits to each centre, since I wanted to follow up some cases and could not have done so without a steady presence in a single centre. After three months at the second centre, however, I did return for a few weeks to the first. As comparisons between them turned out to be fertile, I wanted to compare "backwards" and, by changing environments, limit the effects of excessive socialisation, when too much time is spent in one place. Besides observing consultations, I participated in group activities in both centres, and profited from conversations with physicians and, less frequently, nurses.

The constant comparative method of analysis and its coding procedures were used, first comparing items in each category, then drawing up categories and, finally, comparing categories. For me, these two centres represented a single field of research. A few remarks about field notes are relevant. It is hard to jot down everything said during a consultation with two, often three, persons present. Since my intention was not to do conversational analysis (which would have necessitated noting every word, silence and even gesture), I decided to proceed like an ethnographer. Because some exchanges seemed to be so important that every word needed to be recorded, I always kept a small notebook in full view on my knees. This was not unusual in the teaching hospital setting of these two pain centres and never caused problems. I wrote up selected exchanges verbatim, and noted the sequences during each consultation as well as turning points in conversations and arguments. For instance, I indicated the events preceding intense exchanges and noted whether the clinical examination took place early or late during the consultation. In other words, I tried to signal links in lines of reasoning by jotting down key words so as to help me recall what had happened. Thanks to a physician at the second centre, I was allowed to tape some consultations. By taking notes while recording, I could later compare these two storage techniques and improve my note-taking. Here, excerpts have been taken from among the 326 consultations which were registered in notes or on tape, and coded.

Centre I

"Look for, eliminate, verify, be sure of, make allowance for, determine, logically assume"—this rhetoric of action, which physicians at the first pain centre repeatedly used during consultations, provides an idea of how medical work is performed and made *visible* to patients. This logic, when applied, calls for surveying: What the patient says about the body, what is pointed out, has to be mapped onto the nervous system, turned into a percentage or average. The first task of medical work is to find out whether the pain can be projected onto a body-map, to determine whether "there's something or nothing." Although the terms in this alternative may have quite different contents necessitating different actions, both fit into a single perspective of curing through using technology.

Establishing the Patient's Pain Situation

By this "nothing" they so often use when talking to patients, these physicians do not mean there is no pain. What they actually do is locate the pain, themselves and the patient on one side of the something/nothing alternative. This alternative, which we can use to analyse how they make decisions, is in fact used by them when they switch a patient from one side to the other. It is not horizontal, with equal terms, however. It is vertical, with terms in a hierarchical order.

1. Easy-to-Decide Situations

These physicians can usually determine a patient's pain situation quite easily. They normally receive, from the physician who referred the patient, a letter with a diagnosis, or clear enough indications, for initially defining, thanks to medical semiology and practical experience, the situation even before meeting the patient. The problem is to verify this definition as they interview the patient and examine the medical records he has brought along.

The first consultation with a patient always starts with questions, either specific ("So you've had zoster? Show me where it bothers you now.") or open-ended ("What's the matter?" "What brings you here?" or "Start at the beginning and tell me about it."). If the patient begins talking about physical signs, the physician asks for details right away. Having already had several appointments with other practitioners, patients often use medical terms or talk about previous treatments. In any case, the physician puts the patient on the right track. A patient who said, "I sometimes have severe migraines" was corrected: "No you don't. You have a headache. Where? When? How?" When another started talking about his trigeminal, the physician interrupted, "No, now, tell me how you hurt." If a patient takes up the open-ended invitation and starts telling his story with all the facts, the physician, after a while, interrupts so as to lead away from the pain's context and back to the symptoms:

> *Patient:* I had an accident in 1984—fell backwards in the stairs, couldn't catch myself. Well, I was carrying a bucket. I was used to climbing up on a ladder. So I was laid up three months with infiltrations. I went back to working on roofs for almost a year. In 1985, when it was cold, that was when it was raw out, below zero—I don't know whether it's because of that—I had to stop again.
> *Physician* (cutting him off): So the pain runs down into your leg?
> *Patient:* Yea.
> *Physician:* Where?

The patient is not permitted to wander off interpreting his symptoms. When one patient began, "It all started when I fell two or three times," the physician interrupted, "Maybe. It's very hard to establish the cause." We can sense the determination to specify each party's domain. More importantly, we can see that the physician, at least when he already has the means of deciphering the situation (as in the last interview), considers the patient's causal explanation to be irrelevant.

Physicians look for patterns of pain by asking patients questions about their pain (e.g., what makes it worse or better—standing, sitting, etc.) and about the effects of previous treatments. Questions are not asked in any set order; they might come up before, during or after the checkup, as the physician reacts to the patient's spontaneous declarations. In easy-to-determine cases, the aim is to see whether the referral letter's suggestions are of any use and whether the patient's declarations and medical records are in line with them. During the examination, the physician looks for evidence in support of these leads.

During consultations with cases that could be easily and rapidly determined, what the physician looks for is usually congruous with what the examination along with the patient's reactions and medical records enables him to see. This congruity may sometimes be delayed. In the case of a patient who came about a pain in his back and leg that had persisted since an operation for a slipped disk, the physician had received a letter from a surgeon with whom the centre frequently works. The letter diagnosed the case and requested a "symptomatic treatment." Not doubting this diagnosis, the physician asked the patient to point to where his leg hurt. As he did so, the physician interrupted him, "That's odd. You're not normal. The pain normally shoots up the front." While looking at the X-rays a little later, he said, "Uh-huh, it's clear to see. You have an L5, so that fits, everything fits." By using a means that objectifies the cause of the pain, the physician eliminated a deviation in the patient's experience. Since all the other evidence was congruous, this deviation from the norm could be dismissed as irrelevant.

What the patient says is but an indication. He is not competent to determine what he feels for two reasons. First of all, he has no means of generalizing: "You only know your own experience, while I know several cases." Secondly, he is subject to his sensations; he feels them rather than measuring them.[6]

During the first consultation, the aim is to identify the patient's pain by using both what objective examinations by previous doctors have established and what the patient says. In this effort to find out what the patient's pain corresponds to, the physician draws up, verifies or eliminates hypotheses so as to reduce the number of possibilities. The following case illustrates this process in full. During her first appointment at the centre, a woman stated that her leg pain hurt "like from burning or pinching." She had already gone to a rheumatologist, but a hip X-ray "didn't turn up anything." She thought that her thigh was swollen and that the pain was more intense toward evening. Saying "You think it's bigger?! the physician verified the difference by objectively measuring both thighs with a tape, and said, "We agree." Noticing that the veins were near the surface of the skin, he added, "There's a superficial vein problem, but is that what's causing you trouble?" This became the problem to be solved. The physician proceeded by reducing the number of possibilities. Mentioning the X-ray, he eliminated a possible hip problem. Since he could not establish that the pain followed a nerve, "we can eliminate femoral cutaneous neuralgia." By asking the patient questions about her pain's periodicity and the factors that made it worse, he sought to know whether it had to do with the veins. Given that it stopped during the weekend but increased when she had to stand up for a long time (as she had to at work), he concluded, "So, that's it."

In this case, the only points dealt with were those directly related to the pain: Neither physician nor patient mentioned anything else. This holds for nearly all consultations when the pain situation can be easily identified as being "physical" or, as is said at this centre, "something." What is remarkable about such cases is that the physician nearly never asks questions about the patient's work and life (how it has changed as a result of chronic pain, what the patient can and cannot do, etc.). Many patients talk about the impact of pain on their lives and family relations. They say they are "fed up" or exhausted. Though they listen to them, physicians are not led to open a new line of inquiry or a new field for treatment as long as they can decipher the case by using other resources.

Physicians do not "work" on the information patients deliver about the pain's causes and impact on their jobs, moods, and deepest feelings of self-worth and self-identity. More precisely, when forming their judgement, they do not work on this sort of information as much as on the physical signs and symptoms mentioned by patients. Although these physicians adhere to a theory of pain that does not consider the first sort of information to be irrelevant or merely expressive of personal feelings, such information has a more fragile status than physical evidence because its validity as "facts" is open to question. The gate-control theory of pain fully takes into account both physical and psychological processes in order to explain the modulation of pain messages. It has thus opened the way to two different medical interpretations. As a frame of reference, it has forced all pain centres to construct a discourse with room for the psychological as well as physical aspects of pain. It also forces them to adopt practices that make room for psychology (for instance, by having a psychiatrist or psychologist on staff).

The pain centre under study interprets pain in a way that minimises cognitive and psychological processes. These take second place to physical processes, as the means of qualifying the causes of pain and as objects on which physicians must work. This is what I meant by a hierarchised nothing/

something alternative. This "nothing" is not synonymous with nonexistent. Instead, it refers to something else, the "inorganic side of pain" (as one physician at the centre said), which must be recognised because it opens a field for judging and explaining certain pathologies and can be used to determine difficult cases. This "something else" does not, however, entail specific medical work.

Before exploring a few such cases, we need to establish an inventory of the types of clues that point toward a psychological malfunction. Out of physicians' comments and my observations of consultations, I drew up the following list. It should be emphasised that this list is common to all pain centres—what differentiates centres is the weight assigned to various items.

One set of clues is directly related to the pain itself, or the patient's experience of it: a "wandering" pain ("one day here, the next, there"); a pain with several locations (e.g., cervical and lumbar pain); a pain that stops when the patient goes to sleep but starts again with maximal intensity when he wakes up; a "spontaneous pain" not set off by any traumatic or mechanical factor; more broadly, any pain that remains unexplained after repeated examinations, X-rays or biological tests; pains that a patient describes in very vague or even contradictory terms (e.g., when responding affirmatively to any and all suggestions the physician makes about sensations, or when describing symptoms before or during "a crisis" that do not make sense to the physician—as freezing cold in the lower back before the stomach starts hurting); and a whole series of visible physical signs physicians deem exaggerated (e.g., limping when the elbow hurts or continually touching a sore spot). Other items characterise the patient's relationship to medicine and the medical profession: proclaiming that the pain was caused by or lasts because of mistakes made by doctors or paramedics; being fussy with medicine (e.g., "Today, you hear there's no longer any reason to suffer. That makes me laugh."); and an excessive consumption of medicine (of both drugs and doctors) without any improvement. Finally, there is a set of items having to do with the context wherein the pain arose and, more broadly, with life circumstances: a job-related accident and its financial settlement; and destabilising events (such as unemployment, divorce, bereavement) and situations (such as permanent misunderstanding or constant fighting between spouses, the lack of a spouse, and problems at work or in the family).

For the physician, the clues in certain cases may be so numerous or apply so well that they fall into a pattern that leads him to form an a priori opinion. Hence, the physician retains as relevant the evidence that the patient produces in line with this pattern. For example, one physician read aloud, before receiving the patient, a general practioner's laconic referral letter: "Mrs. X has been suffering from persistent lumbar and cervical pain for several years." The physician told me right away, "A priori, it's a psychological case. You don't drag along with a problem like that for several years while seeing a lot of doctors." The lack of a precise diagnosis in the letter, the pain's double location, the term "persistent" (suggesting that all treatments had failed), the long time that had passed since the pain started, all these clues formed a pattern to which the physician added another, namely "seeing a lot of doctors," which turned out to be false. Regardless of the clues converging toward an a priori opinion, the logic of action stays the same: look for, eliminate, verify, etc.

The decision-making process is nearly reversed when the physician, lacking any basis for an a priori opinion, constructs conclusions in two phases by a delayed treatment of certain pieces of evidence. During the first phase of the consultation, the evidence of a nonphysical problem might add up, but not fall into a pattern before the checkup and tests have made it possible to separate the patient's pain from other physical problems he might have. The separation can then be made, and the possibility of a physical origin eliminated. He or she can then bring together scattered pieces of evidence and try to decipher the patient's complaints in another way.

2. Situations to Be Tested

So far, we have looked at situations that physicians could quite easily define with reference to the "something/nothing" alternative. This is not always so, even though such situations are the most frequent. I have reconstructed two sorts of situation that are not easy to define.

In the first, physicians cannot eliminate without further investigation the possibility of a physical problem, for example when the pain is physically obvious or explicably apparent (if the patient has a serious disease or has undergone major—in contrast to cosmetic—surgery) *but* when these manifestations of pain are contradictory or hard to classify, or point to incompatible processes. To settle such cases, physicians resort to so-called "diagnostic trials."

Although this phrase might refer to additional tests, it more often means that the physician will perform a trial test, such as anaesthetising a nerve or sore spot with a substance having, in principle, fully predictable effects. The patient's reactions can then be compared with averages calculated during pharmacological experiments. Room is thus opened for an interpretation on the basis of the patient's observations of his or her own sensations. When a patient, after being administered an anaesthetic, asked, "Do you want to put it to sleep and study what happens?" the physician replied, "You're going to tell us what happens." Physicians are not at all satisfied with measuring and defining pain like this. Whenever a physician proceeds to a diagnostic trial, a field of judgement is opened about the circumstances wherein the pain originated. This field stays open until the trial's results come in.

In the case of a patient with pain in her feet, the physician was perplexed because the clues found while examining the patient did not clearly point to algodystrophy, which the referral letter suggested. Nor did they—and he dwelled on this with his students—seem to point to any other "physical" track than the algodystrophy. He told the patient, "Since I don't yet have the results (of another test), I don't know what you have because it's apparently not that." Then right away, without letting the patient ask questions, he queried whether "everyone agreed before the operation"—that is, did everyone agree that the operation was a good solution. When she answered affirmatively, he then asked whether her husband, family and close friends had agreed. When she replied, "yes we were told it was nothing," he commented, "Ok, we'll see." In effect, he had opened two tracks of interpretation but would not choose between them until later. He hinted at this to the patient. "Since we don't have proof, we'll have to wait. We won't be able to see till then. The treatment will be either an infiltration (if algodystrophy is confirmed) or an antidepressant (if "something else")."

In the second sort of situation, certain pains, especially when localised in tense muscles, automatically lend themselves to a double reading. For instance, a sore spot in a muscle might be a sequela to both major surgery and the "awful scare" the patient had when facing the mortal risks of the operation. In another example, a patient might have both migraines and tension headaches, two different medical entities even though they may occur together. This situation might call for deciphering the case by concentrating on the patient as a person. Muscle pains are ambiguous in that, despite their obvious physicality, the reasons for them have to be found. They force physicians to adopt a wait-and-see strategy that combines diagnosis and treatment in a so-called "trial treatment." Since such cases do not have to be determined once and for all, physicians face a different problem. They try to order priorities and measure their therapeutic commitment while making it possible to switch back and forth between the terms of the something/nothing alternative. This work of definition is not very clear and may become even harder when the patient reacts to this switching about.

Formulating Advice to Patients: A Logic of Description and Demonstration

Physicians at this centre formulate advice to patients following a logic of description and demonstration. In most cases, the pain situation can be deciphered as a lesion or organic defect. Physicians restrict the description of pain to body sensations. Systematically, at the end of the consultation and in front of the patient, the physician dictates a letter to be sent to the referring doctor. This letter, which *describes* the pain in detail (its periodicity, intensity, concomitant signs, nerve path, etc.), reads like a technical specification.

There is little room for the patient's discourse. Sometimes, the situation is so obvious for the physician that he asks few questions. The patient is peripheral to the formulation of advice about the case. In fact, the letter is used to demonstrate his case to him. The physician often talks about the treatment but not the cause, which he might mention later on—while explaining the treatment or answering a question. This way of omitting the cause, or casually mentioning it, follows from a logic, which the patient is thought to share, that establishes a continuity between cause, treatment and the body as the basis of an explanation.

When formulating advice, the physician uses several resources to make the pain situation visible. He may show the patient the X-rays or test results. He may demonstrate a prescription or treatment with diagrams. A revealing difference between the two pain centres has to do with neurostimulation, a method not yet widely used. In this centre, the physician succinctly explains the treatment to the patient by drawing, on a sketch of the human body, the pain trajectory and marking with two *x*s the approximate places for electrodes. This drawing "objectifies" the pain situation and serves as a demonstration. The physician thus depicts the continuity between a pain, its analysis and treatment.

The physician usually formulates advice as the result of a logical reasoning process founded on medical knowledge. One said, "There are two things we can propose. They can be done in any order: block the root or provide external stimulus. But it's more logical to start with the stimulation." This logic implies a certain progression in the treatment as successive possibilities are eliminated:

"We have to start with the simplest things; and if that doesn't work, we'll go on to complicated ones."

The future is pictured in terms of a possible cure that might be achieved, but with difficulty. For this reason, the physician is unable to give a definitive opinion during the first consultation. He presents the cure as a possibility and usually even as a probability calculated as a percentage. Thanks to this reference to statistics and probability, the patient can already be imagined in various future situations. In effect, the patient's future is a statistical prediction based on the graduated possibilities of the physician's actions. Certain formulas suggest as much: "It's logical to start by . . .," "We'll do this first, then . . .," and "Let's do this to start with, and we'll see afterwards." The conclusion of the letter being dictated in the patient's presence reinforces this idea of a future over which there is little control. As the major lines of action for now and, if these lead nowhere, for later on are being laid down, the patient is reduced to being the spectator of a demonstration that proves the physician's competence and predicts a possible but never certain cure.

This demonstration of a logical reasoning process, of the difficulty of medical work and of the competence of medical professionals, is even more pronounced when the physician shifts to deciphering a case in terms of the patient as a person rather than a body. Here, there is a rupture of continuity, as becomes clear when a physician decides to refer a patient to a psychiatrist. Even if he decides to follow up on the case himself, he makes the patient understand that the pain is something other than physical. One patient was told, "The pain's related to a depressive state, whether conscious or not." Physicians choose an "open awareness context." Since nearly all patients come to the centre to see a physician, not a psychiatrist, they are not ready for this shift. Facing such a case, the physician does not seek so much to understand the psychological nature of the pain as to prove to the patient that it is psychological. This is an essential difference from the second pain centre, as we shall see.

While proving that pain is related to psychological factors, the physician proceeds in several ways. By broadening his discourse from the language of body sensations to talk about the whole person and life circumstances, he can link pain and personality so as to shift the basis for formulating advice. This can be observed during a consultation when the physician repeatedly formulates a patient's problem so as to signal the shift. The physician might also objectify the existence of two types of scientific explanation and give a short lesson as he sets the patient's complaints down to nonphysical factors. He often uses test and X-ray results that show "there's nothing" so as to close the physical realm.

In rare cases, when major diagnostic tests have been performed, the physician tries to prove to the patient that it is impossible to prove the existence of pain objectively. The same procedure is always used, often with the help of the psychiatrist who will, with the patient's consent, follow up on the case. After anaesthetising a sore spot, the physician demonstrates to the patient that his painful sensations are "abnormal" since s/he no longer feels anything when pricked with a pin or pinched but nonetheless still experiences pain. One physician explained this procedure to a student, and myself, as "demonstrating to the patient the inorganicity of his pain, that his pain comes from something else." This demonstration might also involve comparing the patient's results on certain tests with average results. The purpose is to force them to see that their arguments, and insistence on certain sensations, are false, as one physician said, "It must be hard to realize that, during all this time, you were mistaken about your pain." This ultimate form of objectification is intended to motivate the patient to "work on himself," as a psychiatrist told me.

This logic of demonstration meets its limits when a physician's advice switches back and forth from the body to the whole person. Sometimes unable to determine a case with the "something/nothing" alternative, the physician tells patients, "You have two problems" in order to make them realise that they are "too sensitive" and therefore tense and that this is a factor in the pain. Unlike at the second pain centre, however, physicians do not consider this tension to be part of their concern. By making such comments, they open up the possibility for judgement and action, but leave any decision up to the patient, even as they treat the case and continue switching back and forth between medical and lay descriptions.

Face-to-Face Relations and the Work of Justification

This medical work with its logic of demonstration leads to a specific regime of face-to-face relations between physicians and patients. By looking for, eliminating, verifying, determining the pain situation, and demonstrating the irreductibility of their advice, physicians assigned patients a definite place and responsibility: as enlightened consumers. A physician's commitment as a medical expert is thus bounded by voluntary, implicit limits.[7]

Throughout the consultation, the physician draws the borderline between two distinct universes. He acts out the role of scientific expert in front of the patient even as he shows him its limits, difficulties and uncertainty. He does this by asking questions implying that certain parts of a patient's experience are more pertinent. He displays his logic of demonstration by pointing to signs on the body, establishing hypotheses, drawing up a tree diagram of possible causes, eliminating possibilities and laying down operational rules. He establishes the legitimate division of labour.

The patient, at least during the initial consultation, frequently "follows" the physician, especially insofar as the latter limits him to describing his sensations and formulates advice through an explanation based on the body alone. When the patient raises questions reaching beyond these limits, the borderline between the two universes, implicit up to that point, is then explicitly mentioned:

> You're curious. You want to know everything. We don't have a very precise explanation. The drug acts positively or negatively, it depends (the physician continues a vague explanation). Even for *us,* it's complicated, but what's important for *you* is that it works.

As much might be said about the treatment: "*For you,* it'll simply be a shot in the rear end; *for me,* it's a bit more complicated." The physician might hint at this borderline when a patient refuses to follow him as he switches from a physical to a psychological explanation. This happens when one physician described medical duties and the continuity between different specialities:

> Whatever solution I propose, if it takes away your pain, what's the difference to you? It doesn't matter. This is a pain center where several specialists work so that a patient can be referred to the one who can best take care of him. For you, it's a psychiatrist.

For the physician, a consultation is over when, after having defined the pain situation, he draws up a plan of action and explains it, at least partly, to the patient. At this centre, there is no need to obtain the patient's token agreement, especially since, as often happens, the physician insists that, although the treatment may provide a cure, there is "no guarantee." Hence, the question of agreement between the two parties tends to be delayed until the assessment of the treatment's effects.

A point to be emphasized is that the grounding of this face-to-face doctor-patient relationship in two distinct universes does not mean that the patient's role is merely passive. This is seen by the stance physicians adopt about patient's choices as consumers. As in any other medical centre, a patient may, or may not, follow a prescribed treatment without informing the physician. In this centre, however, many treatments call for technical manipulations to be performed during hospitalisation. When proposing such a treatment, the physician spends time emphasising that the patient faces a choice, with full knowledge, to accept or refuse the proposal:

> I'm not the one hurting from your pain. You are. You're the one who'll be relieved. But you're also the one who'll have problems if it doesn't work. I explain things, but you're the one who has to manage. I have the recipes, you have to decide.

By leaving room for decision, the physician refers both parties to their respective universes: himself to his role as a skilled, scientific operator; and the patient to his part as an enlightened consumer who must decide his own fate. The roles are distributed. I take this to mean that patient and physician have separate areas of action.[8] For the physician, providing this information to a patient guarantees that the latter has given his approval.

It appears that this conception of the doctor-patient agreement implies, for physicians, a "market commitment," i.e., an "expert-consumer" relationship. The physician, having provided sufficiently honest information, has fulfilled his moral obligation—this sort of "truth in advertising" about the proposed treatment does not, however, have to cover the reasons for a proposed treatment. What is sought is the patient's global acceptance of the physician's actions in the best interests of both parties. This type of commitment forces the physician to do work justifying the results of his actions. The question of agreement is thus shifted from the initial definition of the pain situation to the assessment of results.

When a patient comes back to the pain centre, s/he is, at best, freed of pain or relieved. In compliance with this centre's approach, the physician tries to measure the improvement and record it as a percentage. The two parties' perceptions often differ because they do not rely on the same criterion to assess progress. The physician reasons in terms of global improvement since the start of treatment; the patient, in terms of the intensity of pain during each crisis. Some patients doubt that results can be assessed because the treatment (as in the case of migraines) is aimed at "blocking" crises. Often, the very idea of measuring painful sensations with numbers seems unrealistic to them.

The physician usually has to work on the very notion of improvement before being able to measure change. The problem is to reach agreement with the patient about whether an improvement has occurred. Patients often start out by saying, "I still hurt," "It's the same" or "It's terrible now"; and physicians have to recall what the pain used to be like ("Remember how you were the last time") or how it has improved ("Now, now, you felt better"). By seeking to prove there has been a positive change for the first time and thanks to the treatment, the physician has entered into the process of justifying his actions. . . . Underlying the assessment of a treatment's effects is the initial definition of the pain situation, a definition with which the patient might not have agreed or that s/he would have liked to discuss. When one woman who came back a month later said, "It's still the same," the physician asked whether the treatment (a painkiller and a small dose of antidepressent) had given relief. She replied that nothing had changed. The physician increased the dose and told her, "We'll see in a month." As they were fixing the next appointment, the following exchange occurred:

> *Patient*: Really though, I'm pretty disappointed. I thought a pain centre would provide relief, that relief would come without taking drugs. So this neurostimulation machine everybody is talking about isn't for me.
> *Physician*: But, Mrs. X, I already explained to you the last time. You hurt in the neck, in the lower back.
> *Patient*: Yes, but if I got relief in my neck.
> *Physician*: But your pain moves around. It's not as though it were localised.
> *Patient*: But it's not the same pain in the neck and elsewhere. It didn't start the same. It hurts a lot worse up here.

The patient started to define her pain in a way that could not be reduced to the physician's. She asked for another treatment, and the physician agreed on it for the future "when we've first taken care of the moodiness and depression."

In more radical situations, there is, lurking underneath the "It stills hurts," a criticism of the physician's definition of the pain situation. One patient was, following the first consultation, prescribed an antidepressant for, she was told, her depression. At that time, neither the patient nor her husband said anything. A month later, there was no improvement. After the physician asked whether she slept well, the patient replied, "Sleep, heavens yes. But the pain's still the same." Pointing to her neck and lower back, she explained that the pain was very intense in the morning when she woke up. When her husband voiced doubts about the need for a sleeping pill since the pain was worse when she woke up, the physician started defending his analysis: "But I didn't give her a sleeping pill. It's an antidepressant, because I thought her pain came from a problem of depression that hasn't ended. I still think so." The tone remained accusatory and vindicatory. Later, when performing the examination, the physician said, "I notice you're limber. When someone can do everything you do, touch the floor, even ski, that doesn't justify looking for anything else." Prescribing a slightly smaller dose of the same antidepressant, he commented, "It's necessary to continue like that." Since the woman and her husband did not seem very pleased, he added, "Don't be disappointed. I think you're doing pretty well. Obviously, you're the one who has to think that." The physician recognised there was a disagreement, but he made sense of it by setting it down to the existence of two different universes.

Centre II

"Understand, ponder, analyse, explain," this is the rhetoric of action in the second pain centre. It is quite different from the one based on looking for, eliminating, verifying, etc. Here, medical work means that physicians recognise both the province of medical knowledge ("It's been established that," "We now know," etc.) and acknowledge the world of the patient and his pain ("I believe you," "Now I never said you weren't in pain"). This work is undertaken in all its logic at the borderline between these two universes. This logic does not call for surveying the body but rather for evaluating the patient's pain by weaving it into a medical classification, namely the "chronic pain syndrome."

Establishing the Patient's Pain Situation

This pain centre is concerned with the specific problem of persistent, durable pain. As at other pain centres, patients who come here already have a long history of pain behind them. Thanks to the chronic pain syndrome, however, the relationship between the patient, the pain and its duration provides a dividing line for locating pain, patient and physician. According to this centre's conception, a lasting pain evolves significantly as it has psychological consequences that become secondary factors in maintaining it. In other words, beyond the variety of its initial causes, lasting pain calls for a work of deciphering that must explain a set of social, behavioural, psychological and physical manifestations as part of a single category, the chronic pain syndrome. When pain, regardless of its aetiology, becomes an illness in itself and is no longer a simple sign of a physical or pathological disorder, pain physicians have, above all, to deal with a behaviour determined by psychological and social factors that are so many causes and/or consequences of the pain itself.

Persistent pain and the chronic pain syndrome are two poles on a continuum along which it is hard to place persons suffering from chronic pain. Not all cases of persistent pain evolve into a "pain illness." The psychological adaptation to illness and pain may be satisfactory. Preventing a persistent pain situation from becoming a chronic pain syndrome is one of the main objectives of medical work. This was stated outright at the end of the following consultation:

Physician: Do you have any questions to ask me?

Patient: If the treatment doesn't work, does that mean I'm going to get worse?

Physician: No, it doesn't. You've experienced the worst pain you'll ever have. This type of pain doesn't evolve, the illness doesn't either. The pain is an aftermath. It doesn't evolve unless you manage it poorly. For sure, it might intensify if you worry, if you don't sleep. At such times, it can hit you with full force. But we'll stop you from heading in that direction.

Every case of persistent pain does not "head in that direction," but it might, hence the strong operational value of the chronic pain syndrome. This syndrome opens the possibility of analysing the patient's pain situation with respect to every possible mechanism maintaining the pain—instead of being taken to be a single, physical or psychological, cause that, once identified, can be cured. Although physicians in this centre distinguish between "somatic" and "psychogenic" pains, the "something/nothing" alternative does not help to analyse how they make decisions. They face the problem not of how to choose between the terms of this alternative, but rather of how to determine, for a given patient's pain, the multiple, deep relations developed over time between these terms. This can then be used to decipher the series of therapeutic failures that has brought the patients to the centre and to understand their involvement with chronic pain. In this sense, a person who comes here always has "something."

This pain centre has chosen a maximalist position with regard to current theories of pain. It has developed an operational definition of pain that comprises cognitive and psychological processes. The patient's pain is never a single, unequivocal phenomenon. It is always multidimensional with numerous—somatic, affective, emotional, cognitive and behavioural—interacting variables. To determine the patient's pain situation entails breaking this complex phenomenon down into parts to be weighed. It also entails, from the start and by definition, working *within* the patient's subjectivity. This has major consequences for medical work, in particular during a patient's first consultation.

At the start of this first consultation (which is called "orientation"), everything is important. In other words, the physician immediately opens two fields of judgement. On the one hand, he has to assess the pain's history (patterns, pathophysiological mechanisms, and previous treatments as well as their results). On the other hand, he has to determine what comes from the person (reactions, thoughts and expectations as well as the way pain has changed life). Both these fields have to be investigated in every case. By using this twofold deciphering process, the physician's aim is not to choose between these fields but rather to interrelate them. He does not seek to eliminate hypotheses but rather to integrate information from the patient into a global judgement about the person and the pain.

It is essential to realise that this global judgement takes shape only through intense interactions with the patient. For this reason, the process of judging is already the first phase of care. In other words, the medical work can be defined as work on the patient's experience of pain and illness. This pain, i.e. illness, is not identified with a lesion. It is seen through a behavioural model that the physician, during the first consultation, uses to decipher the patient's pain behaviour, which might be analysed as "the formation of a chronic pain syndrome" or "an already advanced form." This determines the care to be provided: whether treatment calls for physical and pharmacological as well as behavioural and cognitive means or whether care should be mainly turned toward cognitive, behavioural rehabilitation for learning to live with pain. To determine the pain situation is not to locate the patient in a something/nothing alternative but to weave a web of connections between lesions, sensations, feelings, attitudes and thoughts.

The synthesis of all information garnered during the first consultation is achieved by dynamically weighing each piece. Making this synthesis, rather than establishing the traditional aetiological diagnosis, often causes the most difficulty. This weighing process is illustrated in a letter the centre sent to a patient's private physician in order to explain its definition of the case. On the patient's medical file was written: "mechanical pain by deafferentation, allodynia, chronic pain syndrome." After briefly recalling the problem of the patient, who had been operated on twice on the knee for "chronic laxity," the letter went on to describe the current illness situation:

> This painful symptomatology of a neurological origin *does not alone sum up* the therapeutic problem. Several elements indicate that *the pain has become the illness itself*: thymic repercussions, loss of integration at work. One major element concerns, among others, the periodic reassessment of the degree of handicap (and thus of insurance benefits) as the patient waits for the results. All this leads me to think that the patient must receive as global a care as possible." (My emphasis).

As this excerpt shows, the combination of diverse factors, including financial ones, into a definite syndrome provides the physician with a powerful means for deciphering the pain situation, a means that coexists with a more "classical" interpretation focussed on lesions. At this centre, however, pointing to clues of a psychological malfunction involves more than simply observing whether they are present or not. Clues from the list given earlier take on meaning through a model that integrates all of them into the potential behaviour of a "person in chronic pain."

By using both these means to decipher a case, the physician tries, during the first consultation, to draw up an inventory of the pain situation that can be used to define a therapeutic goal and strategy. As in the first centre, the referral letter provides basic information to be verified, completed or, if need be, corrected. However, the essential difference between these two centres lies elsewhere.

Since everything the patient brings along is important, the "physician's gaze" has to be multifocal. The physician, while looking at the patient's body, has to deliberately concentrate on exploring biography and ideas about pain. This emphasis on "biographical space" colours every consultation differently, so that a typical consultation cannot be described. During the first consultation, the physician is *on the watch*: He keeps his ears and eyes open.

Although they might seem to be improvising, these physicians use a pre-established grid for interviews in order to collect systematically the information necessary for evaluating cases. To help physicians work within their patients' subjectivity, this centre has drawn up an "orientation tree" to be used as a grid for the initial interrogation and examination. The chronic pain syndrome underlying this grid opens a multidimensional space in which a patient's thoughts and words become tools for the eventual diagnosis and therapy. The physician continually elicits the patient's view by saying: "I need to be in your place and understand how you experience this pain," "What do you think about this pain?" or "What bothers you the most? Can you explain it to me?" The referral letter is often used to open the way to this field of interpretation. For instance, one physician said right at the start of the consultation, "Your doctor wrote you have family problems. Is that right?" To obtain all the necessary information, the physician proceeds variously. Of course, the referral letter informs him about the neurophysiology, or perhaps even the psychology, of the patient's case. In addition, there are, of course, the X-rays, test results and other records. The examination is a major source of information too. During it, the physician does not make many comments, however. For instance, he does not transcribe aloud the patient's symptoms onto a nerve path, and he rarely discusses what he sees with students (or with the visiting sociologist). The interview grid and underlying concept of a chronic pain syndrome guide the physician and enable him to adjust his interventions flexibly and seize any opportunity—the referral letter, remarks made by the patient or the person accompanying him, or gestures (such as the way the patient sits down or stands up). Everything has a place in the web of meaning. If no or few opportunities arise, the physician often resorts to direct questions after having created a positive ambiance, in particular by making it clear that he believes in the patient's pain. These questions might be motivated by a search for precise clues, for instance, those signalling a depression.

More often, such direct questions are part of the physician's work of deciphering. . . .

Evidence is brought to light in several ways and gradually woven into the web of meaning. . . .

Following the first consultation, the physician orients the patient. A case might be referred for follow-up by one or two other physicians. If two are chosen, one, a specialist in internal medicine, will have responsibility for prescribing drugs; and the other, specialised in global care as defined by the centre, will teach the patient how to relax and advise him how to live with pain. What leads the co-ordinating physician to choose two colleagues for the follow-up is the degree of difficulty in the case. The principle underlying the practice of medicine at this centre is prudence. For this reason, certain "orientation consultations" are backed up by what we might call an "overspecialised" consultation.

Formulating Advice to Patients: A Logic of Explanation and Conviction

Physicians at this centre formulate advice to patients following a logic of explanation and conviction. Since this centre's conception of pain entails switching attention from the painful stimulus to the person who feels it, medical work must be focussed on the whole person. Though necessary, treating body pain cannot lastingly improve a patient's condition unless a minimal amount of work is also done on his experience of pain over time, the duration itself modifying the experience. In other words, the work of reducing persistent pain always entails modifying the patient's relation with pain. By formulating advice, the physician has to convince the patient to become involved in a dynamic cognitive and behavioural change. "By modifying the way of reacting, we modify the pain" is an assertion that perfectly summarised this point of view. There is no breaking point where the physical becomes psychological, no rupture between "something" or "nothing." This dynamic process depends on the degree of change to be effected. The greater the change, the more the physician has to become involved in convincing the patient—the more he has to work on the latter's convictions. This work is an extension of the explanation.

The explanation must account for three things: the patient's pain, the means of action (the therapeutic programme) and "realistic" expectations about what might be achieved over time. It has to be partly grounded in the patient's experience so as to place him in a gradual future entirely made out of his actions over time, as one physician explained: "So don't say, 'I don't hurt' because it's a matter of degrees, it varies depending on muscle exercises. It'll come along at your pace." The physician tries to involve the patient in this dynamic process by setting up "areas" of negotiation-conviction. For instance, he might have a close talk with a patient about the schedule of possible improvements and about how he will change once feeling better. This way of bargaining about change ("If I took away 20 percent of your pain, what additional activities would you take up?") is one of the most common ways of working on convictions. The patient is thus induced to imagine living differently—managing with less pain, he is often baffled by this work done on his thoughts.

The explanation often links pain to life circumstances, such as a divorce, depression, periods of unemployment, or bereavement. The physician tries to convince a patient that this link accounts for the persistence and/or intensity of the pain. Certain conditions have to be fulfilled before the two parties reach a tentative agreement. The physician has to guarantee that he believes in the patient's pain. He has to finish defining the situation and explicitly close off other therapeutic possibilities (such as an operation). Furthermore, his explanation has to stick close to the patient's experience. For instance, it cannot deny the patient's sensations even if they seem illogical. When, as in cases of "advanced chronic pain syndrome," the physician analyses a patient's pain as a global way of reacting as a person, these conditions become all the more important, since the pain is being linked to the whole person and not just a circumstance. In such a case, the therapeutic strategy induces the person to reinterpret the pain so as to see it as part of reactions to problems, instead of considering it to be the problem itself. The physician tries to make the patient see his pain as part of his everyday life.

To be followed by the patient, the physician must weave a web of meaning between the person's pain sensations, daily situations and global reactions. This work on convictions transforms the explanation into an interpretation that turns the patient as a person into the object on which medical work can be done. Meaning is gradually constructed during the consultation by this deciphering of clues as the physician partly formulates advice to the patient. This switching from the pain to the person is accomplished as the physician successively draws up microhypotheses and as the patient takes these to be pointers of where the physician is heading. By working with ordinary ideas about irritability, worry, aggressiveness, conflict, fear, loss of self-control, stress, etc., the physician gradually makes his interpretation tangible, usually by enacting short scenes that highlight the patient's reactions to problem situations. Through successive "touches," he situates the latter's pain in the daily life, which, more than the body, becomes the focal point of the interpretation.

Once the person thus becomes the object of medical work, the physician can then explain the therapeutic programme and set objectives, mainly in terms of adaptation and pain control. When working so directly on a patient's experiences, on the subjectivity, the physician has to make it clear that he believes in the pain or, even more outright, that he does not think the patient is "crazy." The more the latter is involved as a person in defining his pain situation, especially if he sees himself and not just his body or nervous system as being responsible for his problems, the more precisely the physician has to formulate advice. Attempts to settle this problem take place beside the effort to open a field of interpretation. One physician told a patient:

> Now if we're going to fight and say, "It's the nerves" or "It's not the nerves," I can tell you that's the worst way to become involved, because, if we haggle like that, you on your side of the desk and me on mine, that's the best way not to be any better.

To involve a patient in another interpretation of his pain, the physician draws up hypotheses, which seem more or less convincing. He proposes a fuzzy, precarious proof of these hypotheses, since they are a means not so much of constructing the truth as of performing medical work—even when they come from the patient. One physician proceeded thus:

> So let's follow up a little on your story. In my opinion, your hypothesis that the pain was related to blows that the patient received when she was attacked, (even though she had started hurting earlier) seems important. It's worth taking it into account not in order to say, "It's this" or "It's that" but to ask what we can use it for in the treatment.

Every situation can provide links to be worked on. The problem is not the exactness of a link but rather its capacity to make the patient become involved. The proof is necessarily fuzzy, since everything might have meaning. When one patient said, "There's something odd here. I like to do things like going to the movies or the museum. But I've noticed that, at such times, I get a headache that gets worse while I'm doing them," the physician replied, "But sometimes things are paradoxical. In certain cases, the situations that cause pain are not necessarily the least pleasant ones. I can't prove it each time."

We can see the importance of this sort of link in the follow-up, when patients and physicians work on small graphs that the latter use to show the relations between the former's pain, tensions and activities during a typical day. What this centre "objectifies" is these links between events and not, as the other centre does, the pain itself, nor its diagnosis and treatment.

Mutual Involvement and the Work of Agreeing

This medical work with its logic of explanation and conviction leads to a specific regime of relations between physicians and patients. By seeking to provide explanations to patients, make them understand and involve them in a dynamic change, physicians assign them a definite place and responsibilities: as co-actors in the medical work. This is the division of labour that this centre's physicians have been led to define through their way of working. To develop, this mutual involvement must fit within a universe of shared medical work. Physicians have to create a sense of "us at work." This does not at all mean that patients and physicians are equal, or that the latter cease being experts. Instead, it requires that each party's place be specified in what is called a "contract."

Throughout the consultation, the physician developes a universe of shared work. He repeatedly insists that nothing is possible without the patient's help: "I'm not proposing something where I don't need you. I can get along with handling the medicine, but I'll need you." He implicates the patient in the treatment: "We'll help you, but you have to save yourself." In this universe of shared work, roles and duties are assigned—"You'll have your responsibilities, and we'll have ours"—However the point is not so much that roles should be complementary (as the term "cooperation" might suggest) but rather that a contractual relationship must come out of an agreement. Since the physician has the initiative in striking this agreement, the relationship is not symmetrical.

Sometimes the patient cannot easily be included as an actor in this universe of shared work. They may resist all the harder if they have previously come into conflict with medical professionals, or feel personally implicated in the physician's definition of the situation. To deal with resistance, the physician might proffer the threat that he, in turn, will not implicate himself in the case:

Frankly, I want to say that if I ever feel you have too many good reasons for saying it doesn't work. If you say, "Watch out! It'll have side effects on me" or "I live too far, I can't come," then we won't start the program. To start the program, we have to say to each other, "We got to make an effort, we got to find the right doses." That's our job, but what we need is to create a climate. We need you. We want to give medicine that works, but not anything you can't stand. However you must realise that whether or not a medicine is tolerated or rejected has as much to do with the way it's accepted as with the medicine itself. So, I insist on that because it'll be a little test of the way we'll be able to work together. Your problem is complicated enough for me to tell you, "Listen here, let's not lose any time." If we feel that people are dragging their feet, we give up.

We sense that the physician was committing himself to the case but with the possibility of breaking the commitment later on. His insistence sheds light on the importance of working out an initial agreement and being assured that it has actually been accepted. The physician often seeks this agreement through the patient's adherence to the logic of his approach and through adapting this approach to the patient's problem; as one physician said, "I need to know whether you have the impression it corresponds to your problem." This is all the more important insofar as the problem is defined through hypotheses. One physician queried, "Does that seem worthwhile to you, or do you feel that it's only words?"

This need to work out an agreement with the patient in order to implicate him in a universe of shared work, from the start, implies that the physician makes a conditional commitment. Under this sort of agreement, the medical expert's work goes in hand with the patient's, but the physician takes the initiative not only to make a commitment but also to pursue the relationship. Given this sort of commitment, the physician does not have to justify a treatment's effects. Instead, he must keep the patient involved and, if need be, rework the agreement or withdraw from it.

When the patient comes back to the centre a second time, perhaps soon afterwards, s/he is still probably in pain. The doctor-patient agreement is oriented toward the long term—many therapeutic programmes call for up to ten sessions and even more. The physician has to keep the patient involved on several fronts. This involvement has to be maintained through the length of treatment. Typically, when a patient comes back, s/he says, "I did everything you told me to, but it still hurts." The physician has to "tell the time" by work on the notion of time and "normalising" the length of treatment: "I think things are coming along pretty much like they should. It's too early yet. I'll tell you when you'll be able to have less pain." The physician also has to calm the patient's doubts sparked by new outbreaks of pain.

To deal with discouragement, the physician, besides being sympathetic and trying to make the length of treatment seem normal, might try to reinvolve the patient by striking an agreement about a more limited, attainable objective within the general agreement. In this way, the longterm agreement is better accepted. Here is an example of this agreement within the agreement being worked out with a woman who still had four sessions before the end of her first contract. She felt the same even though she did all the prescribed relaxation exercises, but had not succeeded in doing them without the cassette. The physician insisted that it was an important step in the programme and that she had to do it. But he soon realised that she was discouraged and wanted to stop. So adopting a coaxing attitude and tone of voice he said:

> *Physician*: Come on now. Let's leave that, the problem of doing the exercises without the cassette. Tell me how a day goes by. When does the pain come? When does it bother you the most? (The whole consultation was spent relating moments of intense pain to activities and drawing up a strategy for dealing with the maxima. At the end, an agreement was sought): Does that seem clear to you? Does it seem possible? Do you think it'll work?
>
> *Patient*: Yes, for others, but not for me.
>
> *Physician*: There's where I can help you, I can explain how to do it. That's what we've just done. I can also explain to you how we know that it'll work, because we've studied a lot of people's reactions. We're not improvising for you.

Resorting to an argument like the last one is not always convincing. A physician might then propose additional proof: "If that interests you, I have—if you need to be convinced—testimonies, films of other patients you can watch." In rare cases, he puts the patient in contact with a former patient.

To maintain the patient's agreement, the physician might have to strike compromises about a treatment's strategy. He might agree to prescribe a drug even though he thinks it useless. Or he might modify the priority of a treatment's phases. But the major difficulty during the follow-up is to maintain agreement about the definition of the pain situation. . . .

Conclusion

The main interest of this comparison is to draw attention to an essential, often ignored, level of medical work—operational knowledge or, to put it differently, physicians' practical arrangements of theoretical facts which are resources they use for organising interventions. Table 1 highlights outstanding points of comparison. By examining the mechanisms physicians use to decipher pain

Table 1.1 Comparison Between Centres

Centre I	Centre II
Scientific reference: Gate-control theory	*Scientific reference*: Gate-control theory
Operational knowledge based on the "something/nothing" alternative.	*Operational knowledge based on pain as an illness, as always "something."*
The patient's data arranged in a hierarchy of relevance: Determine the pain situation by eliminating possibilities and seeing clues.	The patient's data all equally relevant: Evaluate by balancing possibilities and listening to clues.
Describe pain and demonstrate advice. Two distinct spheres: Body and person.	Explain pain and convince the patient of advice. A single sphere: The person and his pain in a variable link.
Objective: Cure (do away with) pain. A statistical future, the patient as spectator.	Objective: Heal (control) pain. A gradual future, the patient as actor.
A regime of face-to-face relations	*A regime of relations based on mutual commitment*
Two distinct universes, or fields of separate action (you/us), with parallel logics.	A single universe of shared work. The patient's experience a field for shared action necessitating a single, minimal logic.
No need for an initial agreement; consequence: Justification work about medical care overtime.	Need for an initial agreement; consequence: Work of realigning the initial agreement over time.

situations, this comparison has shown how the operational knowledge under-lying physicians' decision-making gives rise to specific systems of doctor-patient relations. This calls for two comments.

First of all, the world of medicine has boundaries set by a body of theoretical knowledge, which serves as the grounds of theories that medical specialties have developed. Since this theoretical frame of reference is global, it leaves much room for everyday practices. These practices and this central body of knowledge (or theory, as Armstrong has put it), may be linked in many ways, as the following examples show:

— physicians dealing with chronic pain, though using a single theory as starting point, pursue obviously different logics of action, as we have seen;
— physicians specialising in occupational medicine may suspend their role as expert and refer to the patient's judgement in order to make decisions (Dodier, 1991); and
— physicians specialised in pediatric cardiology may switch from a medical model of decision-making to a democratic one when, for

instance, there are limited possibilities for surgery or a choice has to be made between low-risk, palliative surgery and dangerous, corrective surgery (Silverman, 1983).

In what has become a standard work, Armstrong (1984), by analysing professional discourses, has reconstructed two historically differentiated ways of conceiving of clinical work, which perceive illness with different codes.[9] He concluded that these two concepts are both present in contemporary medicine owing to the tension between theory and experience: The discourse which is the vehicle for this new perception necessarily has no immediate or real effects in clinical practice. Most clinical practice today—particularly hospital-based—probably relies on an older scheme of interpretation. Tensions are due to a fundamental conflict between levels of theory and of experience (Armstrong, 1984, p. 243).

The comparison herein has illustrated, with reference to practice, the pertinence of Armstrong's analysis. On the basis of my observations, I have constructed two ways of interpreting chronic pain (with respect to the body or else to "the patient's view"). However, this comparison also raises questions about the tension between theory and practice. Through the examples listed above, we can see that physicians' manifold relations with "theory" are shaped by constructs, by intellectual categories that both depend on but also generate the codes for perceiving illness. If we forget this twofold process, we will always be forced to analyse theory and experience separately, and also to leave the question of operational knowledge as a blind spot or "black box" in the sociology of medical action.

Secondly, this study of contrasting examples of how physicians decipher patients' pain situations sheds light on a central issue: the problem of medical knowledge, of making it operational. The connection from operational knowledge to regimes of doctor-patient relations indicates that there are several ways of postulating the bases of interaction. This knowledge is not replayed every day in medical practice. It serves as a guide for patients and physicians' actions. In other words, this cognitive context partly constrains the actions of actors in medical work and the interactions between them. In this sense, actors' cognitive contexts can be understood as frames in which physicians fit their clinical experiences. Freidson (1970) has shown how physicians base their interventions on personal clinical experiences, which depend on each physician's social characteristics and, even more, on changing factors (such as the type of patients usually treated, the work load or colleague networks) in the work environment. This situationist analysis, with its insistence on the "circumstances of practice," has stimulated much research based on "clinical contexts," a notion with widely divergent meanings, such as: economic determinants in Marxist analyses (Waitzkin, 1979); the sequential organisation of physicians' and patients' discourses during consultations in conversational analyses (Fisher, 1984); and variations in the "ceremonial order" in Strong (1979). Silverman's work, which partly fits into this last line of research, represents, it seems to me, the ultimate achievement in the study of the contexts of practices. Silverman has systematically explored variations in doctor-patient relations, in the forms of consultations and in physicians' decision-making models. He has shown that, to understand these variations, it is important to take into account, among other things: the "patency" of a patient's pathological situation, the trajectories of possible treatments for different pathological problems, and the spatial organisation of consultations. Nonetheless his intent has been to deal with "the social organisation of the discourse in which decisions are announced, disputed or confirmed" (Silverman, 1983, p. 43). This leaves out the operational know-how used to make decisions. Recognising the importance of the cognitive context sheds new light on another aspect of medical actions and doctor-patient relations.

The objective is not to limit physicians and patients to positions as dispensers and recipients of knowledge. Instead, it is to recognise how operational knowledge is central to the medical work that brings these two parties into contact. After examining physicians' work of interpretation (how given practical arrangements of theoretical facts open the way to specific regimes of doctor-patient relations), I shall, during a later study, try to understand how, in these various systems, patients attempt to communicate the "reality" of their pain, which for them too is a problematic fact.

CNRS-CERMES
Paris, France

Acknowledgment

This paper was prepared for "Symbolic Interaction Faces the 90s," a meeting of the Society for the Study of Symbolic Interaction, February 7-9, 1991, San Francisco.

Notes

1. On the construction of scientific facts, see: Latour and Woolgar (1979); and on the construction of private facts, see Claverie (1990).

2. The fact that pain physicians share a theory, even though they have worked it out differently, distinguishes them from the professional group described by Mol and Lettinga (1990), which was split in two segments with different theoretical premises.

3. For a revealing analysis of how various "layers" of knowledge are fitted into contemporary medical discourse, see Armstrong (1984).

4. This work by an emerging professional segment can be compared to the way young practitioners, at the start of careers, put to use the "book knowledge" acquired during medical school. About the construction of a professional world among young general practitioners, see Baszanger (1983). Dodier (1991) has made a similar analysis of occupational medicine.

5. In a research report (1987), I have recounted the history of these two pain centres, and analysed how they are organised and work.

6. The problem of who owns a "true knowledge" of a person's experience is close to some issues raised by Perakyla and Silverman (1991) in a different medical setting.

7. As Strauss et al. (1982) and Baszanger (1986) have insisted, the patient is an actor in medical work. The foregoing pages have alluded to some aspects of this (such as providing information, holding still during checkups, and keeping complaints within reasonable limits). Although my field notes could be analysed from this point of view, my intention here is to explore how the way physicians' work leads them to construct a certain system of relations with patients regardless of the latter's attitudes.

8. This can also be observed when physicians resorted to an interpretation involving both physiological mechanisms and personality traits (sensitivity, nervousness, etc.). However the latter were not considered to be part of their domain, as one of the physicians tried to make a patient realise. "You were born like that, I can't change you." In this case too, the patient was the one who had to manage.

9. Nettleton (1989) has prolonged Armstrong's analysis to pain and fear in dentistry.

References

Armstrong, D. (1984) The patient's view, *Social Science and Medicine,* 18, 737-44.

Baszanger, I. (1983) La construction d'un monde professionnel: entrées des jeunes praticiens dans la medecine générale, *Sociologie du Travail,* 3-83, 275-94.

Baszanger, I. (1986) Les maladies chroniques et leur ordre négocié, *Revue Française de Sociologie,* XXVII, 3-27.

Baszanger, I. (1987) *Entre comprendre et soigner. Les débuts des centres de la douleur en France.* Paris. Rapport de recherche, CNRS-MIRE.

Baszanger, I. (1990) Emergence d'un groupe professionnel et travail de légitimation. Le cas des medecins de la douleur, *Revue Française de Sociologie,* XXVI, 257-82.

Claverie, E. (1990) La vierge, le désordre et la critique. Les apparitions de la vierge à l'age de la science, *Terrain,* mars, 60-75.

Dodier, N. (1990a) Jugements medicaux, entreprises et protocoles de codage, *Raisons practiques,* 1, Les formes de l'action, 115-48.

Dodier, N. (1990b) *How are medical judgements transcribed?* Paper presented at the conference: The social construction of illness, Bielefeld, Germany.

Dodier, N. (1991) Experience privée des personnes et expertises medico-administratives. Une enquéte dans la medecine du travail, *Sciences Sociales et Santé.*

Fisher, S. (1984) Doctor-patient communication: A social and micro-political performance, *Sociology of Health and Illness, 7*(3), 342-74.

Freidson, E. (1970) *Profession of medicine.* New York: Dodd, Mead.

Glaser, B. and Strauss, A. (1967) *The discovery of grounded theory.* Chicago: Aldine.

Latour, B. and Woolgar, S. (1979) *Laboratory life. The construction of scientific facts.* London: Sage.

Mol, A. and Lettinga, A. (1990) *Bodies, impairments and the social construct: The hemiplegia case.* Paper presented at the conference: The social construction of illness, Bielefeld, Germany.

Nettleton, S. (1989) Power and pain: The location of pain and fear in dentistry and the creation of a dental subject, *Social Science and Medicine, 22,* 1183-90.

Perakyla, A. and Silverman, D. (1991) Owning experience: Describing the experience of other persons, *Text.*

Silverman, D. (1983) *Communication and medical practice. Social relations in the clinic.* London: Sage.

Strauss, A., Fagerhaugh, S., Suczek, B. and Wiener, C. (1982) The work of hospitalised patients, *Social Science and Medicine, 16,* 977-86.

Strong, P. (1979) *The ceremonial order of the clinic.* London: Routledge.

Waitzkin, H. (1979) Medicine, superstructure and micropolitics, *Social Science and Medicine,* 13A, 601-9.

Wiener, C. et al. (1980) Patient power: Complex questions need complex answers, *Social Policy,* September-October, 30-8.

2

Identity Dilemmas
of Chronically Ill Men

KATHY CHARMAZ

Commentary

This chapter was written by an extremely skilled researcher who has always used grounded theory in her highly regarded work. Dr. Charmaz has also published articles about grounded theory methodology and methods, including her innovative combining of these with a phenomenological approach. She is known for her valuable contributions about people who suffer from chronic illnesses; indeed, she is one of the few sociologists who have directly written about human suffering. In this particular chapter, her focus is on men's responses to their severe, long, terminal illnesses.

Let us examine the chapter's style of presentation in terms of the author's grounded theory analyses. First, note how clearly and early in the chapter she poses several theoretically oriented substantive questions. Then, she mentions directly (really locating for us) the sources and nature of her data, as well as her use of several grounded theory "steps." The latter consisted of examining

© 1994 by Midwest Sociology Society. Reprinted from *The Sociological Quarterly, 35*(2), 269-288, by permission.

the interviews for gender differences, studying the men's interviews and written accounts for themes, building analytic categories, refining these categories, making comparisons with the women on selected points.

Her analytic and descriptive analysis is simultaneously integrated through discussion of "four major processes in men's experiences of chronic illness." These are explicitly listed in her introductory remarks and soon mentioned as integrating the analysis. Discussion of each is supplemented with a discussion of comparisons of "preserving a public identity" and "changing a private identity." This is followed by another short discussion of "strategies for preserving self." Both discussions are directed at illuminating her principal categories of identity and self (her enduring theoretical interests in her research on experiences with chronic illness). The concluding section of this chapter consists of a brief general "discussion" about male identity and men's responses to their illnesses. The entire chapter incorporates the central emphases of the grounded theory mode of research, emphases on theoretical formulation, constant and multiple comparisons done for theoretical purposes, and undoubtedly a use of theoretical sampling. You should particularly note the clarity of analysis, signaled not only by the overall presentation, but the systematic clarity of her conceptual classifications, labeling, and ordering within each analytic section. From her other works on grounded theory methods, and in this particular chapter, the variety of labeled concepts, we know that she has used the usual ones (coding, memos, and so on), to produce an admirable theoretical analysis.

Chronic illness frequently comes to men suddenly with immediate intensity, severity, and uncertainty. Because men contract more serious and life-threatening chronic illnesses than women, experiencing illness causes men different identity dilemmas. This paper explores men's identity dilemmas by studying how men experience chronic illnesses and by looking at how assumptions about masculinity affected their identity. The paper explores four major processes: (1) awakening to death after a life-threatening crisis, (2) accommodating to uncertainty as men realize that the crisis has lasting consequences for their lives, (3) defining illness and disability and (4) preserving self to maintain a sense of coherence while experiencing loss and change. The data are derived from forty in-depth formal interviews of twenty men, informal interviews with these men, and an extensive collection of published and unpublished personal accounts. The data were analyzed through the strategies of grounded theory.

* * *

Introduction

Chronic illness frequently comes to men suddenly with immediate intensity, severity, and uncertainty. Typically, men contract more serious and life-threatening chronic illnesses than women who experience a higher incidence of degenerative diseases such as arthritis and multiple sclerosis (Conrad, 1987; Verbrugge, 1985, 1989). Hence, men have heart attacks and strokes earlier in life and die significantly more frequently and quickly than women (Verbrugge, 1985). Thus, the suddenness of illness, its intensity, and timing in the life course (usually middle-aged and older) pose special identity dilemmas for men. Identities define, locate, characterize, categorize, and differentiate self from others. Identities develop in stable roles and in emergent situations (Goffman, 1963; Weigert, 1986). Following Hewitt (1989), social identities derive from cultural meanings and community memberships and are conferred upon the person by others. Personal identities define a sense of location, differentiation, continuity, and direction by and in relation to the self. When identities are internalized, they become part of the self-concept, what Turner (1976) defines as the relatively stable, coherent organization of characteristics, evaluations, and sentiments that a person holds about self (cf. Charmaz, 1991; Gecas, 1982).

Identity dilemmas result from losing valued attributes, physical functions, social roles, and personal pursuits through illness and their corresponding valued identities, i.e., positive definitions of self, including socially conferred and personally defined positive identities. These dilemmas include the knotty problems and hard decisions arising as people experience trials, tribulations, and transitions during their illnesses that affect who they are and can become. Serious chronic illness threatens men's taken-for-granted masculine identities and leads to identity dilemmas that can recur again and again. Men's identity dilemmas include the following oppositions: risking activity vs. forced passivity, remaining independent vs. becoming dependent, maintaining dominance vs. becoming subordinate, and preserving a public persona vs. acknowledging private feelings. Whichever direction a man takes has costs. For example, a man may take enormous risks with his health to remain active, independent, and dominant. At each turn, trying to maintain former identities may take more effort while potential social, psychological, and physical losses simultaneously multiply.

To date, the sociological literature has not explicitly addressed the special circumstances that chronically ill men face (see, for examples, Charmaz,

1987, 1991; Corbin and Strauss, 1988; Johnson, 1991; Kelleher, 1988; Kleinman, 1988; Strauss, Corbin, Fagerhaugh, Glaser, Maines, Suczek, and Wiener, 1984). Nor have earlier researchers looked at these men's experience from the standpoint of gender-based conceptions of masculinity. Instead, the literature has largely remained gender-neutral and thus, not only missed seeing the particular emergent structure of men's experience of chronic illness, but also the identity dilemmas that they confront.

This research is an initial attempt to open the discussion of gender and identity in chronic illness. In my depiction of men's identity dilemmas, I build on earlier analyses of (1) experiencing chronic illness first as an "acute interruption" followed by an "intrusive illness" (Charmaz, 1991) (2) developing narratives of self-change through illness (Frank, 1993) and (3) recapturing the past (Charmaz, 1991).

What is it like to be an active, productive man one moment and a patient who faces death the next? What is it like to change one's view of oneself accordingly? Which identity dilemmas does living with continued uncertainty pose for men? How do they handle them? When do they make identity changes? When do they try to preserve a former self?

This research explores these questions by looking at four major processes in men's experience of chronic illness: (1) awakening to death after a life-threatening crisis, (2) accommodating to uncertainty as men realize that the crisis has lasting consequences, (3) defining illness and disability, and (4) preserving self to maintain a sense of coherence while experiencing loss and change. Here, uncertainty means awareness of imminent or eventual recurrence, degeneration, or death. Although uncertainty has long been a key theme in the chronic illness literature, the focus has been on uncontrollable embarrassing, incapacitating, or painful symptoms and further episodes (cf. Reif, 1975; Schneider and Conrad, 1983; Wiener, 1975). By also studying men with potentially life-threatening conditions, uncertainty in relation to death in chronic illness becomes explicit.

Methods and Data

This study is part of a larger qualitative research project on the situations and perspectives of people who have chronic illness.[1] The data are derived from forty in-depth formal interviews of twenty men, seven of whom were interviewed more than once, informal interviews, and a collection of personal accounts.[2] For comparative purposes, the analysis also draws upon eighty interviews with chronically ill women. The criteria for being interviewed included: (1) adult status (over twenty-one years of age), (2) a diagnosis of a serious but not terminal chronic illness, (3) a disease with an uncertain course, and (4) effects of illness upon daily life.

Grounded theory methods were used to analyze the data (Charmaz, 1983; 1990; Glaser, 1978; Glaser and Strauss, 1967; Strauss, 1987; Strauss and Corbin, 1990). The steps included: (1) examining the interviews for gender differences, (2) studying men's interviews and written accounts for themes, (3) building analytic categories from men's definitions of and taken-for-granted assumptions about their situations, (4) conducting further interviews to refine these categories, (5) rereading personal accounts from the vantage point of gender issues (e.g., Fiore, 1984; Hirsch, 1977; Hodgins, 1964; Kelly, 1977; Murphy, 1987; Zola, 1982), (6) studying a new set of personal accounts (e.g., Beisser, 1989; Frank, 1991; Zink, 1992), and (7) making comparisons with women on selected key points. The processes in the major themes served to integrate the analysis.

Awakening to Death

Consider this story. A forty-five year old man had had a serious heart attack three years before while cycling. Being a competitive cyclist had complemented and extended his identities as a hard-driving, no-nonsense businessman, a former military man, and the traditional breadwinner and head of his household. These masculine identities—male athlete, competitive businessman, Viet Nam veteran, and breadwinner—formed the boundaries and content of his self-concept. A business failure just before his heart attack forced his wife to go to work. After his heart attack, his doctor prescribed a rigorous cardiac rehabilitation program. Without my asking, he mentioned, "I didn't know who I was for a while. I'd kind of [think], 'God, if I can do this exercise, I'll die again,' [he saw doing strenuous exercise as risking death]. How to identify?" I asked, "How did you come to identify yourself?" He said:

> Well, what's the alternative? If death is on the one end or do you want repeated heart attacks? We had one of our friends in the group [cardiac rehabilitation] who was in there for the second heart attack and he lasted two and a half years and he's my age but he let himself go—back to smoking and drinking and bad eating habits.

So there is—I've heard this before—you get this invulnerable feeling—this invincible feeling and all of a sudden the hardest thing to accept is, "Hey, you are vulnerable. You can be hurt. You can die." You know, which you never thought of that before, or I never did. So that's still in the back of your mind.

Like other men who participated in cardiac rehabilitation programs, this man had gained a sense of leaving death behind, and regained a feeling of moving on with his life. But reminders of the fragility of life come more frequently and forcefully, as occurred with the sudden death of his friend.

Death. The first identity dilemma comes when men realize that death could occur—now. Clinging to former identities in hope of minimizing the threat of death could risk their lives. Acknowledging the threat of death could cost them their most valued identities. When wholly unanticipated, the threat of death shakes men to their very core. Within moments or brief hours, the disruptive crisis removes them from familiar former identities to that of patient, possibly of dying patient. Crisis can overtake them without earlier warnings. Even illnesses like diabetes or cancer may not become manifest until a crisis.[3] Occasionally, like the athlete above, another man's crisis awakens or reawakens a man to his own vulnerability, aging, and death (cf. Karp, 1988).

Some men invoke gender-based reasoning such as the male midlife crisis (Jaques, 1965; Levinson et al., 1978; Sabo, 1990) to account for what happens to them even as illness develops. One man believed he was having a midlife crisis—that his life was falling apart. "There's a point I was thinking, 'This is a midlife crisis; this is just a state, or this is a stage you're going through.' " Later, his doctor told him that his aorta was literally ripping apart.

Awakening to death comes as an unbelievable shock when a man (1) sees himself as too young to die, (2) defines himself as exceptionally healthy, or (3) has had no earlier episodes or heralding symptoms. A young clinical psychologist, Neil A. Fiore, (1984) sought help for what he believed was an infection on his testicle only to find the physician talking "calcification," "surgery," "cancer," "death." When younger men have heart attacks, particularly the first one, they often do not know what is happening to them (cf. Cowie, 1976; Frank, 1991; Johnson, 1991). The athlete above recounted his heart attack at age 42, "I was on my bicycle going on just a routine ride for me and . . . I just went down. I didn't know what happened. . . . So I had no indication that I [was having a heart attack]—no chest pains, no shortness of breath, no typical [symptoms of] how you feel. I couldn't even tell you what it feels like." This man awoke in the hospital to find himself to be partly paralyzed. The paralysis did not faze him but he became furious when his doctor told him that he had had a heart attack. When I asked him what raised his fury, he juxtaposed the finality of heart disease with the injustice of having paid his dues already by stopping smoking, limiting drinking, getting in shape, and losing weight. All this work and then, the biggest injustice, "It's just I'm too young. . . . Why me?"

Once these men realized or were told what had happened, identity dilemmas emerged. When men believed that they had narrowly survived their crisis, at least at first they assumed it meant vulnerability. A greatly increased risk of dying. A radically altered life. A substantially foreshortened future? Death? Now real and perhaps soon. At this point, they connected death with personal identity. Several men made statements like these: "I know that I am mortal." "We all 'know' that we are going to die, but when you come close to death, you see it is true." "I am not immune to death."

The prospect of immediate death darkens the present and shades the future. While in crisis, men see living and dying as discrete categories. Their sense of betrayal by their bodies evokes anger, self-pity, and envy of the healthy. Once certain futures now look uncertain, even ended. Though premature death now seems possible, these men remain unaware of lasting illness and disability if they are unfamiliar with their diagnoses, their disease process, and other men who have the same condition (cf. Charmaz, 1991).

When men define awakening to death as only a *discrete, immediate event,* they limit the critical period to the initial crisis. Like Speedling's (1982) men who had heart attacks, these men initially saw getting through this crisis as the passage to an unchanged future. Several men who had had bypass surgery or other circulatory procedures questioned whether they should participate in a study of experiencing chronic illness. They believed their surgery had effected the necessary repairs. For them, not only the threat of death was over, but also the illness. A referral to my study, especially if by their nurse, undermined their construction of illness as an acute episode.

Eventually, men's routine interactions and unforeseen daily obstacles turn early glimmers of awareness into growing cognizance that illness remains. They learn lessons in chronicity during everyday routines that have become much more arduous and time-consuming than before. For example, mowing the lawn or simply getting himself bathed, groomed, fed, and dressed for the day can overwhelm a man who has had a heart attack or stroke. Lessons in

chronicity can challenge men's assumptions about male mastery and competence, thereby leading them into depression (cf. Dahlberg and Jaffee, 1977;
Hodgins, 1964). Treating illness and its consequences as problems to solve is
consistent with men's gender-related behavior (Tannen, 1990). Inability to
solve these problems undermines their personal identity. A forty-five year old
man with heart disease disclosed that for six months, "I thought my life was
over. Cardiac Cripple."

The identity issues emerging in awakening to death are not limited to men,
but they are imbedded in the medical diagnoses these men received and the
social conditions they experienced. Women responded similarly when they
found themselves facing unanticipated life-threatening crises. However,
women, even heart patients, reported much more difficulty in getting physicians to view their symptoms as real. Despite severe symptoms, these women
suffered disruption without a legitimizing diagnosis. Subsequently, practitioners, relatives, and the women themselves wondered if they fabricated their
symptoms. Hence, these women met serious diagnoses with relief (cf. Charmaz, 1991). In contrast, men who had crises acknowledged their symptoms
but initially glossed over their meaning and present or potential seriousness.
Further, they seldom had trouble in getting practitioners to attend to their
developing symptoms.[4]

What mitigates the overwhelming implications of awakening to death for
identity? When might a man gain through having a crisis?

Awakening to death can result in direct, positive consequences for identity.
Not only do moments of crisis crystallize when defined and met with a spouse
or partner, so also do identities. During crisis and its immediate aftermath,
most married men felt tremendous affirmation of their valued identities in the
family as they awakened to death (cf. Johnson, 1991; Speedling, 1982). They
received an outpouring of care, comfort, and love from their wives and
families. These men often bragged about how supportive and helpful their
wives had been. Even men who had had troubled marriages felt that their
wives affirmed, valued, and supported them. Statements like these were
common: "Patty was really great through the whole thing." "Marge was right
there every minute; she even stayed at the hospital those first few nights." To
these men, their wives had provided the essence of "being there" for them.
They were vigilantly attentive, helpful advocates, and loving companions
throughout the crisis. The women provided their mates with a continuing link
to both past and future identity through the intensity of their involvement in
the present.

Thus, these men received identity validation, or confirmation of positive social identifications and private definitions of self. More than affirming men's personal identity and worth, this identity validation also implicitly affirmed their gender identities as men in the household. Paradoxically, that validation came when they were most physically dependent but derived from their central positions as husbands (which also validates the wife or partner's identity and role as helpmate and caregiver).

Identity supports to provide validation for single and divorced men, however, usually were much less available. They weathered crises largely on their own. Here, their situations resembled those of single women who often had to fend for themselves during crises and within the health care system. Older widowed and divorced women, however, typically received more caring and comfort from adult children than their male counterparts. The occasional exception occurred when divorced men's first wives, or gay men's friends, gave them care and support through their crises. (The few gay men with whom I talked did not currently have love relationships.) Generally, if single men had no caring children or close friends, they were particularly bereft. Thus, constructing a personally valued, and socially *validated* identity became more problematic for them than for those who had access to families.

Accommodating to Uncertainty

In which ways do men define and handle uncertainty? A casual observer might find that men often accommodate to uncertainty by ignoring, minimizing, or glossing over it. But what do such actions mean to men who do so? Their way of accommodating to uncertainty assumes "bracketing" (Husserl, 1970) the event which elicited it. Bracketing means setting apart this event by putting a frame around it and treating it as something separate and removed from the flow of life. The impact of the event upon identity lessens when this event is separated from social and personal identity. Through bracketing, men define uncertainty as having boundaries—those limited to crisis. Such bracketing coincides with medical definitions when both patient and practitioner use the same measures. For example, when a man has a successful surgery and treatment for cancer, both he and his physician may bracket the earlier uncertainty and limit it to the duration of the five year survival rate. Conversely, the patient's bracketing conflicts with the physician when they invoke different measures. To the extent that men put boundaries on uncertainty and limit it to flare-ups and crises, they avoid letting it permeate their thoughts and alter their identities. Thus, bracketing raises identity dilemmas because it poses maintaining past identity at cost to health against taking illness into account at risk to social and personal identity.

Bracketing reduces awareness of uncertainty. But why might men who remain at least partly aware of continued uncertainty not make the prescribed lifestyle changes because of it? First, these men cannot envision themselves as dead, and may see themselves as risk-takers and winners. Second, their earlier habits merge with their conception of masculine identity. Third, they have lost hope of genuinely effecting change and decide to live on their own terms for whatever time they have left. In each case, they usually do not foresee the possible kind or degree of disability and debility. Rather, they see themselves as remaining the same or as dead. Yet men can use uncertainty to retain power and privilege in their homes. Then, wives who cajole and try to control them get responses like this one: "Why should I care what I eat? I'm going to die anyway." Fertile grounds for marital strife develop in each case (cf. Peyrot, McMurry, and Hedges, 1988). Subsequently, identity dilemmas arise when spouses disagree on bracketing or acknowledging uncertainty.

Eventually most men realize that their bodies have changed. Subsequently, they become aware of uncertainty—uncertain episodes, uncertain treatment effects, uncertain complications—an uncertain life.[5] Awakening to death and *acknowledging* continued uncertainty is sobering. Reappraisals follow. These reappraisals can lead to epiphanies marking major turning points for men and their families (cf. Charmaz, 1991; Denzin, 1989; Gordon, 1990). When men acknowledge continued uncertainty, their reappraisals bring reflection and self-appraisal. Men who had attended much more to work than to their families decided to devote more time to them. Men who described themselves as driven by their "Type A" behavior believed that they had to relinquish it before it killed them. The man above who had viewed himself as a cardiac cripple for six months saw his heart attack quite differently two years later. He said, "I would say, 'Thank you, thank you,' type of thing. But you know, had it not been for my heart attack—I'm grateful it happened now, 'cause it changed my life considerably and so [I] have a lack of words [to describe it]. Yeah, I thank my heart attack for that. In one way I'm grateful."

Reappraisals of productivity, achievement, relationships all altered what these men defined as valuable. Their forced reappraisals led to setting priorities, making decisions, and also, coming to terms with their pasts and presents.

A middle-aged executive regretted his behavior in his first two marriages and resolved to maintain his third. These appraisals lead to assessments of self and identity. The middle-aged attorney reflected:

> When you are on the brink, so to speak, you begin to look at what things in your life are valuable and which aren't. And you begin to—and one of the things is real clear was I was glad that I did work where I tried to help other people rather than having a garage full of Mercedes. And it made me feel not like a saint, or anything, but it made me feel like not a bad person, not even like I was a good person. But I was alright; I was alright.

A resolve to live in the present frequently follows these initial reappraisals. The man above said, "I reflect on the past, leave the sadness and parts of myself that I don't consider functional anymore and try to live in the present." A young man believed that his earlier struggles to sift through and to sort out the past had kept him from attending to the immediate present and from knowing himself within it.

For young men, reappraisal can open paths to self-discovery. Getting a kidney transplant and being released from thrice-weekly dialysis treatments resulted in reappraisal by the young man above. At that point, he suddenly had much more unstructured time. He reflected, "And part of it is getting used to myself. . . . Getting used to *my self,* yeah, two words, because I didn't really have that much time to find out who I was before. I'd get glimpses now and again, and I'd go, 'Oh, yuck,' or 'yeah, far out,' you know, or 'Maybe,' . . . . [I] caught a lot of those [glimpses]."

Not uncommonly, men will be shaken by the initial crisis then gradually resume normal lives. Concurrently, they normalize their symptoms and regimens if they follow one. But before they resettle into a normal routine, they reappraise their lives and their actions.

After awakening to death and defining uncertainty, lifestyles, and also habits, rapidly change—at least for a while. Men quit working, change jobs, renegotiate their work assignments, or retire early. They follow a regimen, lose weight, stop smoking, and reduce drinking. Making permanent changes, however, means *acknowledging* uncertainty and treating its consequences as lasting. Several men with diabetes disclosed that they hadn't attended to their conditions until shocked by a diabetic crisis. One middle-aged manager previously had ignored his diet, his doctor's warnings, and his wife's nagging. After a harrowing struggle against death followed by loss of his foot, he not only acknowledged his own uncertain future, but also tried to instruct unaware relatives and friends about the negative consequences of their lifestyles . . . "because, look what happened to me."

As young men grow older, their accommodations to uncertainty can form the foundation of their identities. As he looked back on having been a diabetic for more than two decades, a professor viewed his regimen not only as the means of reducing uncertainty by staving off further complications but, moreover, as the way he identified himself. He reflected:

> I would not want to have to be preoccupied with it [diabetes] the way I was the first year or so. Ah, but at the same time, it is the ground of my life. *I have no idea who I would be, in a way, if I hadn't become diabetic* . . . Just to have to internalize this regime must have made a great difference to my personality, I think. . . . I was a person who didn't eat unless someone sort of sat him down. And, I like to drink and drink and sometimes got quite intoxicated. Stay up all night, and not sleep, go days without sleeping. And I've now become the opposite of all that, like a field and ground thing (emphasis mine).

Defining Illness and Disability

As they accommodate to uncertainty, how do men define their conditions? How do these definitions affect their personal identity? These men viewed their conditions in four major ways as: an enemy, an ally, an intrusive presence and an opportunity. At different points in time, a man may hold each definition. Similarly, he may view his physical condition as the enemy but the treatment as an ally. Hence, his definitions reflect and simultaneously shape narratives of knowing self through illness (Frank, 1993; Herzlich and Pierret, 1987) and thus can result in raising or resolving identity dilemmas. Definitions of enemies and allies both explicitly create personifications. However, viewing one's illness as an enemy objectifies and externalizes it and thus distances and separates it from at least personal, if not also, social identity (cf. Goffman, 1961, 1963). Viewing illness as an ally emphasizes subjectivity and identification with it and thus, integrates it with personal and, if disclosed, social identity.

Changing definitions and revising the stories that frame them reveal new identifications. Yet these definitions are not always stories of self-change as Frank (1993) describes. Rather, definitions of illness as an enemy typically testify to a man's continuity of self. Here, the narrative framing of the man's definition proclaims that *he* remains the same though his body and situation may have changed.

Definitions of the illness spread to specific symptoms, treatments, and even to the body itself. A young man who had defined the dialysis machine as an enemy tried to make an ally of his new kidney transplant, which his body began to reject. To him, the transplant meant a direct route to his preferred identity as an involved graduate student. He said, "Rejection is a very scary time . . . a very scary time because you have all these hopes and then the kidney—your body is saying, 'Well, I don't agree with you, you don't need—this isn't your kidney.' And you're saying, 'Well, agree with me, this is [my kidney]'—and you get into conversations, I got into conversations with my kidney and my body."

Images of enemies and allies are present, although sometimes implicit, in the competitive discourse of victories and losses that middle-aged and younger men frequently invoke when talking about their illnesses. Norman Cousins (1983) titles his chapter on dealing with his heart attack, "Counter-attack." Lee Foster (1978, p. 526) states, "The record for longevity on a kidney machine, the last time I checked, was fourteen years, and if I stay on dialysis I aim to break the record." Arnold R. Beisser (1989), a psychiatrist who became quadriplegic due to poliomyelitis, took a similar stance toward his disability:

> When I became disabled, I even tried to turn my disability into a competitive sport. I did everything possible to deny the cripple in me. I had no use for him, and no place in my concept of myself for disability. Much of what I have written here has been about my search to find something of worth in that image of the cripple, something with which I could identify without regret. (p. 80)

Beisser wrote his book at age sixty-two; he became ill at twenty-seven. Visible disabilities such as Beisser's wheelchair use result in social identifications that cause or complicate problems in self-definition. If so, definitions of illness and disability as an intrusive presence are likely to follow. Anthropologist Robert F. Murphy had had a productive career before a benign tumor left him progressively paralyzed. He (1987, p. 104) comments:

> From the time I first took to the wheelchair up to the present, the fact that I am physically disabled has been in the background of my conscious thoughts. Busy though I might be with other matters and problems, it lingers as a shadow in the corner of my mind, waiting, ready to come out at any moment to fill my meditations.

> It is a Presence. I too, had acquired an embattled identity, a sense of who and what I was that was no longer dominated by my past attributes, but rather by my physical defects.

Murphy's wheelchair use permeated his consciousness of self, as well as others' consciousness of him, and symbolized his loss of power. Other meanings and symbols emerge when the context and situation are different. When first ill, Beisser (1989) lay flat on his back for a year. He recalled when he first sat in a wheelchair, "I felt as though my power had been restored. I had far greater difficulty in breathing, and it lasted only three or four minutes. But who cared! It was position that counted, and I associated this one with being able to take care of myself" (p. 24).

Visible disability typically becomes a master status and a master identity. It is a master status because this position overrides and subsumes others; it is a master identity because it defines every other identity. Beisser later experienced rudeness, stigma, invaded space, and loss of privacy because of his disability, which raised and reinforced identity issues. Like Beisser, several of my middle-aged and younger interviewees took years to reconcile the identity dilemmas that illness thrust upon them. Older working-class men were resigned to their situations and built lives around illness. Middle-class men sought to make illness and disability meaningful, to recast them into something through which positive identification could be made. Their quest resembled that of the younger and middle-aged women respondents (both middle- and working-class) but these women ordinarily articulated their concerns more directly and arrived at positive conclusions more readily. Nonetheless, by seeking to make illness meaningful, these men changed their definition from illness as an enemy or an intrusive presence to an experience with positive consequences. The professor above first received his diagnosis while he had a diabetic crisis and nearly died. Afterwards, he viewed both his body and his illness as enemies who were trying to kill him. But over the years, his definition changed, "It's [his illness] an enemy that I've made an ally of. Really, I don't think I'd still be here, if I hadn't been diabetic. It's like the paradox of the return of the prodigal son. It kicked me out of Eden alright, having to, you know, be on my best behavior so much and think about when to shoot up and all that. But it was what I needed."

From this vantage point, this man's awareness grew of how central being diabetic was to his sense of identity. He remarked, "Probably if I were less narcissistic and obsessive, I would be a poorer diabetic. It's sort of like diabetes and me, we were made for each other."

By making illness an ally, men can use it as an opportunity for reflection and change. Arthur Frank (1991, p. 1) refers to illness explicitly as "an opportunity, though a dangerous one." He writes, "Illness takes away parts of your life, but in doing so it gives you the opportunity to choose the life you will lead, as opposed to living out the one you have simply accumulated over the years" (p. 1).

Whether men treat their conditions as enemies, allies, intrusions, or opportunities, their definitions are seldom mutually exclusive or static. That is, a man who sees illness as an ally because it led him to set priorities can still see it as an intrusive, even ominous presence in his life. Similarly, a man can treat his illness as an ally for a number of years only to redefine it as an increasingly intrusive presence if it steadily limits his activities. Which definition holds sway depends upon the context and situation, the man's self-definition, and his responsibilities, actions, values, goals, and plans. As a result, many men appreciate what they learn while ill, but still struggle with preserving defining aspects of self from the past before illness.

Preserving Self

Although certain major identities change such as that of worker to part-time retiree, men with chronic illnesses try to lead normal lives. In doing so, they implicitly, and often explicitly, devote much effort to preserving self—aspects of a self known and valued in the past (see also, Charmaz, 1991; Johnson, 1991). Preserving self means maintaining essential qualities, attributes, and identities of this past self that fundamentally shape the self-concept. Thus, ill people relinquish some identities but retain others. By preserving self, men reconcile the identity dilemmas that chronic illness thrusts upon them. Johnson (1991) stresses roles and lifestyles in preserving self, but it means more than that. Rather, preserving self means maintaining a way of being in the world and a way of relating to and knowing self, others, and social worlds. Through preserving self, men maintain continuity throughout the past, present, and future. After he qualified for a disability benefit, Ernest Hirsch (1977), a clinical psychologist with multiple sclerosis, still maintained continuity with the past and forged a future. He retained valued identities through remaining in the same organization, community, and close friendships. His former employer provided him with free office space and clerical help to enable him to do research and writing. Despite earlier worries about losing his masculinity and independence, he managed to preserve essential qualities of self although he endured profound physical and social losses. He writes, "Whatever changes have occurred in me do not touch the core of my 'self,' which has remained pretty much the same. As far as other people are concerned, I think I've remained much as always. Although I realize some changes have occurred, I feel a continuity with the past and have no difficulty recognizing myself as myself, and neither does anyone else" (pp. 169-170).

As men come to terms with illness and disability, they preserve self by limiting encroachments from illness in their lives and controlling definitions of their illness and any disability, as suggested above. They also intensify control over their lives when they can and develop strategies that minimize the visibility and intrusiveness of illness, which I discuss briefly below. This reconciling of identity dilemmas takes illness into account, whether or not others believe that these men do it in a healthy way.

Recapturing the Past Self

Before men learn these new ways of preserving self, many of them assume that they will recapture *the* past self, or explicitly aim to do so. Here, they aim to reclaim the same identities, the same lives that they had before illness. Nothing less will do. For these men, their "real" selves are and must be only the past self (Charmaz, 1991; Turner, 1976). They lapse into invalidism and despondency if they cannot recapture their past selves. Jean B. Zink (1992, p. 60), who has long been disabled, now suffers from post-poliomyelitis syndrome. She compares herself with a male friend:

> Disability came to Bill in his mature life, which was full of fun and freedom, and he feels he was robbed of it. Bill's future is now in the past. Disability robbed me of a carefree youth but not of youth itself, which was full of innocence and idealism. My future was before me. Bill yearns for the past. I prayed for a future.
> . . . Bill lost the life that was precious to him, and now he ages with regret. I age with gratitude, regardless of the struggle, not because I am better than Bill but because my experience as I perceive it has demanded this of me. Bill seems to believe that the way things *were* should be pursued relentlessly. Bill uses his psychic energy to recapture the past. I use my psychic energy to maintain the present.

Except for women whose diseases caused severe mental impairment, women showed more resilience and resourcefulness than men in preserving aspects of self, even though women were less likely to have spouses to bolster their efforts (see also, LeMaistre, 1985; Lewis, 1985; Pitzele, 1985; Register, 1987; Wulf, 1979). Women rarely tied their futures to recapturing their past selves.

Trying to recapture the past self does provide strong incentives to fight illness and to stave off death. When men believe in their doctors and in their treatment, their resolve to struggle maintains their hope. If so, then a man assumes that his past self will be preserved when his physician promises marked improvement. A middle-aged father of young sons commented about having cardiac bypass surgery, "I felt—I was going to do everything I did before; otherwise it wasn't worth having the surgery. . . . I wanted to be just the same as before. And, like for these children, it would be really devastating to them if I were to go ahead and say, 'Well, I can't do this because of my heart; I can't do that,' you know. You don't want to teach young children to be like that."

Attempting to recapture the past self has its pitfalls when all valued social and personal identities remain in an irretrievable past. Being unable to measure up to the past self results in further preoccupation with it, and heightens identity dilemmas. Arnold Beisser (1989, p. 56) recalls how his desire to recapture his past self affected his courtship, "One big thing separated us. I was in love with someone else. That someone else was me, or rather my image of what I used to be. My past was my standard and I carried it with me like a Pepsi generation commercial. And, of course, I assumed that everyone else, including Rita, was attracted to that same image."

Drastic lifestyle changes following illness, such as reduced employment, forced retirement, rigid regimens, and broken marriages erode or collapse former identifies entirely, one after another, like dominoes. Simultaneously, despondency about not recapturing the past self increases and renders preserving valued aspects of self more arduous. A middle-aged man with heart disease felt overwhelmed, immobile, and depressed, when he compared his present precarious physical, financial, and marital statuses with his past fitness, financial security, and stable marriage. His fear of another heart attack, combined with his lassitude, led him to withdraw from everyone. He said, "I'd say I hit rock bottom about October, November last year. I got to where I don't care what happens to me, you know; I don't care what happens to anybody."

The distance increases between a man's past self, by now reconstructed in memory in idealized form, and present identities, as valued former identities collapse and new ones are viewed as negative. With each identity loss from chronic illness, preserving valued past "masculine" identities becomes more difficult. Not surprisingly then, Brooks and Matson (1982) found that the self-concepts of men with multiple sclerosis changed more negatively over time than those of women. Men draw upon the existing cultural logic that currently defines masculinity as they try to make sense of their altered selves and situations (cf. Denzin, 1991). When sexual performance forms the foundation of their conception of masculinity, impotency undermines their identities as men. Preserving a past identity becomes particularly problematic when the basis for that identity is lost. After his heart attack, the man above was financially devastated. Subsequent crises put more responsibility on his wife to get a full-time job, as his identity as *the* wage-earner rapidly eroded. He said, "She was fine throughout that [the financial crisis]—she didn't work [before then]; she worked part-time; now she's working full-time. So yeah, she blamed me for that, me being the provider and that type of thing. That hurts me too, you know."

Under these conditions, illness becomes the symbol of identities lost and the reason why attempts to preserve self flounder. This man explained, "This is the worst year of my life. In one month I lost health, a career. In a year I lost my capital; I almost lost my marriage—you could almost say that year I lost my marriage. My oldest daughter moved."

Problematic health strains an already strained marriage. It also strains a stable marriage when erosion of valued identities continues. Like retirement, chronic illness allows men who cut back or leave work to become new critics of their wives' and children's activities. Loss of control outside of the home leads to efforts to preserve self by exerting more control within it. To the extent that a man takes for granted that masculinity is imbedded in power, the more likely he will tighten his control within the household as access to other arenas decreases. For example, as a retired bartender became house-bound, his scrutiny of his wife's day increased and he became more critical and controlling. She could incur his wrath by failing to anticipate or to satisfy his dictates about the smallest household or personal care task. Such men want to be in control. Illness marginalizes their sense of masculinity (cf. Connell, 1987; Messner and Sabo, 1990). They cannot accept physical dependence, except, perhaps, upon wives. The demeaning nature of seeking help, being evaluated ("his doctor found out he was smoking again and read him the riot act"), of living on new—much less on someone else's—terms does not come easily. Rather than give up old habits, these men may flaunt them. If they cannot control their health, they may try to control someone else's response. To do this, they will take risks—often many of them and, likely, cast their wives and physicians into the role of adversaries to outwit. In this way, they maintain their assumed status in the hierarchy of men and simultaneously, exert dominance over women (cf. Sabo, 1992). At this point, they also risk being identified as obstreperous, unmotivated, and mentally unstable by their practitioners (cf. Albrecht, 1992; Plough, 1986).

Dependency strains relationships and plays havoc with identity. But identity develops and is maintained through interaction. Partners often find themselves in an elaborate dance around dependency. Wives and partners may find themselves anxiously trying to protect shreds of their husbands' former identities while feeling overwhelmed by the escalating demands placed upon them (see, for example, Lear, 1980; Strong, 1988).

These wives and partners provide pivotal identity supports for their husbands that mute the identifying effects of dependency and loss. As illness and disability persist and progress, identity supports dwindle for men in troubled marriages and for single men (cf. Hirsch, 1977). Several single men who became ill in their twenties lost their families of origin through death and divorce. By their thirties, they had become quite isolated. For example, one thirty-eight year old man with multiple sclerosis had markedly deteriorated during the past five years. His parents divorced during his childhood; his father died long ago, and his mother remarried a man in another state and could not afford to visit him. His move to the West Coast at eighteen had weakened his ties with his siblings who did not travel. By the time he became bedridden, his mother's occasional letters provided his only family contact. Like isolated elders, his main support came from a volunteer. After many life and death crises, he felt disconnected from the world and from almost everyone. He said of his illness, "It's everlasting. It's perpetual, and it just goes on and on and on, and it doesn't stop. . . . I don't think of death as gloomy; I see it as a release. I was wishing so much for it. And now it doesn't scare me at all, at all. But I wish and I wonder when it will happen."

This man disdained the self he witnessed in illness. To him, it was not worth preserving. When talking about his teen-aged years, his present immobility contrasted strikingly with his past activity. He said in wonder, "You know, I could do anything I needed to do. Like baseball, or football, or basketball. You know I did all those things—swimming. Now it's no more."

For him, the halcyon days of healthy youth remained in a faded past. But for others, the disparity between past and present identity enfolded the immediate present and foretold the future. A young man whose kidney transplant was failing questioned the value of living on the dialysis machine. The middle-aged attorney above discovered that his condition was far more serious and complicated than he had initially thought and probably had resulted in minimal brain damage. Another surgery became necessary but his health had deteriorated too much to risk doing it. Losses accrued. No stamina for backpacking. Memory losses canceled work. Social Security denied him a disability benefit. A legal victory against Social Security still did not result in processing his benefit. His doctor refused his pleas for more painkillers and less blood pressure medication. The side effects kept him groggy and uncomfortable. He attempted to control his medical care by firing his doctor. Despondent and unable to function as in the past, he said, "I don't do anything but sleep now." Six months later, he hung himself in the room that had come to be his bedroom, office, and sanctuary.

These three men saw their lives shrinking and their chances for creating valued identities diminishing. Under these conditions, they each saw suicide as a reasonable way of resolving the identity dilemmas in which they found themselves.[6] In contrast, possibilities of expanding identities foster hope and support desire to stave off disability and death. The self to be preserved is a developing self, ripe with the potential for new, positive identities. For example, one man had recently won an award in his field which brought him substantial recognition and travel, in addition to renewed friendships. For him, the world was opening up to him, not closing down upon him. Quite spontaneously, he disclosed, "I don't want to die, I'm just a baby, a fifty-two year-old baby boy. I'm just starting; I don't want to die."

Preserving a Public Identity, Changing a Private Identity

Some men claim public identities that reaffirm their pasts and demonstrate continuity with that past. They minimize the effects of chronic illness on their public persona by offering a public narrative of their lives in which chronic illness plays a minor or past role. To keep this narrative creditable, they may have to devote vast amounts of energy to keeping illness contained and disability invisible or less obvious (cf. Charmaz, 1991). Their efforts are founded on assumptions of preserving masculinity. A man struggled to use crutches for far longer than his condition permitted because he wanted to remain in the "manly" position of being on his feet, rather than in a wheelchair. A man with diabetes could not manage both his wheelchair and a tray in the cafeteria. He could not bring himself to ask his co-workers for help and skipped lunch. He risked a coma rather than request help.

Simultaneously, men may maximize the significance of illness and disability in their private identity. At home, the identities derived from illness and disability engulf them and may engulf the entire household. Roger Ressmeyer (1983) revealed that he involved himself in unwise relationships because he needed a partner's support and back-up work. Ironically, the independent public man can transform himself into a dependent patient at home. This stance allows the tyranny of the sickroom, promotes self-pity, and encourages physical dependence. Even when men do not become overly dependent, wives add hours to their day as they manage or collaborate in care by preparing special diets, assisting in bathing, dressing, grooming, completing the daily medical regimen, and providing rides (cf. Corbin and Strauss, 1984; Gerhardt and Brieskorn-Zink, 1986).

Strategies for Preserving Self

Whether or not a complete disjuncture exists between the public and private identities, most men tried to mute the effects of illness on socializing or working. They draw upon both taken-for-granted actions and explicit strategies to preserve their earlier selves and thus, maintain or recreate public and private identities. Their strategies involve careful considerations of timing, pacing, and staging to maintain appearances to others, and often, to self. Wives and partners are often collaborators in preserving self, as well as in care (cf. Corbin and Strauss, 1984, 1988).

When they needed to keep working, men attended closely to ways they could quite literally preserve themselves to do so. These men planned and managed their appearance because looking sick could cost them their bosses' confidence, co-workers' support, or even their jobs. When they felt that they would be disadvantaged in their hierarchy of men, they told no one that they had a serious illness (see also, Ressmeyer, 1983), avoided disclosing further episodes, or minimized their significance. When their co-workers demeaned them or complained that illness brought them special privileges, ill men came to view them as competitors or management spies. One middle-aged man with renal failure worked in a maintenance crew for the county. His cronies of thirty years turned against him for receiving less strenuous tasks for a few months after he had a heart attack. This man decided not to be beaten by his co-workers' attitudes and kept his job. But he refused his supervisor's offers to reassign him to prove that he could still do the strenuous work.[7]

Being able control the *logistics* for doing work, as well as the *amount* and *type* of work itself, allows men to preserve their work and themselves, including their assumptions about masculinity. Part of that control rests on also being able to control other people and the definition of the situation. An executive masked leaving the office early for his dialysis treatments by "attending meetings out of the office." Not even his secretary knew he was a dialysis patient. He believed that knowledge of his illness in the business community would reduce his stature as an aggressive competitor in the hierarchy of businessmen (cf. Sabo, 1992). A salesman completed his sales calls in the morning when he felt and looked fresher, and did paperwork at home in the afternoons when he could take rest breaks. A professor referred questions to several bright students when he felt short of breath. An administrator moved his office to a wing closer to the parking lot. In all these cases, controlling time, pace, space, information, and people gave these men more control over ensuing interaction, impression-management, and identity.

How do men preserve self when they cannot exert this type of control? Their embarrassment about visible markers of illness results in avoiding encounters beyond their inner circles. The executive above maintained a policy of not socializing with business associates. By not attending cocktail or swim parties, he hid his restricted diet and his dialysis shunt. A craftsman with emphysema hid how hard walking had become. He lagged behind anyone who might observe him struggling to climb a few stairs. Later, as his coughing and spitting fractured ordinary conversation, he refused social invitations and reduced his work to a few projects that he could complete alone at home.

Not everyone assumes that illness and disability will become melded with identity. Some men remain strikingly resourceful in finding ways to remain vitally involved and simultaneously to avoid having a stigmatized identity. Wheelchair use, for example, can give rise to developing a host of clever strategies for preserving self. One man arrived at social events early to position himself in an opportune location to see and greet friends. He found that people treated him as a commanding male when seated across from him but did not when they towered over him. When others were seated, he could position his body more forcefully in ways associated with manliness (Connell, 1983; Whitson, 1990). Such strategies preserve self as known in the past and, moreover, preserve assumptions about masculinity.

Discussion

Traditional assumptions of male identity, including an active, problem-solving stance, emphasis on personal power and autonomy, and bravery in the face of danger form a two-edged sword for men in chronic illness. On the one hand, these assumptions encourage men to take risks, to be active, and to try to recover, which certainly can prompt recreating a valued life after serious episodes of illness and therefore bolster self-esteem. On the other hand, these assumptions narrow the range of credible male behaviors for those who subscribe to them. Hence, they foster rigidity in stance and set the conditions for slipping into depression. Men's assumed difference between masculine identity and the "lesser" identities of women and children shrink as they lose ordinary "masculinizing practices" (Connell et al., 1982; Whitson, 1990).

Thus, an uneasy tension exists between valued identities and disparaged, that is, denigrated or shameful, ones. A man can gain a strengthened identity through experiencing illness or can suffer a diminished one. These are not mutually exclusive categories. Men often move back and forth depending on their situations and their perceptions of them. The grieving process in men may be negated or cause those who witness it such discomfort that they cannot give comfort. Men may express their grieving in fear and rage as well as in tears and sorrow. But for many men who experience progressive illness and disability, grieving, instead of being a process, sinks into becoming a permanent depression. Life becomes struggling to live while waiting to die.

What are the conditions that shape whether a man will reconstruct a positive identity or sink into depression? Certainly, whether or not a man defines having future possibilities makes an enormous difference. The men in my study primarily founded their preferred identities in action. Subsequently, if they could define no valued realm of action available to them and no way to preserve a valued self, the likelihood that they would slip into depression increased.

A final point: A more exacting look at the differential experience of men and women who suffer from serious chronic illnesses will deepen sociological and professional understandings of how they make sense of their lives. As the research in chronic illness grows, studying men and women comparatively in conjunction with marital, age, and social class statuses in addition to the type of illness can substantially refine sociological interpretations of the narratives of chronically ill people.

Acknowledgments

A version of this article was presented at the annual meetings of the Society for the Study of Social Problems in Pittsburgh, August 18-20, 1992. I am indebted to Candee Nagle, Norman K. Denzin, David F. Gordon, Mark Mikkelson, Don Sabo, and three anonymous reviewers for their comments on an earlier draft. I thank David F. Gordon and Don Sabo for encouraging me to work in this area.

Notes

1. Chronic illness means experiencing ongoing or intermittent, recurrent, irreversible, and often, degenerative, symptoms of a disease process (cf. Freund and McGuire, 1991). I focus on what it means to have a disease, not on objectivist medical definitions, and address two of Conrad's (1987) subtypes of chronic illness: "lived-with-illnesses" (e.g., multiple sclerosis, chronic fatigue syndrome, renal failure, diabetes, post-poliomyelitis syndrome), which force adapting without immediate life-threat and those "mortal illnesses" (e.g., heart attack, stroke, cancer) that sufferers view as life-threatening and have lasting consequences whether or not they (1) know about these consequences and (2) experience immediate symptoms.

2. When I first met the men, their ages ranged as follows: three below forty; six between forty and fifty; four between fifty and sixty; five between sixty and seventy, and the remaining two men were seventy-three and eighty-five. Ten men worked at least part-time; others had retired or were too ill to work. Their social class statuses include: eight men were working class or poor; six were middle-class, and four were upper-middle class. Ten men were married. Status attributes of the one-half of the sample with whom I kept in touch (5-8 years) changed slightly over time (e.g., financial and marital).

Semi-structured interviews elicited respondents' views of and feelings about their conditions, its course and implications, and effects on daily life (e.g., regimen, limitations, symptom control). These interviews frequently elicited disclosures that the men had not made to family or friends. For guidelines on intensive interviewing, see Lofland and Lofland (1984) and Seidman (1991).

3. Also, men report fewer illnesses and doctors' visits than women; men may not seek early care or routine checks that might result in averting crises (Freund and McGuire, 1991; Nathanson, 1989; Verbrugge, 1989; Verbrugge and Wingard, 1987; Waldron, 1976). Some men disattend to conditions like diabetes or high blood pressure until they become crises.

4. Note that I refer to *initial* crises here. A man who becomes identified as a trouble-maker, crock, mental case, mental incompetent, or an alcoholic will be hard-pressed to have his symptoms and views of treatment taken seriously (cf. Albrecht, 1992; Leiderman and Grisso, 1985; Millman, 1976; Plough, 1986).

7. Most working-class jobs permit little flexibility. Middle-class jobs, in contrast, allow men more control over timing, scheduling, pacing, and using space during work. Kotarba (1983) suggests that working-class laborers may be relatively unconcerned about staying on the job because they can net 80% of their pay if they can claim a job-related disability. Ten years later, many working-class jobs are without access to benefits and even if they are available, workers are hard-pressed to prove that their illness or disability is job-related. Thus, workers try to remain in their jobs.

References

Albrecht, Gary L. 1992. "The Social Experience of Disability." Pp. 1-18 in *Social Problems,* edited by Craig Calhoun and George Ritzer. New York: McGraw-Hill.

Beisser, Arnold R. 1989. *Flying Without Wings: Personal Reflections on Being Disabled.* New York: Doubleday.

Brooks, Nancy A. and Ronald R. Matson. 1982. "Social Psychological Adjustment to Multiple Sclerosis." *Social Science and Medicine* 16: 2129-2135.

Charmaz, Kathy. 1983. "The Grounded Theory Method: An Explication and Interpretation." Pp. 109-126 in *Contemporary Field Research,* edited by Robert M. Emerson. Boston: Little Brown.

_____. 1987. "Struggling for a Self: Identity Levels of the Chronically Ill." Pp. 283-321 in *Research in the Sociology of Health Care: The Experience and Management of Chronic Illness,* Vol. 6, edited by Julius A. Roth and Peter Conrad. Greenwich, CT: JAI.

_____. 1990. "Discovering Chronic Illness: Using Grounded Theory." *Social Science & Medicine* 30: 1161-1172.

_____. 1991. *Good Days, Bad Days: The Self in Chronic Illness and Time.* New Brunswick, NJ: Rutgers University Press.

Connell, R. W. 1983. *Which Way Is Up?: Essays on Class, Sex and Culture.* Sydney, Australia: Allen & Unwin.

_____. 1987. *Gender & Power: Society, the Person and Sexual Politics.* Stanford, CA: Stanford University Press.

Connell, R. W., D. J. Ashenden, S. Kessler, and G. W. Dowsett. 1982. *Making the Difference: Schools, Families and Social Division.* Sydney, Australia: Allen & Unwin.

Conrad, Peter. 1987. "The Experience of Illness: Recent and New Directions." Pp. 1-31 in *Research in the Sociology of Health Care: The Experience and Management of Chronic Illness,* Vol. 6, edited by Julius A. Roth and Peter Conrad. Greenwich, CT: JAI.

Corbin, Juliet M. and Anselm L. Strauss. 1984. "Collaboration: Couples Working Together to Manage Chronic Illness." *Image* 4: 109-115.

_____. 1988. *Unending Work and Care: Managing Chronic Illness at Home.* San Francisco: Jossey-Bass.

Cousins, Norman. 1983. *The Healing Heart: Antidotes to Panic and Helplessness.* New York: Avon.

Cowie, Bill. 1976. "The Patient's Perception of His Heart Attack." *Social Science & Medicine* 10: 87-96.

Dahlberg, Charles Clay and Joseph Jaffe. 1977. *Stroke: A Doctor's Personal Story of His Recovery.* New York: Norton.

Denzin, Norman K. 1989. *Interpretive Biography.* Newbury Park, CA: Sage.

_____. 1991. *Images of Postmodern Society.* London: Sage.

Fiore, Neil A. 1984. *The Road Back to Health.* New York: Bantam.

Foster, Lee. 1978. "Man and Machine: Life Without Kidneys." Pp. 522-526 in *Dominant Issues in Medical Sociology,* edited by Howard D. Schwartz and Cary S. Kart. Reading, MA: Addison-Wesley.

Frank, Arthur. 1991. *At the Will of the Body.* New York: Houghlin-Mifflin.

———. 1993. "The Rhetoric of Self-Change: Illness Experience as Narrative." *The Sociological Quarterly* 34: 39-52.

Freund, Peter E. S. and Meredith B. McGuire. 1991. *Health, Illness, and the Social Body.* Englewood Cliffs, NJ: Prentice-Hall.

Gecas, Viktor. 1982. "The Self-Concept." *Annual Review of Sociology* 8: 1-33.

Gerhardt, Uta and Marianne Brieskorn-Zink. 1986. "The Normalization of Hemodialysis at Home." Pp. 271-317 in *Research in the Sociology of Health Care: The Adoption and Social Consequences of Medical Technologies,* Vol. 5, edited by Julius A. Roth and Sheryl B. Ruzek. Greenwich, CT: JAI.

Glaser, Barney G. 1978. *Theoretical Sensitivity.* Mill Valley, CA: The Sociology Press.

Glaser, Barney G. and Anselm L. Strauss. 1967. *The Discovery of Grounded Theory.* Chicago: Aldine.

Goffman, Erving. 1961. *Encounters.* New York: Bobbs-Merrill.

———. 1963. *Stigma.* Englewood Cliffs, NJ: Prentice Hall.

Gordon, David. 1990. "Testicular Cancer: Passage to New Priorities." Pp. 234-247 in *Clinical Sociological Perspectives on Illness & Loss,* edited by Elizabeth J. Clark, Jan M. Fritz, and Patricia P. Rieker. Philadelphia: Charles Press.

Herzlich, Claudine and Janine Pierret. 1987. *Illness and Self in Society.* Baltimore: Johns Hopkins University Press.

Hewitt, John. 1989. *Dilemmas of the American Self.* Philadelphia: Temple University Press.

Hirsch, Ernest. 1977. *Starting Over.* Hanover, MA: Christopher.

Hodgins, Eric. 1964. *Episode: Report on the Accident Inside My Skull.* New York: Atheneum.

Husserl, Edmund. 1970. *The Crisis of the European Sciences and Transcendental Phenomenology.* Evanston, IL: Northwestern University Press.

Jaques, Elliot. 1965. "Death and the Mid-Life Crisis." *International Journal of Psychoanalysis* 46: 502-514.

Johnson, Joy L. 1991. "Learning to Live Again: The Process of Adjustment Following a Heart Attack." Pp. 13-88 in *The Illness Experience,* edited by Janice M. Morse and Joy L. Johnson. Newbury Park, CA: Sage.

Karp, David. 1988. "A Decade of Reminders: Changing Age Consciousness Between Fifty and Sixty Years Old." *The Gerontologist* 28: 727-738.

Kelleher, David. 1988. "Coming to Terms with Diabetes: Coping Strategies and Non-Compliance." Pp. 155-187 in *Living With Chronic Illness,* edited by Robert Anderson and Michael Bury. London: Unwin Hyman.

Kelly, Orville E. 1977. "Make Today Count." Pp. 181-194 in *New Meanings of Death,* edited by Herman Fiefel. New York: McGraw-Hill.

Kleinman, Arthur. 1988. *The Illness Narratives: Suffering, Healing, & the Human Condition.* New York: Basic Books.

Kotarba, Joseph A. 1983. *Chronic Pain: Its Social Dimensions.* Beverly Hills, CA: Sage.

Lear, Martha. 1980. *Heartsounds.* New York: Simon & Schuster.

Leiderman, Deborah B. and Jean-Anne Grisso. 1985. "The Gomer Phenomenon." *Journal of Health and Social Behavior* 26: 222-231.

LeMaistre, Joanne. 1985. *Beyond Rage: The Emotional Impact of Chronic Illness.* Oak Park, IL: Alpine Guild.

Lewis, Kathleen. 1985. *Successful Living With Chronic Illness.* Wayne, NJ: Avery.

Levinson, Daniel J., C. Darrow, E. Klein, M. Levinson, and B. McKee. 1978. *The Seasons of a Man's Life.* New York: Knopf.

Lofland, John and Lyn H. Lofland. 1984. *Analyzing Social Settings.* Belmont, CA: Wadsworth.

Messner, Michael A. and Donald F. Sabo. 1990. "Toward a Critical Feminist Reappraisal of Sport, Men, and the Gender Order." Pp. 1-15 in *Sport, Men, and the Gender Order: Critical Feminist Perspectives,* edited by Michael A. Messner and Donald F. Sabo. Champaign, IL: Human Kinetics Books.

Millman, Marcia. 1976. *The Unkindest Cut.* New York: William Morrow.

Murphy, Robert F. 1987. *The Body Silent.* New York: Henry Holt.

Nathan, Laura E. 1990. "Coping With Uncertainty: Family Members' Adaptations During Cancer Remission." Pp. 219-233 in *Clinical Sociological Perspectives on Illness & Loss,* edited by Elizabeth J. Clark, Jan M. Fritz, and Patricia P. Rieker. Philadelphia: Charles Press.

Nathanson, Constance A. 1989. "Sex, Illness, and Medical Care: A Review of Data, Theory, and Method." Pp. 46-70 in *Perspectives in Medical Sociology,* edited by Phil Brown. Belmont, CA: Wadsworth.

Peyrot, Mark, James F. McMurry, Jr., and Richard Hedges. 1988. "Marital Adjustment to Adult Diabetes: Interpersonal Congruence and Spouse Satisfaction. *Journal of Marriage and the Family* 50: 363-376.

Pitzele, Sefra Kobrin. 1985. *We Are Not Alone: Learning to Live With Chronic Illness.* New York: Workman.

Plough, Alonzo. 1986. *Borrowed Time: Artificial Organs and the Politics of Extending Lives.* Philadelphia: Temple University Press.

Register, Cherie. 1987. *Living With Chronic Illness.* New York: Free Press.

Reif, Laura. 1975. "Ulcerative Colitis: Strategies for Managing Life." Pp 81-88 in *Chronic Illness and the Quality of Life,* edited by Anselm L. Strauss. St. Louis: Mosby.

Ressmeyer, Roger. 1983. "A Day to Day Struggle." In *California Living, San Francisco Examiner and Chronicle,* July 10: 1-5.

Sabo, Don F. 1990. "Men, Death Anxiety, and Denial: Critical Feminist Interpretations of Adjustment to Mastectomy." Pp. 71-84 in *Clinical Sociological Perspectives on Illness & Loss,* edited by Elizabeth J. Clark, Jan M. Fritz, and Patricia P. Rieker. Philadelphia: Charles.

———. 1992. "Rethinking Men's Health and Illness: The Relevance of Gender Studies." Paper presented, Society for the Study of Social Problems, Pittsburgh, August 18-20.

Schneider, Joseph W. and Peter Conrad. 1983. *Having Epilepsy.* Philadelphia: Temple University Press.

Seidman, I.E. 1991. *Interviewing as Qualitative Research: A Guide for Researchers in Education and the Social Sciences.* New York: Teachers College Press.

Speedling, Edward J. 1982. *Heart Attack: The Family Response at Home and in the Hospital.* New York: Tavistock.

Strauss, Anselm. 1987. *Qualitative Analysis for Social Scientists.* New York: Cambridge University Press.

Strauss, Anselm and Juliet Corbin. 1990. *Basics of Qualitative Research.* Newbury Park, CA: Sage.

Strauss, Anselm L., Juliet Corbin, Shizuko Fagerhaugh, Barney G. Glaser, David Maines, Barbara Suczek, and Carolyn Wiener. 1984. *Chronic Illness and the Quality of Life,* 2nd ed. St. Louis: Mosby.

Strong, Maggie. 1988. *Mainstay.* Boston: Little Brown.

Tannen, Deborah. 1990. *You Just Don't Understand: Women and Men in Conversation.* New York: Ballantine.

Turner, Ralph. 1976. "The Real Self: From Institution to Impulse." *American Journal of Sociology* 81: 989-1016.

Verbrugge, Lois M. 1985. "Gender and Health: An Update on Hypotheses and Evidence." *Journal of Health and Social Behavior* 26: 156-182.

_____. 1989. "The Twain Meet: Empirical Explanations of Sex Differences in Health and Mortality." *Journal of Health and Social Behavior* 30: 282-304.

Verbrugge, Lois and Deborah L. Wingard. 1987. "Sex Differentials in Health and Mortality." *Women and Health* 12: 103-145.

Waldron, Ingrid. 1976. "Why Do Women Live Longer Than Men?" *Social Science and Medicine* 10: 349-362.

Weigert, Andrew J. 1986. "The Social Production of Identity: Metatheoretical Foundations." *The Sociological Quarterly* 27: 165-183.

Whitson, David. 1990. "Sport in the Social Construction of Masculinity." Pp. 19-30 in *Sport, Men, and the Gender Order: Critical Feminist Perspectives*, edited by Michael A. Messner and Donald F. Sabo. Champaign, IL: Human Kinetics Books.

Wiener, Carolyn J. 1975. "The Burden of Arthritis." Pp. 71-80 in *Chronic Illness and the Quality of Life*, edited by Anselm L. Strauss. St. Louis: Mosby.

Wulf, Helen Harlan. 1979. *Aphasia, My World Alone*. Detroit: Wayne State University Press.

Zink, Jean B. 1992. "Adjusting to Early and Late-Onset Disability." *Generations* 16: 59-60.

Zola, Irving K. 1982. *Missing Pieces: A Chronicle of Living With a Disability*. Philadelphia: Temple University Press.

3

A Social Worlds
Research Adventure

The Case of Reproductive Science

ADELE E. CLARKE

Commentary

Grounded theory methodology and methods are so much a part of some
researchers' thinking that they don't bother especially to address them when
writing up their research. Their attention is elsewhere—on theory or substance, for instance. The chapter by Adele Clarke is one example of this. She
was a student of Anselm Strauss and when he retired replaced him at the
Department of Social and Behavioral Sciences, San Francisco, carrying on
the same research tradition.

In this unusual chapter, her emphasis is on the development, through her
research, of theories about both social worlds and work. She describes this
development of theories in combination with the narrative of her own "research

© 1990 by Indiana University Press. Reprinted from *Theories of Science in Society,* S. Cozzens
and T. Gieryn (Eds.), pp. 15-35, by permission.

adventure." Her discussion in the Conclusions section of the chapter addresses the relationship of existing theory and her specific research, touching explicitly also on the role of theory in discovery, and the fun of doing research, as well as noting that "scholars are thinkers and keep thinking, which is, after all, the exciting part [of your research]." These are all major emphases of grounded theory methodology (see Strauss & Corbin, 1990).

The body of Clarke's chapter explicitly addresses or touches on all of those issues, and several others such as variation, "openness," and insight. You can see her creativity in using different kinds of material—documents (such as relevant historical ones and laboratory records, and autobiographies). She also uses interviews, and field notes taken from observations at biological laboratories. You can sense her making comparisons along provisionally significant dimensions: "Wondering whether important differences existed in the kinds of problems pursued in biological, medical, and agricultural research settings, I charted major research problems in each. The organization of the problem structure of reproductive science did vary across the three professions that addressed it. Problems in the life sciences can be considered analytically by organism, by organ system, by location (e.g., biogeography), by environment . . . and so on. . . . These different foci . . . " Note also her acute theoretical sensitivity to symbolic interactionism, and some of its assumptions, such as about interaction itself, and her explicit attempt to elaborate the principal concepts and thrust of social world theory.

Her attitude toward and use of social worlds theory is especially admirable; she is stimulated and guided by it, but not in the slightest subservient to it. Yet, in this chapter we can see writ large that theory does not just "emerge" from data; rather, data itself is constructed from many events observed or read about or heard about, constructed in a highly selective series of actions, and interpreted all along the course of the research project. For the research interpretations, actors' own words and interpretations are necessary, respected, but recast in new and analytic terms.

* * *

Introduction

All research is guided by an approach and a perspective—assumptions about how one can learn and know, the nature of causality, concepts of change, and the proper unit of analysis. Theoretic and methodological principles thus guide and inform researchers in the sociology of science in their processes of discovery (e.g., Collins and Restivo, 1983; Gerson, 1983). This essay is a research adventure story about how one such approach and perspective—social worlds theory—guided my research on the emergence of reproductive science in the United States before World War II.[1]

Blumer (1954) finds two basic approaches used in sociological research. In the first, the goal is to develop precise and fixed procedures that will yield stable and definitive empirical content. To this end, data are abstracted from their social milieus and standardized techniques, experimental arrangements and mathematical categories are used to generate *definitive concepts.* The goal is to return to the natural social world with these definitive concepts which refer precisely to what is common to a class of objects with a clear definition of attributes. Such concepts can then be interrelated to build theory.

The second basic approach involves direct study of the natural social world and data are not abstracted from it. Rather, the research is guided by a set of *sensitizing concepts*—less specific suggestive ideas about what might be potentially fruitful to examine and consider, an emergent meaningful vocabulary that alerts the researcher to promising avenues of investigation. Here the empirical data are then used to refine and improve the sensitizing concepts and their interrelations to build theories that better capture and reflect the empirical terrain. It is important in this approach to attend carefully to the range of variation of a given phenomenon and to any negative cases, as these are strong sources for revising concepts and refining understanding of their interrelations (Blumer, 1969; Glaser and Strauss, 1967; Glaser, 1978; Schatzman and Strauss, 1973; Strauss, 1987). The researcher should also investigate all the domains in which the phenomenon is embedded. What are often elsewhere considered "surrounding" contexts are, in this approach, viewed as the intrinsic *structural conditions* under which the phenomenon exists and therefore central to understanding it. Such structural conditions are immediately *within* the situation.

Blumer (1954) argues, and I agree, that most sociological concepts are sensitizing rather than definitive. Moreover, while definitive concepts are useful in many areas, they remain removed from social life while naturalistic research has the advantage of remaining in close and continuous contact with the natural social world. In my research, I used the concepts of social worlds theory as sensitizing concepts in Blumer's terms.

The conceptual roots of social worlds theory lie in the Chicago School of symbolic interactionist sociology (e.g., Blumer, 1978; Hughes, 1958, 1971; Park, 1952; Strauss, 1971). In this tradition, social groups of some kind structurally situate individuals in society. W. I. Thomas (1914; Thomas and Znaniecki, 1927) argued persuasively that the proper unit of analysis for sociology was "social wholes." Initially focused on local communities, Chicago interactionists now address such "social wholes" as medicine (e.g., Freidson, 1968; Strauss et al., 1985), the arts (Becker, 1982; Faulkner, 1971, 1983), and sciences (Busch, 1982; Busch and Lacy, 1983; Fujimura, 1987, 1988a; Gerson, 1983; Glaser, 1964; Star, 1989; Strauss and Rainwater, 1962; Volberg, 1983).

In a fundamental sense, the sciences serve as substantive areas—social wholes or social worlds—through which to pursue classic Chicago School sociological research in work, organizations, occupations, and professions. New approaches to the study of work (discussed below) have been developed and integrated with social worlds approaches toward enhancing our understanding of scientific work organization (Clarke and Gerson, 1990).

Because social worlds theory is itself a relatively recent development in the Chicago symbolic interactionist tradition and moves it in new directions, I next provide a brief overview of its origins and development followed by a discussion of social worlds theory applied to the sciences. Then, once you the reader are "sensitized" to the concepts, we embark upon a research adventure into the uncharted territory of reproductive science before World War II. Here I discuss my research processes as I constructed the first sociological map of this terrain and outline my major conclusions. The usefulness of social worlds theory for the sociology of science and vice versa is taken up in the conclusions.

Developing Social Worlds Theory

Chicago School sociology begins from certain assumptions in pragmatist philosophy. I have italicized the major concepts generated by contributors to social worlds theory to highlight them for readers to whom this may be a new territory.

The Chicago Tradition

Pragmatist philosophy and sociology of the Chicago tradition "insisted on the unity of thought and action, of theory and the real world" (Kurtz, 1984:2). The meanings of phenomena, including social worlds, are to be found in their embeddedness in relationships—in society. For something to be socially (including scientifically) significant or "true," pragmatists emphasized, a number of people must go along with it—agree at least in principle and for whatever reasons. In the words of James (1914:202), " . . . Pragmatism insists that truth in the singular is only a collective name for truths in the plural, these consisting always of a series of definite events. . . . " Whatever "truth" exists lies at the intersection of multiple perspectives on a given phenomenon. "Truth" then is relative to perspective.

Mead (1938/1972:518) emphasized the social nature of the organization of meaning: "The universality of meanings implies, then, the organized medium within which it obtains and prevails, what is logically referred to as a universe of discourse." "Truth," then, is a social phenomenon. Or, in the words of Lily Tomlin's wonderful bag lady in her "Search for Intelligent Life in the Universe": "What is reality anyway? Nothing but a collective hunch."

At the heart of the notion of a *universe of discourse* is the assumption that people would not concern themselves with a given phenomenon if they were not intending to *do* something with it or about it. "Pragmatism defines 'agreeing' to mean certain ways of 'working,' be they actual or potential" (James, 1914:218). Work or collective action of some kind is the business of a universe of discourse—a social world.

Pragmatist philosophers also emphasized the ultimate significance of the interrelations of phenomena and the processual aspects of knowing. As Dewey stated (1910:117-18, emphases in original).

> All knowledge, all science . . . aims to grasp the meaning of objects and events, and this process always consists of taking them out of their apparent brute isolation as events, and finding them to be parts of some larger whole *suggested by them*, which, in turn, *accounts for, explains, interprets them;* i.e., renders them significant.

The "larger whole suggested by them" draws our attention to the need to examine the contexts or structural conditions of given phenomena. But Dewey is pushing us even further, implying that these are actually the relationships through which meaning is constructed and which we as investigators must grasp in order to interpret the phenomenon.

In practice, early Chicago sociology focused on breaking new empirical ground and linking theory and research in a comprehensive approach encompassing multiple levels of analysis—from micro through macro. Investigators sought patterns of organization of "social wholes" within natural areas of Chicago, their "sociological laboratory" (Kurtz, 1984:4). Their work centered on the nature of *communities* of different types and temporal durations. These communities included gangs (Thrasher, 1927/1963), ghettos (Wirth, 1928), taxi dancehalls (Cressey, 1932), and peasant immigrant communities (Thomas and Znaniecki, 1927). Unpublished Chicago theses addressed such topics as the stockyards community, the "higher life" of social elites, a strike, and a real estate board (Faris, 1967:135-50). These studies of "social wholes"—communities, collective activities, and occupations—centered on the *group nature of the interaction.* Eubank noted in 1927 (Meltzer, Petras, and Reynolds, 1975:42) that it was characteristic of the "newer" sociology "to make the group the focal center and to build up from its discoveries in concrete situations, a knowledge of the whole. . . . [T]his newer approach stresses intensive examination of the interactions that take place in the group." Researchers in this tradition continued the study of groups through studies of work, occupations, and professions of many kinds during the 1950s and 1960s; these studies also moved from (Bulmer, 1984) local to national and international groups (Fisher and Strauss, 1978a:11, 1978b), and increasingly attended to the relationships of those groups to other "social wholes," the interactions of collective actors.

Social Worlds Theory

Shibutani (1955, 1962) transformed community studies into social worlds studies and initiated explicit social worlds theory development. For him *reference groups* became the organizers of social life and individual commitments. Reference groups generate shared *perspectives* which form the basis for collective action organized through the construction of *social worlds.*

Becker (1960) extended sociological understanding of the concept of *commitment* as a basis for social action. In a sense, commitments imply the notion of a "going concern" (Hughes, 1971) in which certain assumptions about what activities are important and what will be done can be taken for granted. Becker (1974, 1982) and Strauss (1978) then defined social worlds as groups with shared commitments to certain *activities* sharing resources of many kinds to achieve their goals. Social worlds form fundamental "building blocks" of collective action and are the principal affiliative mechanisms through which people organize social life. A social world is an interactive unit, a "universe of regularized mutual response," communication or discourse; it is not bounded by geography or formal membership "but by the limits of effective communication" (Shibutani, 1955:566). "Society as a whole," then, can be conceptualized as consisting of a mosaic of social worlds that both touch and interpenetrate. More specifically, in Strauss's words (1978:122).

In each social world, at least one primary *activity* (along with related activities) is strikingly evident, i.e, . . . researching, collecting. There are *sites* where activities occur; hence space and a shaped landscape are relevant. *Technology* (inherited or innovative means of carrying out the social world's activities) is always involved. . . . In social worlds at their outset, there may be only a temporary division of labor, but once underway, *organizations* inevitably evolve to further one aspect or another of the world's activities.

People typically participate in a number of social worlds simultaneously (Unruh, 1979).

There are three major types of social worlds (Gerson, 1983; Kling and Gerson, 1977, 1978):

1. *production worlds* where the activities produce something (e.g., manufacturing and industrial worlds; scholarly and scientific worlds producing knowledge);
2. *communal worlds* where the activities focus on the establishment and mainte- nance of communities of people committed to each other and to their shared goals (e.g., ethnic communities, hobby worlds);
3. *social movements* where the activities focus on shared commitments to alter the larger world in which they are embedded (e.g., the birth control movement, the antinuclear movement).

Mixed worlds are both possible and common. For example, the wide social world of the life sciences is both a production world (producing knowledge) and a communal world (producing shared commitments to the advancement of scientific work). Social worlds characteristically generate *ideologies* about how their work should be done and *debates* about both their own activities and others' activities that may affect them (Strauss et al., 1964; Becker, 1982).

Participation in social worlds usually remains highly fluid. Some partici- pants cluster around the core of the world and mobilize those around them (Hughes, 1971:54). These *entrepreneurs* (Becker, 1963) typically remain at the core over time while others move in and out of participation or situate themselves more peripherally.

The structure of social worlds is also highly fluid. Every complex social world characteristically has subdivisions or subworlds. Two or more worlds may *intersect* to form a new world, or one world may *segment* into two or more worlds (Strauss, 1982).[2] Such structural changes generally derive from processes of negotiation, conflict, and exchange. In fact, social worlds are structural units—the structural framework—within which the *negotiated social order* (Strauss, 1979) is itself constructed and reconstructed.

In the social world perspective of Shibutani (1955, 1962), individuals are the units of analysis and are studied in relation to their social worlds. In contrast, for Strauss (1978), Becker (1974, 1982), Gerson (1983), and myself (Clarke, 1985, 1988a, 1990a,b), the social worlds and subworlds themselves become the units of analysis in the study of collective action. Individual actors, of course, compose social worlds, but commonly act as part of or on behalf of their social worlds. Personal interests are also at stake, but key sociological differences emerge when investigators focus on studying the social world's *work activities* and their organization rather than individuals. Placing work in the analytic foreground permits the analysis of social worlds qua worlds.[3]

Industries are social worlds organized around the production of a group of related goods or services—a core production activity (Kling and Gerson, 1977, 1978). Particularly important intersections for production worlds are the *markets* for the goods or services. An important question here is "[W]hat is the pattern of markets in which the world is engaged, and how do these 'map' onto the pattern of [interactions and] intersections among subworlds?" (Gerson, quoted in Strauss et al., 1985:288).

Both within and across social worlds an *arena* of concern may form where all the groups that care (in the pragmatist sense) about a given issue come together. Worlds involved in an area may be knowledge producers, audiences, sponsors, consumers, markets, industries, policymakers, governmental regulatory bodies, and so on. In the arena "various issues are debated, negotiated, fought out, forced and manipulated by representatives" of the worlds or subworlds (Strauss, 1978:124). The analyst needs to elucidate which worlds and subworlds come together in a particular arena and why. For production worlds, all of their markets are typically involved in arenas as organizational entities because of their sensitivity to changes in production patterns. Such changes typically promote a realignment or reorganization of the worlds and subworlds involved in the arena (Gerson, 1983). In fact, market structures are actually a specialized subtype of arena for production worlds wherein the core questions concern "buying" and "selling," broadly conceived.

Very important activities within all social worlds are establishing and maintaining *boundaries* between worlds and gaining social *legitimation* for the world itself (Strauss, 1982: cf. Gieryn, 1983). These processes involve the social construction of the particular world and a variety of claims-making activities (Becker, 1970, 1974). The very history of the social world is commonly constructed or reconstructed in the process (Strauss, 1982).

A *natural history,* career, or trajectory approach is useful in analyzing both scientific and nonscientific worlds—at some stage of becoming, maintaining, expanding, or deteriorating. Some worlds become *going concerns* (Hughes, 1958, 1971), established and viable social groups with collective commitments, actions, and activities. Production worlds are *enterprises* embedded in specific product and service markets with established audiences, sponsors, and consumers (Clarke, 1985).

Sociologists can examine the fluidity of social worlds via social movements analyses. Bucher and Strauss (1961) and Bucher (1962, 1988) extended social movements analysis to include changes *within* professions and disciplines. Blumer (1978) alerted us to the origins of movements in social dissatisfaction, unrest, and agitation. Social worlds commonly contain conflict, contention, and dissatisfaction and are open to change through both internal and external social movements. Reform movements within a discipline or profession provide examples, such as the movement for "scientific" medicine within the medical profession and the life sciences at the turn of the century (e.g., Numbers, 1980; Sabin, 1934).

Scientific Social Worlds

Scientific social worlds are primarily *production worlds* in which the product is knowledge and its actual or potential applications. Production worlds—be they in art or computing or biology—shape and organize the work commitments and conventions or "standard operating procedures" of their participants (Becker, 1970:261-74, 1982; Kling and Gerson, 1977, 1978).

Scientific social worlds shape the development and direction of scientific research traditions (Gerson, 1983). Solving the problems scientists seek to address shapes and organizes all the other activities in a field of scientific inquiry. It forms the touchstone against which all decisions are ultimately made and around which essentially all conflicts are fought out.

Scientific work, then, centers on problem solving. How shall we examine this work? Over the past decade, a number of investigators who had focused on occupations and professions have turned their sociological eye toward concrete work and its organization and have attempted to distinguish these concerns from earlier studies (e.g. Clarke, 1987; Clarke and Fujimura, in preparation; Freidson, 1976; Fujimura, 1986, 1987, 1988b; Gerson, 1983;

Strauss, 1985, 1988; Strauss et al., 1985). They argue that basically what have passed for studies of work have actually been studies of occupations and professions and/or examinations of work problems only in relation to problems of occupations or professions. Work tasks and activities have not been examined directly in their own right.

These analysts offer a fresh alternative approach that centers on studying concrete tasks and activities—what is actually done. Their efforts have revealed types of work not previously viewed as work per se (e.g., patients' work in medical settings), hidden work (Hazan, 1985), the complex organization of work tasks and activities, and the negotiation of the actual division of labor (rather than, for example, professional claims-making about it). While not necessarily integral to social worlds theory, this new focus has certainly been central to the Chicago interactionist study of scientific social worlds to date.

To integrate social worlds theory with this emerging interactionist sociology of work in order to focus on science, forms of work organization must be laid out. All activities that address a given set of coherent and cohesive problems constitute a *line of work*—a scientific social world (Gerson, 1983). The concrete work of scientific social worlds is generally organized as shown in the table below. While we can pull them apart analytically, these forms merge, blend, fuse, and muddle in actual practice and in terms of the emergence of meaning.

Forms of Work Organization	*Example in Science*
Production-based social world	Line of work (subdiscipline or specialty) with an established problem structure
Programs	A set of problems to be studied in a long-term, somewhat organized fashion
Projects	Shorter-term sets of related experiments
Activities	Single experiments, report preparation
Tasks	Sets of tasks to achieve completion of an activity

Lines of work are themselves organized into larger scientific social worlds—disciplines and professions. In fact, lines of work initially derive from subparts of those worlds that have cohered around new or emergent families of related problems. Scientist entrepreneurs then construct the lines of work into identifiable subworlds as specialty areas.

Whether X is a world or subworld depends upon one's analytic focus of the moment. The sociological goal is to understand the organization and realignment of work and relationships within and among lines of work and the transformation of one kind of work into another over time as scientists solve, shelve, refocus, and reorganize problems. Change—the reconstruction of meaning—is the constant.

Discovering Reproductive Science: A Research Adventure

Now that you are "sensitized" to the concepts, we are packed and ready to embark on a research adventure. Here I attempt to tell two stories: one about the emergence of reproductive science in the United States and another about my processes of discovery using social worlds theory as a guide and its sensitizing concepts to light the way. This reflexive effort relates very partial stories. The processes I describe were not always clear to me at the time, nor painless. Moreover, I could not have written the earlier sections of this paper then as clearly as today because the research process itself rendered social worlds theory vital and valid for me and laid bare the interconnections and overall coherence of the approach.

I focus here on concepts in social worlds theory that helped to illuminate basic social processes in disciplinary, subdisciplinary, and professional emergence and development, an important and growing area of science studies.[4] My goal was to generate what Robert Ezra Park (Fisher and Strauss, 1978a:12) called "The Big News" about the emergence of reproductive science. I was constructing the first sociological map of the pre-World War II American reproductive science territory, and I sought to chart the land masses, bodies of water, deserts, mountains, and fertile areas. My highly open-ended guiding research questions were suggested by Strauss (1978:92): "What was the social world of reproductive science before World War II all about?" and "What was the structure of relationship among the various related social worlds?" Reproduction refers here to sexual reproduction of predominantly mammalian species. I eventually had to limit the scope of research I analyzed to "basic" research (e.g., Restivo, 1974; Graham et al., 1983), excluding most clinical and applied investigations.

What did I have to work with? Very little attention had been paid to the historical development of reproductive science in the United States. Major contributions in the secondary literature had focused on Great Britain (Borell, 1976, 1978, 1985, 1987; Hall, 1974, 1976), earlier eras (Farley, 1982), endocrinology (e.g., Medvei, 1982), citation analyses (Studer and Chubin,

1976), and related lines of research (e.g., Churchill, 1979; Greep et al., 1976, 1977; Maienschein, 1984). In addition to published scientific reports, major contributions in the primary literature consisted of "insider histories"—accounts of events, biographies, and autobiographies by participating scientists.[5]

In pursuing this topic I was intentionally following the dictum of Strauss (1967) to "study the unstudied." I was also "unstudied" in biology in general, much less reproductive science in particular. I did have some background in the histories of biology and medicine and these provided obvious starting points. My first question was "When and how did modern reproductive science get off the ground as a coherent scientific social world?" Initially I assumed that early reproductive scientists would have framed their pursuits as a line of work with an explicit problem structure in the late nineteenth century (c. 1880-1900) as physiological research in biology and medicine had focused on various other organ systems at that time. I began reading on the life sciences in that era. I was wrong.

An Intersection

Modern reproductive science initially got off the ground in Great Britain with publication in 1910 of the first English-language book on reproductive science, Marshall's *Physiology of Reproduction*. My somewhat belated discovery and analysis of Marshall's book was my first big breakthrough. From a pragmatist philosophical perspective, Marshall (1910:1-2, emphasis added) laid out in crystal-clear language both *who* cared enough about reproductive problems to do something about them and *what* needed to be done:

> Yet generative physiology forms the basis of gynaecological science, and must ever bear a close relation to the study of animal breeding. In writing this volume . . . I have attempted . . . to co-ordinate or give *a connected account* of various groups of ascertained facts which hither to have not been brought into relation. . . . [The book is addressed] primarily to the trained biologist, but it is hoped that it may be of interest also to medical men engaged in gynaecological practice, as well as veterinarians and breeders of animals.

Upon reading this, my sociological ears perked up, for to both Marshall and me the *social world* of reproductive science included biological, medical, and agricultural investigators and practitioners. Reproductive science *mattered* to all of them, whether they were centrally or peripherally engaged.

Given this and much other evidence, I realized not only that Marshall's book signaled the emergence of a multidisciplinary reproductive science but also that reproductive science was itself a cross-professional effort. In social worlds theory, it was an *intersection* that "arise[s] when two or more lines of work come together—more precisely, when a single activity or cluster of closely related activities simultaneously comes to be part of two or more lines of work" (Gerson, 1983:363).

Of course, considerable prior scientific research on reproductive problems had been done on a piecemeal basis in the professional and institutional contexts of biology, medicine, and agriculture. What occurred during the emergence era from 1910 to 1925 was the development of both a newly framed problem structure and an intersection among the subworlds focused on reproductive science in each profession—a new social world.

I will discuss the intersectional nature of the reproductive research enterprise first. Participation in an intersectional effort depends upon who can and who cannot afford to make commitments to it, individually, collectively, and structurally. The key sociological questions here were "What made this intersection possible at this time?" and "Why was the intersection so intimate and harmonious?"

I gradually came to understand that it was the relative institutional and professional autonomy of scientists in biology, medicine, and agriculture that greatly facilitated the intersection. Each field was sufficiently established with its own special markets, audiences, sponsors, and consumers bound to them by tradition and interest. They could intersect to create a broader, stronger, and more legitimate endeavor while simultaneously retaining their particular institutional and general professional independence, autonomy, and economic market bases. For each group during this period, the social structure of the intersection made the others *allies* (Latour, 1987) more often than competitors. Moreover, very little was known about reproductive processes. It was a newly opened territory with lots of problems to explore and room for many investigators. This also helped to make the intersection intimate and harmonious.

Largely through archival research (examination of correspondence, grants, course listings, and other documents) I found that this intersection constituted relatively stable milieus through which resources flowed. Investigators shared both scientific and practical information and resources. For example, they shared skills and techniques: obstetric and gynecologic texts helped researchers perform surgeries on laboratory animals. They shared live and fresh research materials and specimens and information on means of acquiring and maintaining them as well as on their surgical manipulation (Clarke, 1987). The classic example here is the hypophysectomized rat (that is, rats from which the researcher has removed the anterior pituitary gland), which became a key laboratory animal in reproductive science.[6] And they shared research ideas and papers. In fact, early in this century many university libraries did not receive all the major journals, so the archival record reveals constant requests for papers.

When, in 1921, the Rockefeller Foundation began its fiscal support of reproductive science through the National Research Council's Committee for Research on Problems of Sex (NRC/CRPS), money flowed fairly widely, although groups of investigators rather than lone individuals received the bulk of the funds (Aberle and Corner, 1953). In addition, support and sentiments such as prestige and loyalty flowed among the varied work and professional settings.

A Problem Structure

Returning to Marshall's book (1910), the "facts" that he "brought into relation" formed the first statement of the *problem structure,* the long-term problem foci of reproductive science. In the apt words of one of Marshall's students many years later (Parkes, 1952/1966:x), the book "mapped the present and pointed the way to the future." Marshall's map showed that the study of basic reproductive physiology was just getting under way in 1910 and that "internal secretions" (as hormones were often called) might play significant roles in reproductive processes. But Marshall was an agriculturally oriented British physiologist and I wanted to study American reproductive science! What had happened in the United States?

Insider histories and published research again provided my initial clues. I soon found the first statement by an American of the problem structure of reproductive science. Frank R. Lillie presented it to the NRC/CRPS in 1922 (Aberle and Corner, 1953:102-4), the same year the second edition of Marshall's text came out. When I compared Lillie's and Marshall's statements of the problem structure (and other research), the increasing importance of endocrinological problems and the decreasing focus on physiological problems showed vividly across the three decades 1910-1940. A clear shift in the *core activity* of reproductive science had occurred. The title of the second major book on reproductive science. *Sex and Internal Secretions* (Allen, 1934), demonstrated the extent of this shift. This later edited volume also demonstrated that a single investigator could no longer provide a sophisticated grasp of the entire field (Maienschein, 1990). The publication of this "Bible" of reproductive science, supported by the prestigious NRC/CRPS, also demonstrated the shift of preeminence in reproductive science from Britain to the United States.

Wondering whether important differences existed in the kinds of problems pursued in biological, medical, and agricultural research settings, I charted major research publications in each. The organization of the problem structure of reproductive science did vary across the three professions that addressed it. Problems in the life sciences can be conceived analytically, by organism, by organ system, by location (e.g., biogeography), by environment (e.g., ecology), and so on. Reproductive biologists tended to focus on analytic problems (sex determination, sex differentiation, fertilization). Medical researchers by and large focused on functions of the organ system (reproductive system) ultimately significant for humans, especially in the treatment of pathology (e.g., infertility). And agricultural scientists focused on the reproductive system in particular *domestic organisms* toward improving reproductive capacity, largely through technological innovations.

These comparative foci reflected the different *markets*—audiences, institutional sponsors, and consumers—for the research produced by each profession. Biologists' emphasis on analytic problems reflected their commitments to developing and moving through "basic" scientific problem structures. Their unit of analysis was in some senses the species, but more fundamentally—and sociologically—it was the problem itself. Physicians' emphasis on reproductive organ systems reflected the established division of labor in medicine and its patterns of specialization by organ system in both research and the organization of delivery of clinical services. Their units of analysis were individual humans and human populations. Agricultural scientists' focus was also based on the extant division of labor in animal agriculture based on type of organism. Their unit of analysis was populations of organisms with high economic value.

A Shift of Core Activity

By 1925, then, investigators in biology, medicine, and agriculture had fully initiated reproductive research as a modern line of scientific work. The cutting edge in reproductive science c. 1925 centered on sex hormones, having shifted from classic physiological work to a biochemical endocrinological focus. Over the next fifteen years the scientific world of reproductive research coalesced around this new work and became a full-fledged scientific enterprise.

Insider histories confirmed this as the model work and core activity of the enterprise. Guy Marrian (Parkes, 1966b:xx) called the years c. 1926-1940 the "heroic age of reproductive endocrinology," while Alan Parkes (1962:72) termed it the "endocrinological gold rush." They did so because during this period the chief naturally occurring estrogen, androgens, and progesterone were isolated and characterized, and the anterior pituitary, placental, and endometrial gonadotropins were discovered.

But, I argued with myself, endocrinology did not become the core activity of reproductive science c. 1925-1940 solely because these major hormones were implicated in reproductive phenomena and therefore were pursued and discovered. This was a social phenomenon and deserved a sociological explanation. Placing endocrinology at the center of the reproductive science enterprise involved a series of choices and commitments by investigators from many countries. Developments could have been otherwise or emphases different.

Establishing *legitimacy* is one of the fundamental tasks in developing emergent social worlds into going concerns or enterprises. It gradually became apparent to me that endocrinology became the centerpiece of reproductive science because it provided the emerging enterprise with a series of structural and strategic advantages for entrepreneurial development and coalescence. These included:

- scientific legitimacy and fashionableness via association with one of the most promising research worlds in the life sciences—general endocrinology;
- a core research activity that was therefore immediately recognizable to their various markets;
- a sophisticated biochemical instead of a merely physiological thrust and strong working alliances with biochemists;
- a common denominator and language across the intersection of biology, medicine, and agriculture that would further enhance the usefulness of these allies.

The endocrinological focus thus brought scientific legitimacy to the enterprise vis-à-vis multiple markets.

"Lateness," Markets, and Segmentations

Though I could now lay out the basic story of reproductive science after 1910, I still gnawed at the questions of why reproductive science developed so "late" in comparison with the physiology of other major organ systems (e.g., Brooks, 1959) and why it emerged when it did. After all, this question concerned the structural conditions of disciplinary emergence, important to historians of science as well as to sociologists (e.g., Rosenberg, 1979a, 1967). I will take you along my convoluted path toward answering these questions.

Insider scientist-historians had proposed several explanations that worried me. Was Corner (1981; Aberle and Corner, 1953) right in attributing the "lateness" to the association between reproduction and sexuality, which made it prohibitive to pursue reproductive science in Victorian times? Was there a "chilling effect," as the term has been used in studies of discrimination? What about the more "internalist" argument (e.g., Medvei, 1982), that the lateness of reproductive science was determined by the intellectual or cognitive need for endocrinology, which did not get off the ground until the turn of the century (Borell, 1976)? Were there other salient issues or events in the life sciences of the era? Did the massive social changes going on that we think of as the industrialization of the United States and the reformist social responses to it known as the Progressive movement have anything to do with the emergence of reproductive science? I knew I had to deal with the embeddedness of the social world of reproductive science in society in order to answer these questions. I knew too that I wanted to specify the relationships and not merely presume some "invisible hand" or mutter vaguely about "social forces."

If Corner was right, at least in part (and I thought he was), what could have turned the illegitimacy of the situation around? Or, more generally, what had changed at the turn of the century that might have had a positive effect on reproductive science? Here the concept of the *arena* guided my thinking and research. I began by listing and reading about who—what other social worlds—cared about reproductive science. To whom would it make a difference in the pragmatist sense? Who were the audiences of reproductive science and what were its markets? Contiguous worlds were also in the picture, even if doing reproductive science was not their direct concern. My informal question was "Who were the players and what was the game?" My extensive reading about the life sciences at the turn of the century was finally going to pay off—it was not "too early" after all.

The social worlds participating in the broader arena in which reproductive science emerged included universities, biology, genetics, embryology, animal scientists and the animal agricultural industry, birth control movements, medicine, obstetrics, and gynecology—a wide array of scientific and nonscientific worlds. I had all the major puzzle pieces and merely had to establish their interrelations! After much reading, reflection, and discussion, what follows is my answer to the question of "lateness" or "why then?"

The turn of the century era, when modern reproductive research emerged, was one of fundamental changes in the professions, academia, and the life sciences. The basic social processes characteristic of *both* the changing structural conditions of and the actual approaches used in the life sciences during this period were those of industrialization—rationalization, professionalization, specialization, and technical development in terms of improving market value and effectiveness. The professions consolidated as market-based occupations (e.g., Larson, 1977; Starr, 1982). Universities were transformed into knowledge-production industries or corporations as well as teaching and training institutions (e.g., Light, 1983; Machlup, 1962; Servos, 1976; Oleson and Voss, 1978). The sciences were professionalized and industrialized (Beer and Lewis, 1974; Birr, 1979). Science qua institution became more akin to an industry or set of industries with specialized markets both within and outside academia (Clarke, 1988a). The approaches scientists brought to bear on their work were also rationalized as life scientists reconstructed their work around analytically based problems, sought reductionist approaches, and realigned their professional and disciplinary organization to match (Busch and Lacy, 1983; Clarke, 1988b; Pauly, 1987).

Specific demand for reproductive science was also requisite for it to emerge on its own terms, to reduce its illegitimacy. These demands took the shape of new or emergent *markets*—participants in the reproductive arena. The accompanying figure summarizes the market structure of the reproductive science enterprise, which included academia (biological, agricultural, and medical worlds), birth control movements, clinical medicine, and applied agriculture. There were also scholarly and applied markets in the social sciences which typically sought biological explanations for social phenomena and biological solutions for social problems in psychology and criminology. I did not address these social science markets in my research because of the usual necessary limitations of scope.

At the turn of the century, birth control, eugenics, and neo-Malthusian movements emerged and were themselves growing into established social

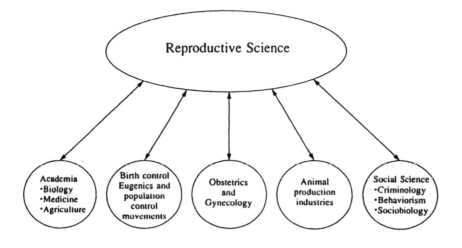

Figure 3.1. Reproductive Science and Its Emergent Market Structure

worlds. They aided reproductive science initially by placing reproductive topics at the center of public discussion, bringing them "out of the closet" of impropriety through the development of a public forum on human reproductive issues c. 1900-1920. The stature of many such advocates—elite groups of scientists, physicians, and educated middle classes in other professions— also served to legitimate reproductive topics, including reproductive science (e.g., Borell, 1987; Gordon, 1976; Reed, 1984). Gradually these separate social movements merged under a population research and control banner, accompanied by the development of an academic population research establishment with an ambitious institutional infrastructure. These birth control-population control worlds became powerful and well-funded consumer markets and constituencies for the products of reproductive science after World War II.

In agriculture, structural conditions were also becoming supportive of research that would lead to improved plant and animal food resources for growing urban populations. During the last decades of the nineteenth century, research supported and conducted by the Bureau of Animal Industry in the U.S. Department of Agriculture focused on the control and prevention of contagious diseases in farm and ranch animals (Sandgren, 1987). Production was thereby improved by keeping more animals alive and healthy. Well into this century the quality of the animals could be only minimally addressed through rudimentary breeding practices (Lush, 1951). Expanding the quantities of animals produced through enhanced control over reproductive processes was the logical next step. Both quality and quantity concerns were addressed simultaneously through the development between the wars of modern technologies of artificial insemination, which were widely applied in the United States after World War II (Herman, 1981). Thus industrialized approaches were brought to bear on animal agricultural production as they had been in other agricultural domains (e.g., Busch, 1982; Busch and Lacy, 1983).

Both the birth control—population control movements and the animal-production industries were, then, at the forefront of articulation of goals of *control over reproduction* throughout the "Chain of Being," the ancient metaphor connecting all life forms, with "man" at the apex. As the means and mechanisms of industrialization passed from the factory into agricultural and social life, the laws of God or nature were to be replaced by the scientific ingenuity of humans. The fundamental feature of this transformation was the shift of *control* over the means of reproduction from nature, God, and religion to humans. Arguments for scientifically based "progress" also challenged the illegitimacy of reproduction as a social topic and scientific pursuit. The means of control over reproduction were to be provided by reproductive science.

At the turn of the century, structural conditions in biology and medicine also changed in directions helpful to the emergence of reproductive science. In addition to the broad development of the "new biology" after 1890 with its emphases on experimental, physiological, and biochemical approaches (e.g., Allen, 1978; Farber, 1982b; Maienschein, 1981, 1985), there were two distinctive developments that promoted reproductive research as a distinctive line of scientific work.

First was the discovery c. 1890 of internal secretions as "chemical messengers" regulating bodily processes, which challenged the reigning view that neurological mechanisms were fully responsible. This led to the concept of "hormones" in 1905 and the development of endocrinology. By the 1920s endocrinology was at the cutting edge of life sciences research (Borell, 1976, 1978). Endocrinology was important to reproductive science not only in terms of explaining basic reproductive function but also because its prestige lent legitimacy to lines of work in which hormones were "actors" (Latour, 1988).

Second, since Darwin's work in the mid-nineteenth century, most life scientists had focused their attention directly on heredity, a considerably more legitimate set of scientific problems than those posed by reproduction. The heredity enigma centered on a nexus of undifferentiated scientific problems of the nature and mechanisms of heredity, evolution, sex determination, fertilization, and development (e.g., Churchill, 1979, 1981; Cravens, 1978; Maienschein, 1984). In the two decades after the "rediscovery" of Mendel's ratio work in 1900, investigators decomposed this complex of scientific problems into separate and distinctive problem structures.

In my work I have called this decomposition a *trilateral segmentation* of subdisciplines within the biological sciences. It involved the emergence of newly bounded and structured lines of work or scientific worlds in genetics, developmental embryology, and, last but not least, reproductive physiology. Despite considerable historical research on the disciplinary development of genetics and embryology, no one had remarked on the fact that these segmentations in biology had also framed a third territory—reproductive science—that centered neither on heredity nor development though contiguous with both (Clarke, 1990a).

My early reading had shown that such scientific specialization was characteristic of the turn of the century era (e.g., Geison, 1981; Reingold, 1979; Rosenberg, 1979b; Rossiter, 1976). Armies of brand new scientists invaded frontier territories bent on staking claims and establishing jurisdiction over new problem domains. I also knew that in each of the three professional fields in which reproductive science developed from 1910 to 1940—biology, medicine, and agriculture—the reproductive system had been relatively unexplored, especially compared with other organ systems, and was therefore a research frontier. The insider histories then confirmed that this open territory factor offered such advantages that it too acted against the social and scientific illegitimacy of pursuing reproductive science.

In 1934 Warren Weaver of the Rockefeller Foundation asked (Kohler, 1976:291):

> Can man gain an intelligent control of his own power? Can we develop so sound and extensive a genetics that we can hope to breed, in the future, superior men? Can we obtain enough knowledge of physiology and psychobiology of sex so that men can bring this pervasive, highly important, and dangerous aspect of life under rational control?

In other words, can we industrialize human reproduction in terms of quality and quantity (Clarke, 1988b)? Reproductive scientists answered in the affirmative, and extensive foundation support helped secure the results (Aberle and Corner, 1953; Greep et al., 1976).

Prompted by Wertz (1983), I asked, "What then did reproductive science do for biology, medicine, and agriculture?" The answer is that it provided multiple benefits to each profession, establishing each as an appropriate academic science and providing each with offerings attractive to its markets. Reproductive science provided biologists with a new line of research as they sought to expand their discipline. It provided medicine with a wide array of nonsurgical diagnostic categories and therapeutic interventions for functional reproductive problems and eventually for birth control and treatment of infertility. It provided agriculture with revolutionary reproductive technologies that drastically improved animal production. Last but not least, it provided a fundable set of research problems for scientists in all three professions in the decades before World War II.

In sum, the changes we term industrialization processes acted to organize previously unorganized markets for reproductive science—in biology, medicine, agriculture, and birth control-population control worlds—thereby legitimating it. This was further demonstrated by the fact that biological research centers waned and applied medical and agricultural centers came to predominate in reproductive science in both Great Britain and the United States by 1950 (Clarke and Borell, 1987).

My long-term worry about the "late" emergence of reproductive science ultimately paid off in the most fundamental way. While changes in *both* the internal-cognitive dimensions of science and its external-institutional conditions were requisite for the emergence of reproductive science, my research takes this further. First, the internal and external dichotomy dissolves as we see the inextricable interrelations of the elements to which they refer and as we come to understand that they cannot be pulled apart without violating the phenomena under study in their natural historical states. Second, we can therefore begin to specify how *both* so-called internal and external dimensions of science are simultaneously organized by market structures, at least since the turn of this century.

Conclusions

What do theories and research traditions do in sociology? Basically they provide a conceptual vocabulary and thereby frame a focus: they emphasize certain aspects of social life while deemphasizing others; they set the stage of sociological concern, both foreground and background; and they draw our attention to particular actors (individuals or collectivities) and their activities and interrelations. We use research traditions like auctions, purchasing a few items or many. We may be involved briefly or for long periods, and we may draw on quite different aspects of the same tradition (Fisher and Strauss, 1978a:5). Both ideally and pragmatically, research traditions promote research.

What I have tried to do in this essay is delineate an emergent research tradition in Chicago-style symbolic interactionism, trace its roots, and discuss and illustrate its usefulness in the sociology of science. What is important to me as a pragmatist is whether social worlds theory helps in the process of discovery, opens analytic doors, and provides entree into chaotic data and a useful analytic framework. If it does so, the theory will continue to be built and refined on firm empirical foundations.

The usefulness of social worlds theory for the sociology of science is multifaceted. First, it provides an open but strongly structural framework for conceptualizing scientific work and its organization into disciplines and subdisciplines. This framework then advances sociological conceptions by permitting the researcher to analyze scientific social worlds as the units of analysis.

Second, social worlds theory offers particular advantages in terms of analytically tolerating the porous boundaries between and among various lines of scientific work specifically because of the very openness of its conceptual framework. Segmentation and intersection processes are typically messy, with loose ends of problem structures slipping between the cracks and disappearing, only to reappear again later, perhaps elsewhere. The social worlds framework allows the researcher to keep track over time not only of what *is* being done in a line of work but also what *isn't*—often equally interesting. For there are "bandwagons" in science as elsewhere (Fujimura, 1986, 1988a) and too few studies of nonreigning research traditions. (There was, in fact, such a tradition in reproductive science that continued to emphasize physiological problems despite the shift to an endocrinological focus; that tradition remains lively and has led to a recent resurrection of comparative reproductive science [e.g., Nalbandov, 1978; Fujimura, 1988b].)

Third, because social worlds theory promotes comparative analysis, it can make us think better sociologically. We can easily compare the social worlds of taxi dancehalls, manufacturing industries, ethnic communities, gangs, and lines of scientific work and surprise ourselves by thinking in fresh ways about our data. This obviously is a very different way of looking at science! I also compared reproductive science with other lines of scientific work, both historical and contemporary. In addition to helping me ask better questions, this deepened my grasp of the fate of reproductive science vis-à-vis other lines of work. It is such comparisons that ultimately enable the refinement of concepts and theory.

Fourth, social worlds theory, through its simultaneous attention to scientific problems, concrete scientific work, institutional settings, and structural conditions, dissolves the "internal" (cognitive/intellectual) versus "external" (institutional/economic) distinction in science studies. The social worlds approach leads the researcher directly to questions about the relationships and interactions between research programs or problem structures, their institutional bases and conditions, and the content of scientific work. It brings a natural history approach to bear on the development of social structure *in relation to* scientific problem structure and vice versa.

The arena concept is especially salient here. Because analysts must attend to the other players in the game, our span of perception is widened to grapple with the meanings other social worlds have in the situation. In historical science studies we can see the increasing importance of audiences (markets, sponsors, and consumers) of scientific work (Clarke, 1988a). This can permit better framing of our own future research as we study particular substantive areas.

Fifth, the interactionist sociology of work approach in conjunction with social worlds theory can also yield high payoffs and generate new areas of sociological concern. For example, by paying close attention to concrete work in medical contexts, Strauss et al. (1985) discovered that patients do a considerable amount of work yet had never been included in discussions of the division of medical labor. Similarly, by attending to the daily work of reproductive scientists as recounted in biographical materials, I noticed that they spent considerable time acquiring and maintaining research materials and I began to investigate this (Clarke, 1987; Clarke and Fujimura, in preparation). No one had explicitly studied the development of organized access to research materials as part of the requisite infrastructure of the life sciences. Through similar analyses, Star (1986, 1989) delineated triangulation patterns within basic and clinical research in localizationist neurological theory. Fujimura (1986) focused on the construction of doable problems in basic cancer research laboratories as involving the ongoing alignment and realignment of several levels of work organization with different kinds of concrete work.

Most of all, social worlds theory promotes sociological insight by providing a framework for discovery. It invites researchers to play fun—and productive—sociological games. It makes one think and keep thinking, which is, after all, the exciting part of being a sociologist.

Last, what does the sociology of science offer to social worlds theory and researchers? In a fundamental sense, the sciences are substantive areas in which to pursue basic sociological problems in the study of work, organizations, occupations, and professions. The sciences are, from a sociological point of view, comparatively small, accessible, manageable, and highly interesting social worlds amenable to a variety of historical and contemporary studies that can feed into one another toward building robust sociological theory. One might even say facetiously that the sciences are excellent laboratories for basic sociological research. And, like reproductive science early this century, the sociology of science is largely an unexplored territory. What more could one ask?

Notes

1. I am grateful to Kathy Charmaz, Nan Chico, Joan Fujimura, Elihu Gerson, Anna Hazan, Marilyn Little, Theresa Montini, Kathy Slobin, and S. Leigh Star for conceptual and editorial assistance. K. E. Studer and Daryl Chubin kindly gave permission to use their unpublished work. Support of various kinds was provided by the University of California, San Francisco, the Rockefeller University, and the NIMH Postdoctoral Program, Department of Sociology, Stanford University.

2. Studer and Chubin (1980) use the term *convergence* to refer to certain kinds of intersectional processes.

3. The connections between various network theories and social worlds theory deserve comparative consideration elsewhere (e.g., Latour 1987; Law and Lodge, 1984; Callon, 1986; Wellman and Berkowitz, 1988).

4. See, for example, Farber, 1982a; Geison, 1981, 1983; Haraway, 1983; Kimmelman, 1983; Kohler, 1982; Larson, 1977; Law, 1976; Lemaine et al., 1976; Light, 1983; Maienschein, 1985; Pauly, 1984; Rosenberg, 1979a, 1976, 1967, Rossiter, 1979; Servos, 1976; Star, 1983; Volberg, 1983; Woolgar, 1976).

5. See, for example, Aberle and Corner, 1953, Cole, 1977; Corner, 1981; Parkes, 1966a, b; Price, 1972; Vollman, 1965.

6. Roy Greep (personal communication, 1987), a renowned reproductive investigator, told me that he intentionally learned how to do effective hypophysectomies in the 1930s, rightly reasoning that this skill might help him obtain a position during the Depression.

References

Aberle, Sophie D., and George W. Corner. 1953. *Twenty-Five Years of Sex Research: History of the National Research Council Committee for Research in Problems of Sex, 1922-1947.* Philadelphia: W. B. Saunders.

Allen, Edgar (Ed.). 1934. *Sex and Internal Secretions.* 1st ed. Baltimore: Williams and Wilkins.

Allen, Garland. 1978. *Life Sciences in the Twentieth Century.* New York: Cambridge University Press.

Becker, Howard S. 1982. *Art Worlds.* Berkeley: University of California Press.

_____. 1974. Art as Collective Action. *American Sociological Review* 39(6):767-76.

_____. 1970. *Sociological Work: Method and Substance.* New Brunswick: Transaction Books.

_____. 1963. *Outsiders: Studies in the Sociology of Deviance.* New York: Free Press.

_____. 1960. Notes on the Concept of Commitment. *American Journal of Sociology* 66:32-40.

Beer, John B., and W. Daniel Lewis. 1974. Aspects of the Professionalization of Science. In Sal P. Restivo and Christopher K. Vanderpool (eds.), *Comparative Studies in Science and Society.* Columbus: Merrill.

Birr, Kendall. 1979. Industrial Research Laboratories. In Nathan Reingold (ed.). *The Sciences in the American Context: New Perspectives,* pp. 193-207. Washington: Smithsonian Institution.

Blumer, Herbert. 1978. Social Unrest and Collective Protest. In Norman K. Denzin (ed.). *Studies in Symbolic Interaction* 1, pp. 1-54. Greenwich: JAI Press.

_____. 1969. *Symbolic Interactionism: Perspective and Method.* Englewood Cliffs: Prentice Hall.

_____. 1954. What Is Wrong With Social Theory? *American Sociological Review* 19(February): 3-10.

Borell, Merriley. 1987. Biologists and the Promotion of Birth Control Research, 1918-1938. *Journal of the History of Biology* 20(1):57-87.

_____. 1985. Organotherapy and the Emergence of Reproductive Endocrinology. *Journal of the History of Biology* 18:1-30.

_____. 1978. Setting the Standards for a New Science: Edward Schafer and Endocrinology. *Medical History* 22:282-90.

_____. 1976. Organotherapy. British Physiology and Discovery of the Internal Secretions. *Journal of the History of Biology* 9(2):235-68.

Brooks, Chandler McC. 1959. The Development of Physiology in the Last Fifty Years. *Bulletin of the History of Medicine* 33:249-62.

Bucher, Rue. 1988. On the Natural History of Health Care Occupations. *Work and Occupations* 15(2):131-47.

_____. 1962. Pathology: A Study of Social Movements Within a Profession. *Social Problems* 10:40-51.

_____, and Anselm L. Strauss. 1961. Professions in Process. *American Journal of Sociology* 66:325-34.

Bulmer, Martin. 1984. *The Chicago School of Sociology: Institutionalization, Diversity and the Rise of Sociological Research.* Chicago: University of Chicago Press.

Busch, Lawrence. 1982. History, Negotiation and Structure in Agricultural Research. *Urban Life* 11(3):368-84.

_____ and William B. Lacy. 1983. *Science, Agriculture and the Politics of Research.* Boulder: Westview.

Callon, Michel. 1986. The Sociology of an Actor-Network: The Case of the Electric Vehicle. In Michel Callon, John Law, and Arie Rip (eds.). *Mapping the Dynamics of Science and Technology,* pp. 19-34. London: Macmillan.

Churchill, Frederick B. 1981. In Search of the New Biology: An Epilogue. *Journal of the History of Biology* 14(1):177-91.

_____. 1979. Sex and the Single Organism: Biological Theories of Sexuality in Mid-Nineteenth Century. In William Coleman and Camille Limoges (eds.), *Studies in the History of Biology* 3. Baltimore: Johns Hopkins University Press.

Clarke, Adele E. 1990a. Embryology and the Rise of American Reproductive Science, 1910-1940. In Keith Benson, Ronald Rainger, and Jane Maienschein (eds.), *The Expansion of American Biology.* New Brunswick: Rutgers University Press.

_____. 1990b. Controversy and the Development of Reproductive Science. *Social Problems* 37.

_____. 1988a. Getting Down to Business: The Life Sciences, c. 1890-1940. Presented at meetings of the Society for Social Studies of Science. Amsterdam.

_____. 1988b. The Industrialization of Human Reproduction, c. 1890-1990. Plenary address, University of California Systemwide Conference of Women's Programs, Davis.

_____. 1987. Research Materials and Reproductive Science in the United States, 1910-1940. In Gerald L. Geison (ed.), *Physiology in the American Context, 1850-1940,* pp. 323-50. Bethesda: American Physiological Society.

_____. 1985. *Emergence of the Reproductive Research Enterprise, c. 1910-1940: A Sociology of Biological, Medical and Agricultural Science in the United States.* Dissertation in Sociology. University of California, San Francisco.

_____, and Merriley Borell. 1987. The Comparative Development of Reproductive Science in the U.S. and Great Britain. Presented at meetings of the Society for Social Studies of Science, Worcester.

_____, and Joan H. Fujimura (eds.). In prep. The Right Tools for the Job: Materials, Instruments, Techniques and Work Organization in Twentieth-Century Life Sciences, Princeton: Princeton University Press.

_____, and Elihu M. Gerson. 1990. Symbolic Interactionism in Science Studies. In Howard S. Becker and Michael McCall (eds.), *Symbolic Interactionism and Cultural Studies.* Chicago: University of Chicago Press.

Cole, Harold H. 1977. *Adventurer in Animal Science: Harold H. Cole.* Oral History Center, Shields Library. University of California, Davis.

Collins, Randall, and Sal Restivo. 1983. Development, Diversity and Conflict in the Sociology of Science. *Sociological Quarterly* 24:185-200.

Corner, George W. 1981. *Seven Ages of a Medical Scientist: Autobiography.* Philadelphia: University of Pennsylvania Press.

Cravens, Hamilton. 1978. *The Triumph of Evolution: American Scientists and the Heredity-Environment Controversy, 1900-1941.* Philadelphia: University of Pennsylvania Press.

Cressey, Paul G. 1932. *The Taxi Dancehall: A Sociological Study in Commercialized Recreation and City Life.* Chicago: University of Chicago Press.

Dewey, John. 1910. *How We Think.* Boston: Heath.

Farber, Paul L. 1982a. *The Emergence of Ornithology as a Scientific Discipline.* Boston: D. Reidel.

_____. 1982b. The Transformation of Natural History in the Nineteenth Century. *Journal of the History of Biology* 15(1):145-52.

Faris, Robert E. L. 1967. *Chicago Sociology, 1920-1932.* Chicago: University of Chicago Press.

Farley, John. 1982. *Gametes and Spores: Ideas About Sexual Reproduction, 1750-1914.* Baltimore: Johns Hopkins University Press.

Faulkner, Robert. 1983. *Music on Demand.* New Brunswick: Transaction.

_____. 1971. *Hollywood Studio Musicians.* Chicago: Aldine.

Fisher, Berenice, and Anselm L. Strauss. 1978a. The Chicago Tradition and Social Change: Thomas, Park and Their Successors. *Symbolic Interaction* 1(2):5-23.

_____. 1978b. Interactionism. In Tom Bottomore and Robert Nisbet (eds.). *A History of Sociological Analysis,* pp. 457-98. New York: Basic Books.

Freidson, Eliot. 1976. The Division of Labor as Social Interaction. *Social Problems* 23:304-13.

_____. 1968. The Impurity of Professional Authority. In Howard S. Becker, Blanche Geer, David Reisman, and Robert Weiss (eds.). *Institutional Office and the Person: Essays Presented to Everett C. Hughes.* Chicago: Aldine.

Fujimura, Joan H. 1988a. The Molecular Biological Bandwagon in Cancer Research: Where Social Worlds Meet. *Social Problems* 35:261-83.

_____. 1988b. The Institutional Construction of Mavericks in Science. Paper presented at the meetings of the Society for Social Studies of Science. Amsterdam.

_____. 1987. Constructing Doable Problems in Cancer Research: Articulating Alignment. *Social Studies of Science* 17:257-93.

_____. 1986. *Bandwagons in Science: Doable Problems and Transportable Packages as Factors in the Development of the Molecular Genetic Bandwagon in Cancer Research.* Doctoral dissertation in Sociology. University of California, Berkeley.

Geison, Gerald L. 1981. Scientific Change, Emerging Specialties and Research Schools. *History of Science* 19:20-40.

_____ (ed.). 1983. *Professions and Professional Ideology in America.* Chapel Hill: University of North Carolina Press.

Gerson, Elihu M. 1983. Scientific Work and Social Worlds. *Knowledge* 4:357-77.

Gieryn, Thomas F. 1983. Boundary-Work and the Demarcation of Science From Non-Science: Strains and Interests in Professional Ideologies of Scientists. *American Sociological Review* 48:781-95.

Glaser, Barney G. 1978. *Theoretical Sensitivity: Advances in the Methodology of Grounded Theory.* Mill Valley: Sociology Press.

_____. 1964. *Organizational Scientists: Their Professional Careers.* Indianapolis: Bobbs-Merrill.

_____, and Anselm Strauss. 1967. *The Discovery of Grounded Theory.* Chicago: Aldine.

Gordon, Linda. 1976. *Woman's Body, Woman's Right: A Social History of Birth Control in America.* New York: Penguin.

Graham, Loren, Wolf Lepenies, and Peter Weingart (eds.). 1983. *Functions and Uses of Disciplinary History.* Dordrecht and Boston: D. Reidel/Kluwer.

Greep, Roy O., and Marjorie A. Koblinsky. 1977. *Frontiers in Reproduction and Fertility Control: A Review of the Reproductive Sciences and Contraceptive Development.* Boston: MIT Press (Ford Foundation).

_____, and F. S. Jaffe. 1976. *Reproduction and Human Welfare: A Challenge to Research.* Boston: MIT (Ford Foundation).

Hall, Diana Long. 1976. The Critic and the Advocate: Contrasting British Views on the State of Endocrinology in the 1920s. *Journal of the History of Biology* 9(2):269-85.

_____. 1974. Biology. Sex Hormones and Sexism in the 1920s. *Philosophical Forum* 5:81-96.

Haraway, Donna. 1983. Signs of Dominance: From a Physiology to a Cybernetics of Primate Society: C. R. Carpenter, 1930-1970. *Studies in History of Biology* 6:129-219.

Hazan, Anna. 1985. *A Study of Shrinking Institutions: The Transformation of Health and Human Services Work After Proposition 13.* Doctoral dissertation. University of California, San Francisco.

Herman, Harry A. 1981. *Improving Cattle by the Millions: NAAB and the Development and Worldwide Application of Artificial Insemination.* Columbia: University of Missouri Press.

Hughes, Everett C. 1971. *The Sociological Eye.* Chicago: Aldine Atherton.

_____. 1958. *Men and Their Work.* Glencoe: Free Press.

James, William. 1914. *The Meaning of Truth.* London: Longmans.

Kimmelman, Barbara A. 1983. The American Breeders' Association: Genetics and Eugenics in an Agricultural Context, 1903-1913. *Social Studies of Science* 13:163-204.

Kling, Rob, and Elihu M. Gerson. 1978. Patterns of Segmentation and Intersection in the Computing World. *Symbolic Interaction* 2:25-43.

_____. 1977. The Dynamics of Technical Change in the Computing World. *Symbolic Interaction* 1:132-46.

Kohler, Robert E. 1982. *From Medical Chemistry to Biochemistry: The Making of a Biomedical Discipline.* Cambridge: Cambridge University Press.

_____. 1976. The Management of Science: The Experience of Warren Weaver and the Rockefeller Foundation Programme in Molecular Biology. *Minerva* 14:279-306.

Kurtz, Lester R. 1984. *Evaluating Chicago Sociology.* Chicago: University of Chicago Press.

Larson, Magali Sarfatti. 1977. *The Rise of Professionalism: A Sociological Analysis.* Berkeley: University of California Press.

Latour, Bruno. 1988. Mixing Humans and Nonhumans Together: The Sociology of a Door-Closer. *Social Problems* 35(3):298-310.

_____. 1987. *Science in Action.* Cambridge: Harvard University Press.

Law, John. 1976. The Development of Specialties in Science: The Case of X-ray Protein Crystallography. In Gerard Lemaine, Roy MacLeod, Michael Mulkay, and Peter Weingart (eds.), *Perspectives on the Emergence of Scientific Disciplines,* pp. 123-52. The Hague/Chicago: Mouton/Aldine.

_____, and Peter Lodge. 1984. *Science for Social Scientists.* London: Macmillan.

Lemaine, Gerard, Roy MacLeod, Michael Mulkay, and Peter Weingart (eds.). 1976. *Perspectives on the Emergence of Scientific Disciplines.* The Hague/Chicago: Mouton/Aldine.

Light, Donald W. 1983. The Development of Professional Schools in America. In Konrad Jarausch (ed.), *The Transformation of Higher Learning,* 1860-1930, pp. 345-66. Chicago: University of Chicago Press.

Lush, Jay L. 1951. Genetics and Animal Breeding. In L. C. Dunn (ed.), *Genetics in the Twentieth Century,* pp. 493-525. New York: Macmillan.

Machlup, Fritz. 1962. *The Production and Distribution of Knowledge in the United States.* Princeton: Princeton University Press.

Maienschein, Jane. 1990. Edmund V. Cowdry's *General Cytology* and the Emergence of the Collaborative Textbook. In Keith Benson, Ronald Rainger, and Jane Maienschein (eds.), *The Expansion of American Biology.* New Brunswick: Rutgers University Press.

_____. 1985. History of Biology. *Osiris* (Second Series) 1:147-62.

_____. 1984. What Determines Sex? A Study of Converging Approaches, 1880-1916. *Isis* 75(278):457-80.

_____. 1981. Shifting Assumptions in American Biology: Embryology, 1890-1910. *Journal of the History of Biology* 14(1):89-113.

Marshall, F. H. A. 1922. *The Physiology of Reproduction.* 2d ed. London: Longmans, Green.

_____. 1910. *The Physiology of Reproduction.* London: Longmans, Green.

Mead, George Herbert, 1938/1972. *The Philosophy of the Act.* Chicago: University of Chicago Press.

Medvei, Victor C. 1982. *A History of Endocrinology.* Lancaster, England: MIP.

Meltzer, Bernard N., John W. Petras, and Larry T. Reynolds, 1975. *Symbolic Interactionism: Genesis, Varieties and Criticism.* Boston: Routledge and Kegan Paul.

Nalbandov, A. V. 1978. Retrospects and Prospects in Reproductive Physiology. In Charles H. Spelman and John W. Wilks (eds.), *Novel Aspects of Reproductive Physiology.* New York: Halsted/Wiley.

Numbers, Ronald (ed.). 1980. *The Education of American Physicians: Historical Essays.* Berkeley University of California Press.

Oleson, Alexandra, and John Voss (eds.). 1979. *The Organization of Knowledge in Modern America, 1860-1920.* Baltimore: Johns Hopkins University Press.

Park, Robert Ezra, 1952. *Human Communities.* Glencoe: Free Press.

Parkes, A. S. 1966a. *Sex, Science and Society: Addresses, Lectures and Articles.* London: Oriel Press.

———. 1966b. The Rise of Reproductive Physiology. 1926-1940: The Dale Lecture for 1965. *Journal of Endocrinology* 34:xx-xxxii.

———. 1962. Prospect and Retrospect in the Physiology of Reproduction. *British Medical Journal.* July 14, pp. 71-75.

———. 1952-1966. *Marshall's Physiology of Reproduction.* 3d ed. New York: Longmans, Green.

Pauly, Philip J. 1987. *Controlling Life: Jacques Loeb and the Engineering Ideal in Biology.* New York: Oxford University Press.

———. 1984. The Appearance of Academic Biology in Late Nineteenth Century America. *Journal of the History of Biology* 17(3):369-97.

Price, Dorothy. 1972. Mammalian Conception, Sex Differentiation, and Hermaphroditism as Viewed in Historical Perspective. *American Zoologist* 12:179-91.

Reed, James. 1984. *The Birth Control Movement and American Society: From Private Vice to Public Virtue.* 2d ed. Princeton: Princeton University Press.

Reingold, Nathan. 1979. *The Sciences in the American Context: New Perspectives.* Washington: Smithsonian Institution.

Restivo, Sal P. 1974. The Ideology of Basic Science. In Sal P. Restivo and Christopher K. Vanderpool (eds.), *Comparative Studies in Science and Society.* Columbus: Merrill.

Rosenberg, Charles E. 1979a. Toward an Ecology of Knowledge: On Discipline, Contexts and History. In Alexandra Oleson and John Voss (eds.), *The Organization of Knowledge in Modern America,* pp. 440-55. Baltimore: Johns Hopkins University Press.

———. 1979b. Rationalization and Reality in Shaping American Agricultural Research, 1875-1914. In Nathan Reingold (ed.), *The Sciences in the American Context: New Perspectives,* pp. 143-63. Washington: Smithsonian Institution.

———. 1976. *No Other Gods: On Science and American Social Thought.* Baltimore: Johns Hopkins University Press.

———. 1967. Factors in the Development of Genetics in the United States: Some Suggestions. *Journal of the History of Medicine and Allied Sciences* 22(1): 27-46.

Rossiter, Margaret. 1979. The Organization of the Agricultural Sciences. In A. Oleson and J. Voss (eds.), *The Organization of Knowledge in Modern America, 1860-1920,* pp. 211-48. Baltimore: Johns Hopkins University Press.

———. 1976. The Organization of Agricultural Improvement in the United States, 1785-1865. In Alexandra Oleson and Sanborn C. Brown (eds.), *The Pursuit of Knowledge in the Early American Republic: American Scientific and Learned Societies From Colonial Times to the Civil War,* pp. 279-96. Baltimore: Johns Hopkins University Press.

Sabin, Florence Rena. 1934. *Franklin Paine Mall: The Story of a Mind.* Baltimore: Johns Hopkins University Press.

Sandgren, Erik. 1987. The Bureau of Animal Industry and Research on Infectious Diseases. Presented at meetings of the American Association for the History of Medicine.

Schatzman, Leonard, and Anselm L. Strauss. 1973. *Field Research: Strategies for a Natural Sociology*. Englewood Cliffs: Prentice Hall.

Servos, John. 1976. The Knowledge Corporation: A. A. Noves and Chemistry at Cal Tech, 1915-1930. *Ambis* 23(3):175-86.

Shibutani, Tomatsu. 1962. Reference Groups and Social Control. In Arnold Rose (ed.), *Human Behavior and Social Processes*, pp. 128-45. Boston: Houghton Mifflin.

_____. 1955. Reference Groups as Perspectives. *American Journal of Sociology* 60:562-69.

Star, S. Leigh. 1989. *Regions of the Mind: Brain Research and the Quest for Scientific Certainty*. Stanford: Stanford University Press.

_____. 1986. Triangulating Clinical and Basic Research British Localizationists, 1870-1906. *History of Science* 24:29-48.

_____. 1983. Simplification in Scientific Work: An Example From Neuroscience Research. *Social Studies of Science* 13:208-26.

Starr, Paul, 1982. *The Social Transformation of American Medicine*. New York: Basic Books.

Strauss, Anselm L. 1988. The Articulation of Project Work: An Organizational Process. *Sociological Quarterly* 29:163-78.

_____. 1987. *Qualitative Analysis for Social Scientists*. Cambridge: Cambridge University Press.

_____. 1985. Work and the Division of Labor. *Sociological Quarterly*.

_____. 1982. Social Worlds and Legitimation Processes. In Norman Denzin (ed.). *Studies in Symbolic Interaction 4*, pp. 171-90. Greenwich: JAI Press.

_____. 1979. *Negotiations: Varieties, Contexts, Processes and Social Order*. San Francisco: Jossey-Bass.

_____. 1978. A Social Worlds Perspective. In Norman Denzin (ed.), *Studies in Symbolic Interaction I*, pp. 119-28. Greenwich: JAI Press.

_____. 1971. *Professions, Work and Careers*. San Francisco: Sociology Press.

_____. 1967. Strategies for Discovering Urban Theory. In Leo E. Schnore and Henry Fagin (eds.), *Urban Research and Policy Planning*. vol. 1. Urban Affairs Annual Reviews. Beverly Hills: Sage.

_____, and Juliet Corbin, 1990. *Basics of Qualitative Research*. Newbury Park, CA: Sage.

_____, S. Fagerhaugh, B. Suezek, and C. Wiener, 1985. *The Social Organization of Medical Work*. Chicago: University of Chicago Press.

_____, Leonard Schatzman, Rue Bucher, Danuta Erlich, and Melvin Sabshin. 1964. *Psychiatric Ideologies and Institutions*. Glencoe: Free Press.

_____, and Lee Rainwater, 1962. *The Professional Scientist: A Study of American Chemists*. Chicago: Aldine.

Studer, K. E., and D. Chubin, 1976. The Heroic Age of Reproductive Endocrinology: Its Development and Structure. Unpublished manuscript.

Thomas, William I. 1914. The Polish-Prussian Situation: An Experiment in Assimilation. *American Journal of Sociology* 19:624-39.

Thomas, William I., and Florian Znaniecki. 1927. *The Polish Peasant in Europe and America*. 2d ed. New York: Knopf.

Thrasher, Frederick M. 1927/1963. *The Gang: A Study of 1,313 Gangs in Chicago*. Chicago: University of Chicago Press.

Unruh, David R. 1979. Characteristics and Types of Participation in Social Worlds. *Symbolic Interaction* 2(2):115-30.

Volberg, Rachel A. 1983. *Constraints and Commitments in the Development of American Botany, 1880-1920*. Dissertation in Sociology. University of California, San Francisco.

Vollman, Rudolph P. 1965. *Fifty Years of Research on Mammalian Reproduction: Carl G. Hartman.* USDHEW, Public Health Service Publication 1281.

Wellman, Barry, and S. D. Berkowitz (eds.), 1988. *Social Structures: A Network Approach.* Cambridge: Cambridge University Press.

Wertz, Dorothy C. 1983. What Birth Has Done for Doctors: A Historical View. *Women and Health* 8(1):7-24.

Wirth, Louis, 1928. *The Ghetto.* Chicago: University of Chicago Press.

Woolgar, Steve. 1976. The Identification and Definition of Scientific Collectivities. In Gerard Lemaine, Roy MacLeod, Michael Mulkay, and Peter Weingart (eds.), *Perspectives on the Emergence of Scientific Disciplines,* pp. 233-46. The Hague/Chicago: Mouton/Aldine.

4

The Molecular Biological Bandwagon in Cancer Research

Where Social Worlds Meet

JOAN H. FUJIMURA

Commentary

This is another chapter, whose author participated in our seminar, which also does not explicitly mention using grounded theory as its main method. The methodology and at least its basic procedures, and probably subsidiary ones, however, inform both Dr. Fujimura's doctoral research and this particular publication, which was adapted from it. We include the article here principally because of this researcher's extensive and systematic conceptualization of a huge amount and variety of descriptive data. These data called for dense description, especially as most of her readers (primarily, sociologists and historians of science) were not very familiar with much of the substantive detail about cancer research and genetic theory. The researcher's conceptualization weaves in and out of her description, ordering and interpreting it, and

© 1988 by the Society for the Study of Social Problems, Inc. Reprinted from *Social Problems,* 35(3), 261-283, by permission.

using the hallmark techniques of grounded theory: theoretical conceptualization, constant comparisons (of activities and organizations and their strategies,
sets of conditions and consequences), and theory-driven sampling to attain,
among other things, systematic theory about her subject matter. The entire
chapter is organized around a central concept pertaining to the phenomenon
of "a scientific bandwagon."

Disciplinary literature, principally from both sociology and the sociology
and history of science, is used with great effectiveness, in conjunction with
her own field observations, interviews, and reading of substantive materials.
A general interpretive framework rests on clearly spelled out sociological
concepts of work, social worlds, intersection, careers and negotiation, mostly
drawn from the writings and research of the University of Chicago interactionists. Other perhaps "closer to the ground" concepts include "standardization," "technology," "theory" (genetic and medical), "package" (of
techniques and theory), "risk," "doable work and problems." The core category or central phenomena that she is analyzing is "a scientific bandwagon."

This exceptionally effective analysis is another example of grounded
theory presentation. It is adapted to the complexity of her problem and data,
but also to multiple audiences of sociologists and historians of science,
medical biologists, and of sociologists in general. It is important also to realize
that Fujimura's interactionist emphasis on work and allied concepts was
relatively new to her main audience of sociologists/historians of science
whose own approaches were, and still are, ideational rather than action
oriented. Above all, the participants in a scientific bandwagon are *actors,*
including laboratories and other organizations, engaged in doing *work* within
complicated networks of intersecting *social worlds.*

* * *

Introduction

This paper analyzes the development of a scientific bandwagon in cancer
research using a social worlds perspective and qualitative methods. It shows
that a "standardized" package of oncogene theory and recombinant DNA
technologies served as a highly transportable interface among many different
laboratories and lines of research. That is, the package promoted intersections
among different social worlds which, in turn, facilitated the rapid develop-

ment of oncogene research and the larger molecular biological cancer research bandwagon. The paper proposes the bandwagon as one process by which conceptual shifts in science occur and shows that the process of such change is inseparable from both the local and broad scale organization of work and technical infrastructures.

A scientific bandwagon exists when large numbers of people, laboratories, and organizations commit their resources to one approach to a problem. A package of theory and technology is a clearly defined set of conventions for action that helps reduce reliance on discretion and trial-and-error procedures. This paper analyzes the development of such a bandwagon and package around a molecular biological approach in the study of cancer in the United States.

The data, collected through 1986, come from formal and informal interviews, observation in academic and private industrial cancer research laboratories, participant observation in tumor biology courses, and various documents. I examined journal articles, books, biological materials and instruments catalogues, laboratory manuals, and information on organizations sponsoring cancer research. I attended colloquia, public lectures, and a cancer research conference. Respondents included cancer research scientists, technicians, students, administrators of cancer research institutes and funding organizations, and management of a commercial biotechnology company.

My main premise is that science is work and that scientific information is constructed through negotiations among actors working in organizational contexts. Changing conventionalized and embedded work organizations involves a lot of convincing and persuading, buying and adopting, teaching and learning. Conceptual change in science, in turn, is based in individual and collective changes in the way scientists organize their work. The task of sociology of science is to shed light on these activities, contexts, and processes through which scientific knowledge is constructed and changed.[1]

The development and maintenance of this particular bandwagon was facilitated by a package consisting of a theoretical model for explaining cancer, the oncogene theory, and recombinant DNA technologies for testing the theory. Oncogene proponents hold that cancer is caused by normal cellular genes called "proto-oncogenes" that somehow turn into cancer genes, loosely called "oncogenes." I focus on the construction and marketing of the theory-methods package by oncogene researchers and the buying and importing of the package by their colleagues, members of other lines of research, funding agencies, and suppliers. Early oncogene researchers used this package to push their lines of research and generated a bandwagon that redefined the work organization in many cancer research laboratories. The collective commitments of resources made by early bandwagon joiners set the conditions for gaining new adherents (scientists, laboratories, and organizations) through a "snowball effect." By 1984, the bandwagon was sustained by its own momentum and researchers climbed on primarily because it *was* a bandwagon.

Intersecting Social Worlds in Cancer Research

Scientific problem solving and fact making are collective enterprises organized generally along different lines of research, research traditions, and disciplines (Gerson, 1983). When individuals and organizations commit their resources to a line of research, they are committing themselves to a particular set of problems and oftentimes methods.

Changes in commitment are expensive and require new investments of resources. Moreover, these changes in the conventions of work, including scientific work, occur only through the cooperation of people from diverse social worlds (cf. Becker, 1982; Shibutani, 1955; Strauss et al., 1985). Why would scientists and organizations with existing resource investments in different lines of research be willing to commit their resources to this particular new approach? And how do these members from different social worlds come to practice a common approach to studying cancer?

We can begin to understand these changes by borrowing Everett Hughes's (1971) view of the workplace as "where [diverse] peoples meet." Work gets done in these places only through the conflict, struggle, and negotiations over a set of conventions to guide action and interaction at this meeting of worlds. Here, cancer research is the workplace, the arena where different social worlds meet, and he negotiations are about how one should approach solving the problem of cancer (see Shibutani, 1955; and Strauss, 1978b on arenas). Beginning in the late 1970s in the United States, participants from many different lines of work came to agreement on how best to study cancer. The molecular biological approach has gained an increasing proportion of cancer research commitments although basic, clinical, and epidemiological research with no ties to molecular biological methods continue. That is, in the struggle to define their common object, cancer, molecular biologists and tumor virologists have won acceptance of their definition of the situation by other researchers, sponsors, suppliers, and diverse participants in the cancer research arena. Cancer has become defined for many people as a disease of the DNA, to be studied through oncogene theory and recombinant DNA technologies. The story of this bandwagon's development then is also the story of how molecular biologists managed to impose their definition of the situation on much of the larger world of cancer research.

In the battle over whose "fact" is more "factual," Callon (1985) and Latour (1987) argue that actors enroll allies much as military leaders enlist armies and weapons. A major strategy used by scientists in fact making is to translate others' interests into their own interests. More generally, translation is the mechanism by which certain entities gain control over the way society and nature are organized, by which "a few obtain the right to express and to represent the many silent actors of the social and natural worlds they have mobilized" (Callon, 1985:224).

Packages in Bandwagon Development: From Custom Tailoring to One-Size-Fits-All

Scientists' commitments are organized into three major interdependent sets of activities that define their work: problem solving, career building, and line-of-research-building. Problem solving in basic science is rarely standardized and requires enormous amounts of work to sort through all the combinations of variables. Results are never assured. Constructing "doable" problems, or successful research projects, is an uncertain process (Fujimura, 1987). For any project to succeed, scientists must negotiate tasks ranging from convincing funding agencies of the project's worth to making or buying necessary supplies to experimental manipulations of DNA. For example, to carry out an experiment, scientists must pull together diverse elements including funds, laboratory space and infrastructure, staff, skills, technologies, research materials, and audiences for the experimental results. This has been called articulation work (Bendifallah and Scacchi, 1987; Fujimura, 1987; Gasser, 1984; Star, 1985; Strauss, 1988; Strauss et al., 1985). Uncertainty and ambiguity reign at every turn in research paths and require constant surveillance, discretionary decision making, regular reorganization of activities, and more (Fujimura, 1986a; Gasser, 1984; Zeldenrust, 1985; Star, 1985).

At the same time, scientists are constrained by the requirements of career building. Since the end of the nineteenth century, industrialization has changed the organization of scientific work in American universities into a rationalized system of production of new knowledge and technologies for "market" consumption. Basic scientists became "professionals" who were located in research universities. In the university context, scientists are now judged by the amount and quality of their publications and by their students. University molecular biologists, for example, build careers primarily by publishing papers based on the results of laboratory experiments. Even molecular biologists located in private biotechnology companies still build careers through publications (Fujimura, 1986b). They require funds to build their labs and conduct experiments. Further, time scales for experimental results have shrunk in recent years. No scientist today can spend five years to produce results and publications and still expect to win research grants. A tumor virologist with whom I spoke said:

> Researchers have to convince the funding sources that their studies will produce progress, results, within a political time span. . . . If you tell them not to expect progress in five years, they won't fund you. . . . The whole structure of science is pushing for quick results.

Organizations and institutions also have careers. University departments, universities, research institutes, and biotechnology and pharmaceutical companies are betting resources on molecular biological cancer research with the goal of ensuring or increasing productivity, maintaining their own existence, and increasing their power and credibility (Latour and Woolgar, 1979).

Problem solving under highly uncertain conditions and career building in the context of rationalized knowledge production seem diametrically opposed. Under these conditions, scientists and organizations make commitments to particular lines of research. They aim to construct doable problems which will produce novel information and marketable products within short time frames.

The careers of research traditions can vary in duration, growth or decline, amount and degree of participant support, and kinds of activities and concerns. Scientists, supplying and sponsoring organizations, and academic and commercial research enterprises are committed to the continuance and growth of a line of research because the careers of these lines of research are tightly tied to individual and organizational careers.

In this context, one way to attract adherents to one's approach to a problem and to build up a line of research is to provide a way of organizing work that facilitates the construction of doable problems for scientists, research institutes, and commercial laboratories. Latour (1987:109) argues similarly that the first and easiest way to find people who will immediately believe the statement, invest in the project, or buy the prototype, is to *tailor the object* in such a way that it caters [to] these people's *explicit interests* . . . "[I]nterests" are what lie *in between* actors and their goals, thus creating a tension that will make actors select only what, in their own eyes, helps them reach these goals amongst many possibilities [first emphasis added].

In the case studied here, one approach succeeded in quickly "translating the interests" of many members of different social worlds. However, diverse worlds usually have diverse problems and concerns. Tailoring the "object" for each world is a very expensive strategy, requiring much negotiation and many resources. The question then is how the molecular biological approach to understanding cancer succeeded in winning the commitments (or "translating the interests") of members of these different worlds.

The following case study of the molecular biological cancer research bandwagon tells the story of the efforts of certain scientists who constructed a "package" and then convinced members of diverse social worlds that they could use it to construct doable problems.

The Molecular Biological Bandwagon in Cancer Research

Since 1978 the National Cancer Institute has awarded an increasing amount of its basic research funds (versus clinical and educational funds) to molecular biological studies of cancer. Before 1983 the National Institutes of Health (NIH) had no category for oncogenes (or cancer genes) in its computer databank of funded projects.[2] In 1983, the NIH instituted an oncogene category and listed the number of sponsored projects at 54 and the number of dollars disbursed to oncogene projects at $5.5 million. By 1987 the NIH was distributing $103.2 million to 648 oncogene projects. NIH support for projects on genetic manipulation in cancer research grew from $16.3 million in 1977 to $194.4 million in 1987.

Molecular biological cancer research articles increasingly crowded the pages of general science journals like *Science* and *Nature* as well as journals specializing in biochemistry, molecular biology, and cancer research. By 1984 the journal *Science* wrote that "the evidence implicating oncogenes as causes of human cancers, although still circumstantial, has been accumulating rapidly during the past few years" (Marx, 1984:2). In 1984 even popular weekly magazines like *Newsweek* carried articles on oncogenes (Clark, 1983; Clark and Witherspoon, 1984; Clark et al., 1984).

New investigators chose to study oncogenes, and even established investigators shifted their research agendas to include oncogene or oncogene-related problems. Cancer research institutes changed their agendas by hiring molecular biologically trained researchers and establishing the proper facilities. The Memorial Sloan-Kettering Cancer Center, the country's oldest and largest research and hospital complex devoted exclusively to cancer, recently shifted from immunology to molecular biology. A molecular biologist, Paul Marks, was appointed to head the organization, and he replaced the old leadership with molecular biologists. A respondent outside the organization commented to me on Marks's agenda: "So now you have Memorial Sloan-Kettering in lockstep going toward molecular biology." Marks himself states:

> You have the feeling now that this research is making inroads toward the control and cure of the disease. . . . Most of the answers to cancer lie down on the level of the genes, in our understanding of how cells differentiate and divide. . . . You have to work with people who've been trained to think like that. (quoted in Boffey, 1987:27)

How did this bandwagon develop, and why did it develop at the intersection of molecular biology and cancer research? I present the story of the bandwagon's development in seven broad stages, beginning with a description of the state of cancer research before the 1970s. Later stages include the development of recombinant DNA technologies, the standardization of recombinant DNA technologies, oncogene theory development, marketing the package of oncogene theory and recombinant DNA technologies, buying the package, and, finally, bandwagon maintenance through the snowball effect.

The State of Cancer Research Before the 1970s

Cancer is the name given to over a hundred different diseases, all of which have one property in common: uncontrolled cell growth. Scientists have studied cancer for a century from many different perspectives and using many different technologies (Bud, 1978; Cairns, 1978; Fujimura, 1986b; Rather, 1978; Studer and Chubin, 1980), yet except for some success at treating a few leukemias, there are no cures or reliable treatments for solid tumors, which form the large percentage of human cancers. Still the hundreds of millions of dollars spent on cancer research by the National Institutes of Health (including the NCI), the American Cancer Society, and other private foundations make it an attractive area of research. The search for the elusive "magic bullet" goes on.

Prior to the development of recombinant DNA technologies in the mid-1970s, cancer research was populated by endocrinologists, immunologists, classical geneticists, biochemists, chemotherapists, and medical researchers of all kinds. Molecular biologists played a limited role. Many researchers pursued the causes of cancer at the cellular and whole organism level. These lines of research included studies of the roles of chemicals, hormones, and radiation in cell transformation. Classical geneticists studied the role of genes in cancer using inbred mice strains and tumor transplantation experiments. Tumor virologists examined the roles of various types of animal viruses and viral oncogenes in cell transformation, often using established cell lines (for a review of these approaches, see Shimkin, 1977). However, until the mid-1970s, researchers had no technologies for testing theories of cancer at the molecular level.

The Development of Recombinant DNA Technologies

Recombinant DNA technology provided a method for manipulating eukaryotic cell DNA. Molecular biologists had previously focussed their research on prokaryotes (simple organisms like bacteria, viruses, and algae whose cells have no defined nuclei). The new methods permitted research on higher organisms whose DNA are enclosed in structurally discrete nuclei (eukaryotes). Since the ultimate goal of this research is to find a cure for human cancer and since humans are mammals with complex eukaryotic DNA, no molecular biological research on human cancer was possible until the mid-1970s.

In 1973, molecular biologists artificially recombined the DNA of two different species, a prokaryote and a eukaryote (Morrow et al., 1974). According to Wright (1986:315),

> the impact of this new capacity to move pieces of DNA between species at will was immediately understood by molecular biologists in the dual scientific and practical terms that characterized the perceptions of its inventors. On the one hand, they saw the ability to do controlled genetic engineering experiments as a powerful means to open up new lines of inquiry into the structure and function of DNA. . . . On the other hand, industrial applications were also anticipated.

Recombination by itself, however, did not allow scientists to do controlled experiments at the molecular level. Molecular biologists needed other techniques, including the cloning, sequencing, mapping, and expressing of genes, before they could easily manipulate DNA to do controlled genetic engineering experiments. By 1977, molecular biologists had developed cloning techniques that allowed them to insert eukaryotic DNA into and among bacterial DNA. They could then grow the bacteria to produce more copies of the isolated foreign piece of DNA in order to analyze it. By 1977 they had also developed faster and more efficient sequencing techniques, which they used to delineate the location of genes on the genome (the complete genetic message of an individual organism) and later to map out the structure of entire genomes, or at least of smaller genomes. Finally, molecular biologists also developed new methods to make the recombined eukaryotic genes, especially mammalian genes, express themselves in bacterial systems. Gene expression is the transformation of the genetic code into the proteins which make the cell function. Gene transfer was one of these new methods. While some molecular biologists used cloning and sequencing techniques to study the DNA structure and the location of genes on the DNA, others used gene transfer techniques—introducing foreign DNA sequences into living cells—to study the functions of genes and gene fragments. However, the techniques were still not standardized enough for researchers other than recombinant DNA methodologists to use efficiently in pursuing other biological problems.

Standardization of Recombinant DNA Technologies

The bandwagon was further developed with the standardization of recombinant DNA technologies. Even if scientists want to incorporate new technologies into their work, they may not be able to do so for lack of funding, available skills, time, or other needed resources. Scientists working in existing laboratories and institutions have made major commitments of resources to particular problems and approaches to those problems. Altering current problem paths requires making changes in ongoing organizations of work: acquiring new skills and knowledge, hiring new staff, and buying new instruments and supplies. Yet, scientists in both university and commercial laboratories tend to work within relatively stable resource allotments that can rise or fall in small increments. They can gain additional resources only through the expenditure of other resources (time and effort taken away from experimental work to write grants or put on "roadshows"). Thus, preferred changes are relatively inexpensive. Investing in standardized technologies is, in fact, an economical way around resource constraints, if entry costs are low enough.

Standardized technologies are tacit knowledge made explicit and routine via simplification and the deletion of the contexts in which the technologies were developed (Kling and Scacchi, 1982; Latour and Woolgar, 1979; Star, 1983). They are conventions for action that are carried with little or no change from one context to another. Standardized technologies take the form of prefabricated biological materials (reagents, probes), procedural manuals (often called "cookbooks") spelling out "recipes" for action, industrial standards, computing protocols, and instruments that automate many procedures (Fujimura, 1987; Kling and Gerson, 1977, 1978).

Because they are explicit and routine procedures, standardized technologies are highly transportable. They reduce the amount of tacit knowledge, discretionary decision making, or trial-and-error work needed to solve problems. What is done to which material for what reason or purpose and with what outcome are all built into the "black box" of transportable technologies. Thus, they are easier to learn and cost less time and effort in retraining and monitoring laboratory staff. To illustrate, before the development of standardized electrophoresis procedures and equipment, a molecular biologist would need "golden hands" to separate DNA lengths of different molecular weights using the centrifuge. Most researchers found the centrifuge too clumsy a tool for such delicate work. Thus, few researchers performed experiments requiring separation techniques until the development and marketing of electrophoresis procedures and equipment. With the development of standardization, experiments requiring the technique flourished.

Finally, these technologies have to be financially affordable in many laboratories for a bandwagon to roll. Standardized technologies allow for rationalized production and distribution of the materials, techniques, and instruments. This reduces the costs of consumption, while economies of scale in production firms reduces the unit cost of the goods. The net result is reduced entry costs.

By saving in training efforts, time, trial-and-error procedures, and/or material costs, standardized technologies reduce the costs of importing them into uninitiated laboratories and the costs of doing research in each laboratory. Reduced costs increase the number of experiments that can be done in a given laboratory with a given budget.

By 1980, recombinant DNA technologies had become conventionalized ways of organizing work (cf. Becker, 1982).[3] Conventionalized tools are relatively stabilized ways of doing work that reduce the uncertainties of daily bench work and the number of "moments" of discretion. Conventions effectively designate some steps in the work processes as taken-for-granted or unproblematic, so that scientists can concentrate on the problematic (Latour and Woolgar, 1979).

First, a few researchers had refined methods for recombining and manipulating DNA into a set of standardized technologies that other molecular biologists and even nonmolecular biologists could also use. The developers of recombinant DNA technologies had codified the technologies in three forms: standardized sequences of standardized tasks, standardized materials, and standardized instruments. By 1982, "cookbook" manuals containing technical "recipes" were available. Cold Spring Harbor Laboratory—a leading institution in molecular biology directed by James Watson, who delineated the structure of DNA in 1953—had compiled and published its first edition of *Molecular Cloning: A Laboratory Manual* (Maniatis et al., 1982) and, by 1984, many other manuals and textbooks were available.

Walter Gilbert spoke of the relative ease of learning the new Maxam-Gilbert DNA sequencing method as he accepted a Nobel Prize in 1977:

> To find out how easy and accurate DNA sequencing was, I asked a student, Gregor Sutcliffe, to sequence the ampicillin resistance gene . . . of Escherichia coli. . . . All he knew about the protein was an approximate molecular weight, and that a certain restriction cut on the [pBR322] plasmid inactivated that gene. He had no previous experience with DNA sequencing when he set out to work out the structure of DNA for his gene. After 7 months he had worked out about 1000 bases of double-stranded DNA, sequencing one strand and then sequencing the other for confirmation. . . . The DNA sequencing was correct. Sutcliffe then became very enthusiastic and sequenced the rest of plasmid pBR322 during the next 6 months, to finish his thesis. (quoted in Cherfas, 1982:124)

Second, materials used in recombinant DNA technologies (restriction enzymes, oncogenes, DNA probes, herring sperm DNA, reverse transcriptase, cell lines, antibiotics, many kinds of chemical reagents, agarose and polyacrylamide gels) are easily available due to the commitments of many organizations. Nonprofit organizations like the American Type Culture Collection (ATCC), located in Rockville, Maryland, collect and maintain recombinant DNA research material samples from laboratories for distribution on demand. Among other materials, researchers can order plasmids and DNA sequence probes (including cloned human DNA) and pay only maintenance and shipping charges.

Scientists can also mail order from private companies high quality biological materials used in recombinant DNA experiments. These materials range from standard to customized products. For example, instead of purifying or constructing their own materials, scientists can purchase restriction enzymes, modifying enzymes, and vectors required for DNA cloning from New England Biolabs (NEB) and Bethesda Research Laboratories (BRL).

Information for using recombinant DNA technologies is also readily available. DNA, RNA, and protein maps and sequences have been published in journal articles and books. Even more helpful are the centralized, systematic databases holding DNA and RNA sequence information on many organisms, including humans.

Finally, instruments automating standardized procedures are well-developed in recombinant DNA technologies, including DNA synthesizers and sequenators, centrifuges, and electrophoresis systems. A "gene machine," or automated DNA synthesizer, exemplifies the prodigious efforts that molecular biologists, commercial entrepreneurs, and venture capitalists have invested in recombinant DNA technology. A DNA synthesizer manufactures customized synthetic oligonucleotides, or short segments of DNA (or RNA). Synthetic DNA is useful to both applied genetic engineering and to basic research scientists. For example, an article in *High Technology* describes a common task in molecular biological laboratories which can be accomplished by the DNA synthesizer:

> Perhaps the most common use of DNA synthesis today is to make "probes" that help locate a natural gene of scientific or commercial interest—such as that for human growth hormone, insulin, or interferon—among thousands of different genes in the DNA of a cell. . . . [f]inding a particular gene is akin to searching for the proverbial needle in a haystack. Fortunately, the ability to make pieces of [complementary] synthetic DNA has greatly simplified the search. (Tucker, 1984:52)

The first automated DNA synthesizer was introduced in 1981. By 1984 seven more reliable machines were on the market and operating in biotechnology companies. A 1986 article reported: "[t]he chemistry has been refined to such a degree that the synthesis of oligonucleotides up to 50 bases in length has become *routine* and oligonucleotides longer than 100 bases have been synthesized" (Smith, 1986:G63).

In 1986, automated DNA sequenators took the facility and efficiency described by Gilbert one step further. The operator need only know what solvents and reagents to put into the instruments. The sequenators thus reduce training requirements even more. Sets of tasks that once were considered thesis problems are now routinely performed by machines.

Thus, even researchers who were not at Harvard University, Massachusetts Institute of Technology, Stanford University, or Cold Spring Harbor Laboratory, the institutions where the "state-of-the-art" technologies were being developed, were able to easily acquire the materials and tools needed for recombinant DNA research. Standardization has also allowed for rationalized production and distribution of the materials, techniques, and instruments used in recombinant DNA research. Thus, the cost of the research has been reduced to affordable levels.

The Oncogene Theory: One-Size-Fits-All

The development and standardization of recombinant DNA and other molecular biological technologies, however, were not solely responsible for the molecular biological cancer research bandwagon. Theories of cancer framed around DNA were also part of the package. Researchers used such theories to guide their use of recombinant DNA technologies and to interpret the results of such applications. Oncogene theory is an important example as it played an ideological role in the initial bandwagon formation.

While some molecular biologists tinkered at improving recombinant DNA technologies, others further explored the structure of DNA, and still others applied the techniques to long-standing questions in almost all biological disciplines (Kumar, 1984:ix). Molecular biologists regarded recombinant DNA technologies and eukaryotic cell genes as the keys to the previously locked doors in normal differentiation and development, cell proliferation, cancer, and even evolution. A group of molecular biologists and a group of tumor virologists took the opportunity to apply the techniques via the oncogene theory to build new lines of research on human cancer.

In the late 1970s, a few molecular biologists and tumor virologists were engaged in two separate lines of research on the molecular mechanisms of cancer causation. The tumor virologists claimed they had found a class of genes in the normal cell that can be triggered to transform the normal cell into a cancer cell (Bishop, 1982; Fujimura, 1986b; Weinberg, 1983). In 1983, Weinberg, a molecular biologist, and his associates claimed their oncogenes to be in the same class as those found by tumor virologists:

> Two independent lines of work, each pursuing cellular oncogenes, have converged over the last several years. Initially, the two research areas confronted problems that were ostensibly unconnected. The first focused on the mechanisms by which a variety of animal retroviruses were able to transform infected cells and induce tumors in their own host species. The other, using procedures of gene transfer, investigated the molecular mechanisms responsible for tumors of nonviral origin, such as those human tumors traceable to chemical causes. We now realize that common molecular determinants may be responsible for tumors of both classes. These determinants, the cellular oncogenes, constitute a functionally heterogeneous group of genes, members of which may cooperate with one another in order to achieve the transformation of cells. (Land et al., 1984:391)

Although their data came from two different areas of research, both groups used recombinant DNA technologies to try to prove their claims. They posited several types of triggering mechanisms. There are many little debates among oncogene researchers about specifics, but the general oncogene theory has become the most popular theory of cancer causation in the 1980s.

These tumor virologists and molecular biologists framed the oncogene theory in a way that they claimed encompassed and unified many other areas of cancer research. They claimed that further investigation using the oncogene framework would produce explanations at the molecular level for problems previously pursued in classical genetic, chemical, radiation, hormonal, and viral lines of research on cancer. They also proposed connections between their theory and other work in the molecular biology of normal growth and differentiation. At the time (and at present), the oncogene theory was the only coherent theory for activities at the molecular level in oncogenesis. The claims were quite grandiose. For example, Robert Weinberg (1983:134), one of the first researchers who claimed to have found cellular oncogenes in human tumor cell lines, said in 1983 that the oncogene theory accounted for findings in many lines of cancer research:

> What is most heartening is that the confluence of evidence from a number of lines of research is beginning to make sense of a disease that only five years ago seemed incomprehensible. The recent findings at the level of the gene are consistent with earlier insights into carcinogenesis based on epidemiological data and on laboratory studies of transformation.

The claim of oncogene theorists to have found one set of causal elements that unified all pathways fell on welcoming ears. *Newsweek* (Clark & Witherspoon, 1984:67) ends one article on oncogenes with the following acclamation:

> Such discoveries shed important light on the fundamental processes of cancer as well as the growth and development of all forms of life. In the future, they will surely lead to better forms of diagnosis and treatment. The presence in cells of abnormal amounts of proteins caused by gene amplifications, for example, could lead to sensitive new tests for certain kinds of cancer. As for treatment, scientists envision the development of drugs designed to specifically inhibit oncogenes. These would be far better than anticancer drugs that indiscriminately kill normal cells along with cancerous ones. "We would," says Frank Rauscher of the American Cancer Society, "be using a rifle rather than a shotgun."

The unifying theory appealed to scientists because of its elegance, a term they use to describe a theory that can precisely and simply explain many disparate observations.

Oncogene theory proponents claimed to have developed a "one-size-fits-all," molecular explanation for many different types (classifications) and causes (causal explanations) of cancer. The ultimate claim was that their research might lead to a common cure, a "magic bullet" for cancer.

Marketing the Package

Claiming that one's theory unifies many lines of research, however, does not mean that others will agree with the claim and rush to pursue experiments based on the theory. In the fifth stage, tumor virologists and molecular biologists jockeyed for position and finally joined forces to construct and promote the package of the oncogene theory and recombinant DNA technologies. They marketed the package as a tool by which other researchers could transmute their work organizations and construct doable problems. Incentives for "old-fashioned" cancer researchers included a chance to use "hot," new recombinant DNA technologies. Molecular biologists were offered a chance to attack the *human* cancer problem through the oncogene theory. These incentives contributed to the development of the bandwagon.

Oncogene theory proponents enrolled allies behind their package not only by claiming to have accounted for findings in many other lines of cancer research, but also by framing and posing new doable problems on oncogenes for other researchers to investigate. That is, they posed questions which: (1) scientists could experimentally investigate using recombinant DNA and other molecular biological technologies; (2) laboratories were already organized and equipped with resources to handle, or could relatively easily import the requisite resources; and (3) satisfied significant audiences.

The proposed problems were both specific and general. Researchers could immediately begin experimentation on specific problems, while thinking of possible ways to translate more general problems into specific experiments.

J. Michael Bishop's (1983:345–48) article on "Cellular Oncogenes and Retroviruses" in the 1983 *Annual Review of Biochemistry* is an excellent example of the rallying cries used to market the package. The article proposed problems that mapped onto established laboratory organizations and available technical skills. Bishop first summarized work in several other lines of cancer research and then presented proposals for research that linked oncogenes with these other lines of work in cancer research and in biology generally, including experimental carcinogenesis, evolutionary biology, normal growth and differentiation, medical genetics, and epidemiology. Bishop (1982:91) states:

> Medical geneticists may have detected the effects of cancer genes years ago, when they first identified families whose members inherit a predisposition to some particular form of cancer. Now, it appears, tumor virologists may have come on cancer genes directly in the form of cellular oncogenes.

In a volume entitled *RNA Tumor Viruses, Oncogenes, Human Cancer and AIDS: On the Frontiers of Understanding,* the editors Furmanski, Hager, and Rich (1985:xx) proclaimed that

> we must turn these same tools of molecular biology and tumor virology, so valuable in dissecting and analyzing the causes of cancer, to the task of understanding other equally critical aspects of the cancer problem: progression, heterogeneity, and the metastatic process. These are absolutely crucial to our solving the clinical difficulties of cancer: detection, diagnosis and effective treatment.

Oncogene theorists also used other strategies to gain allies. For example, in 1984 they established the first of annual national meetings devoted entirely to oncogene research. At a more hands-on level, they distributed their probes for oncogenes to other laboratories and to suppliers, thus facilitating the spread of oncogene research by providing standardized tools. One oncogene researcher told me:

We've had so many requests for our probes for [two cellular oncogenes] that we had one technician working full-time on making and sending them out. So we finally turned over the stocks to the American Type Culture Collection.

These probes were more than physical materials. They were "black boxes," designed with reference to specific hypotheses about their involvement in cancer causation. Any researcher can call or write to ATCC to order the probes at the cost of maintenance and shipping. In other words, oncogene researchers made the tools for testing and exploring their theory available and accessible to a host of other researchers.

Oncogene theory proponents taught and talked about their work to students and researchers in other biological disciplines. A respondent described the positive response of cell biology conference participants to an oncogene promotion talk. Most of the conference participants, uninitiated in the complexities of oncogene research, were awed by the promotion and unable to evaluate the difficulties in the data. Proponents also spoke about their work in the popular media. On October 6, 1987 the *New York Times* published an article headlined "Young Science of Cancer Genes Begins to Yield Practical Applications."

Efforts to build lines of research and to gain allies for particular perspectives, theories, and research are common. The issue here is not that tumor virologists and molecular biologists attempted to gain allies but how they did it and why they succeeded. I have discussed their strategies for gaining allies here. Next I discuss why they succeeded.

"Buying" the Package: Many Prizes in the Box

The decisions of individual researchers, funding agencies, research institutes, and private companies to pursue oncogene research were based on their goals: to construct doable problems, build careers, produce marketable products, and build successful "going concerns" (Hughes, 1971).

Researchers do not readily alter successful research programs just to pursue new opportunities. As I argued elsewhere (Fujimura, 1986a), they redirect, shift, or add to their problem paths when opportunities outweigh costs or when they cannot work around contingencies that block further progress. New recruits decided to import the package and change the course of their research because: (1) the oncogene theory offered the chance to pursue research on human cancer; (2) the package of oncogene theory and recombinant DNA technologies provided a pathway to exploring new, uncharted territory ("sexy" problems); (3) researchers could incorporate the new, "hot" standardized recombinant DNA technologies into their laboratories at relatively economical start-up costs; (4) work in some laboratories had led to "dead-ends" or "roadblocks," while work in some cancer research institutes had been criticized as "old-fashioned." The package of oncogene theory and recombinant DNA technologies fit both organizationally and intellectually with the requirements, goals, and conditions of the work of researchers in several different lines of work.

Incentives for Tumor Virologists. Tumor virologists decided to shift to or augment their research with oncogenes questions in order to work more closely with human cancer etiology. This concern grew in prominence during the 1970s because tumor virology research had come under fire for its lack of payoff in human cancer terms.

Using traditional virological methods to investigate RNA tumor viruses, tumor virologists had found specific genes in the viruses that transformed cultured cells and caused tumors in laboratory animals. These viral oncogenes, however, caused cancer only in vitro and in laboratory animals. No naturally occurring tumors in animal and human populations were credited to viral oncogenes although researchers have argued that they have confirmed suspected links between some human cancers and retroviruses (see especially Gallo, 1986).

Most of the tumor virology research was funded by the National Cancer Institute's Viral Cancer Program, which was established on the premise that many human cancers were virally induced. The VCP, initiated as a contract program in 1964, was thereafter heavily funded. In 1971 the National Cancer Act continued to fund allocations to virus cancer research despite heavy criticism from biological and biomedical scientists (Chubin and Studer, 1978; DeVita, 1984; Rettig, 1977; and Studer and Chubin, 1980). After further protests and controversy, the ad hoc Zinder committee was constituted to review the VCP. In 1974 the committee, headed by Norton Zinder of Rockefeller University, submitted an extremely critical report to the National Cancer Advisory Board (NCAB), which oversees the work of the entire NCI (Rettig, 1977). In 1980, as a further consequence of this and other in-house controversies, NCI leaders decided to break up the VCP and integrate the pieces into other NCI programs. This overhaul had cumulative negative effects on viral cancer research funds.

In response to criticism and to NCI cutbacks in support, many tumor virologists decided to shift their research toward cellular oncogenes. The oncogene theory and recombinant DNA technologies provided the means for tumor virologists to construct doable problems on a group of genes in normal cells in all eukaryotes (including human) that were suspected of causing cancer. The possible impact of this research on human cancer satisfied sponsor demands and thus increased its marketability.

Incentives for Molecular Biologists. As I noted earlier, molecular biologists were not participants in cancer research until very recently. Molecular biologists used recombinant DNA technologies and the oncogene theory as a means to insert themselves into cancer research, especially into work on the human cancer problem. Weinberg (1982:135; emphasis added), an important player in this field, spelled this out clearly: "The study of the molecular biology of cancer has *until recently* been the domain of tumor virologists."

Incentives for the National Cancer Institute. NCI administrators "bought" the package for reasons similar to those of the tumor virologists. Their sponsors were Congress and the publics they represented, including other scientists. The oncogene theory and recombinant DNA technologies provided them with both the justification for past research investments in the Viral Cancer Program, then under heavy criticism, and with a product to market to Congress.

Efforts to use oncogenes to justify past investments in viral oncology are evident in the following statement by Vincent T. DeVita, Jr. (1984:5), director of NCI:

> We have often been asked if the NCP [National Cancer Program] has been a success. While I acknowledge a bias, my answer is an unqualified "yes." The success of the Virus Cancer Program which prompted this essay is a good example. Since its inception, this Program has cost almost $1 billion. If asked what I would pay now for the information generated by that Program, I would say that the extraordinarily powerful new knowledge available to us as a result of this investment would make the entire budget allocated to the NCP since the passage of the Cancer Act worthwhile. There may well be practical applications of this work in the prevention, diagnosis, and treatment of cancer that constitute a significant paradigm change. The work in viral oncology has indeed yielded a trust fund of information, the dividend of which defies the imagination.

Indeed, DeVita used the oncogene theory to justify the entire National Cancer Program. Similar justificatory statements were made by leading oncogene theorists, such as J. Michael Bishop (1982:92), and leading molecular biologists, such as James D. Watson (DeVita, 1984:1).

DeVita told me he also used oncogenes to sell their general future program of molecular genetic research on cancer to Congress:

> Molecular genetics is a term nobody in Congress understands. Oncogenes they know. How do they know? I tell them. I can explain oncogenes to them much better than I can explain molecular genetics. When I point my finger at a Congressman, I say, "Mr. So-and-So, you and I both have genes in us, which we believe are the genes that are responsible for causing cancer." It gets their attention. They say, "My God! What do you mean I have genes in me . . . ?" I have to explain it to them. If I tried to explain molecular genetics, they'd fall asleep on me.

The statement that we all have genes that can be triggered to cause cancer can engender great fear in congressional members and their constituents. This fear, however, was laid to rest by the claim that a unifying pathway to all cancers may exist and that there may be ways to intervene in this pathway.

The National Cancer Institute bought completely the oncogene theory and molecular genetic approaches to cancer in general. DeVita summarized for me NCI's investments in molecular genetic cancer research for 1984:

> [In 1984] we had $198 million in molecular genetics. . . . [That figure] includes oncogenes, but it also includes people who are walking up and down the genome, tripping on oncogenes but looking for something else. And they're going to find the regulatory elements that control the oncogenes, [which is] really the major step. Oncogenes have told us something very important, but now what you want to find out is what regulates these genes so that you can use this information to turn them on and off.

In addition, in 1981, while NCI leaders were in the process of reorganizing research at the Frederick Cancer Research Facility, they decided to similarly shift the facility's emphasis. "We put three or four crackerjack oncogene scientists up there, and they're up there cranking out the data and having a fun old time," said one administrator.

NCI appointed a viral carcinogenecist who had worked with George Todaro, one of the originators of an early version of the oncogene theory, to the position of associate director of the entire NCI. He oversaw the Frederick

Cancer Research Facility and specifically kept track of oncogene research progress (Shapley, 1983:5). Finally, NCI committed funds to a supercomputer to facilitate oncogene and other molecular biological cancer research.

The NCI focus on oncogenes and other molecular biological cancer research studies meant cutbacks in other basic research lines, as a 1983 article (Shapley, 1983:5) in the journal *Nature* indicates:

> If NCI allows spending on oncogene research to expand naturally, does this mean less prominence for important traditional fields such as chemotherapy? DeVita says that some other work must obviously go, given the fact that NCI is unlikely to receive any budget increases in the next few years. He notes that chemotherapy has been cut by about 30 percent in the past six years on scientific grounds: "some things we didn't need to do any more," he says. And, as explained by Alan Rabson, director of NCI's division of cancer biology and diagnosis, "if you understand oncogenes you may learn where to go in chemotherapy. It may open up whole new areas of chemotherapy."

Although chemotherapy was the only area mentioned in the article, other areas of research were also neglected just by the fact that Congress did not increase their budget while oncogene research expanded.

Incentives for Students, New Investigators, Established Researchers. The growing commitments of tumor virologists, molecular biologists, and the NCI to oncogene and related molecular biological cancer research became, in turn, further incentives for students, new investigators, and even researchers established in other lines of work to frame their theses and research problems in these terms.

Besides interesting intellectual questions and the problem of curing cancer, new researchers had to attend to career development contingencies in making problem choices. The immediate foreground was filled with the exigencies of their daily work lives: researching and writing Ph.D. theses, establishing and maintaining laboratories and staff, publishing and gaining tenure, writing grant proposals, attracting and training students. Constructing doable problems that produce results that someone will publish is a practical and pressing concern. Thus, desirable "cancer research" becomes "doable research."

Students and beginning researchers gained major advantages for establishing their careers and laboratories by choosing to investigate problems under the rubric of oncogene research. By 1982 these advantages included clearly articulated experiments, research funds, high credibility, short-term projects, increased job opportunities, and the promised generation of down-stream doable problems.

By 1982, the package of oncogene theory and molecular biological tech-nologies provided clear problem and experiment structures. At the end of 1983, a researcher in an oncogene laboratory explained his work to me as a set of logical steps:

> Everyone knows that it would be worthwhile to sequence this gene. It's obvious what should come next. There are logical steps in this work. 1. Identify the protein [involved in transforming normal cells into cancer cells]. 2. Clone the gene associated with the protein. 3. Sequence the gene. You can always find money to sequence. We get enough grant money to sequence what we want to. It may not solve the cancer problem, but it will give some information.

By 1982 oncogene research was a "hot" area, consisting of several lines of research. NCI had made substantial funding allocations to oncogene research. Here a graduate student who had been studying cellular immunology and shifted his thesis problem to investigate an oncogene talks about the growth of commitment to the new line of work:

> I studied cellular immunology and am now doing c-myc [cellular myc oncogene] research. My professor said, "There's the funding, go for it." So I did. I wrote a grant to fund this oncogene research project. When you write a grant, it also forces you to get into it, to think up innovative ways of approaching the problem. Why not go for it? It makes sense to use the funding that's there to do your work. If it turns out to be significant work, then good. If not, you can always change later.

Oncogene research uses skills in molecular biology, including recombinant DNA technologies. These technical skills were, by then, standardized and available to new researchers at affordable investment costs.

Moreover, new researchers raised the credibility of their work by con-structing problems using molecular biological technologies. Latour and Wool-gar (1979:242) note that

> credibility is a part of the wider phenomenon of credit, which refers to money, authority, confidence and, also marginally, to reward. . . . [For example,] the mass spectrometer is . . . an actual piece of furniture which incorporates the majority of

an earlier body of scientific activity [in physics]. The cost of disputing the generated results of this inscription device [is] enormous.

Very few biologists would be willing to attack findings based on results from a mass spectrometer, often used in molecular biological experiments, because physics ranks high among scientific hierarchies of credibility (Becker, 1967). Although power is negotiated, the relative power of the negotiating parties matters (Strauss, 1978a). Since many molecular biological methods came from physics and chemistry, oncogene researchers increase their negotiating power and credibility by enrolling recombinant DNA and other molecular biological technologies. That is, they are adding the appeal, legitimacy, and credibility of molecular biology, physics, and chemistry to the construction of their "facts." For these reasons, oncogene research problems were extremely good bets in the early 1980s for gaining marketable problems, skills, support, and products.

In addition, new researchers increased their chances for successful future careers by enrolling molecular biological technologies. Molecular biology has steadily expanded its boundaries during the past two decades. There are very few fields of research and biological disciplines that molecular biologists have not entered. University biology departments, research institutes, commercial biotechnology companies, and pharmaceutical companies all continue to vie for the best molecular biologists in the world (Stokes, 1985; Wright, 1986). Expansion of genetic screening programs for inherited diseases have extended the impact of molecular biology to the public, including private citizens, insurance companies, and governments (Duster, 1981, 1987, in press). If only for the chance to gain highly marketable molecular biological skills, then, oncogene research became a good bet for graduate and postdoctoral students. A postdoctoral student training in an oncogene laboratory specifically stated his view that his research on oncogenes, with one foot in cancer and the other in molecular biology, would definitely get him a job in either the university or in industry.

Cancer research similarly was a well-funded arena, with a $1.2 billion budget in 1984 for the NCI alone ($1.3 billion for 1987). With additional funds from other National Institutes of Health, National Science Foundation, American Cancer Society, and other private foundations, cancer research was a thriving enterprise. At the intersection of the molecular biology and cancer research, oncogene research provided new researchers with important resources for building careers.

Oncogene problems also provide the advantage of results in relatively short time frames. Most oncogene researchers publish from two to fifteen articles a year depending on their professional status, the size of their laboratories, and the number of collaborations. These short time frames fuel the oncogene bandwagon and draw attention away from other areas like cell biology. One respondent said: "The reason that oncogene research is surging is that the work is doable. There is a productive methodology. And you get results quickly. . . . " He argued that the fault for this focus on short-term payoff lay with the supporters of research rather than with the researchers themselves.

Another senior investigator concurred that bandwagons develop because of time and task constraints on new investigators:

> How do waves get started and why do they occur? I think the reason for that has to do with the way science is funded. And the way young scientists are rewarded. . . . [A] youngster graduates and . . . gets a job in academia, for instance. As an assistant professor, he's given all the scut work to do in the department. . . . In addition, he must apply for a grant. And to apply for a grant and get a grant . . . nowadays, you have to first show that you are competent to do the [research], in other words, some preliminary data. So he has to start his project on a shoestring. It has to be something he can do quickly, get data fast, and be able to use that data to support a grant application . . . so that he can be advanced and maintain his job. Therefore, he doesn't go to the fundamental problems that are very difficult. . . . So he goes to the bandwagon, and takes one little piece of that and adds to that well-plowed field. That means that his science is more superficial than it should be. And that's bad for the field of science.

Thus, if it takes many more years to construct a doable problem using one approach versus another, most researchers choose the shorter, surer bet.

At this stage of the bandwagon's development, early oncogene researchers had circulated claims that problems framed in terms of their package were fast, highly doable, highly credible, and highly productive. They had lined up sponsors, integrated transportable recombinant DNA technologies, worked their way into the human cancer and normal cell genomes, and connected oncogenes to many other lines of research, including the "hot areas" of evolutionary biology and normal growth and differentiation. They had connected such heterogeneous things as human cancer, a class of genes called oncogenes, recombinant DNA technologies, normal growth and differentiation, and the National Cancer Institute. They had persuaded other researchers and funding agencies that, because of these connections, oncogene research would satisfy their interests and the demands put upon them by their sponsors, colleagues, students, and university administrations. With respect to many worlds within cancer research and molecular biology, then, the oncogene theory held high privilege. Presented with such a highly privileged theory as an incentive in a race for time, new investigators jumped on the bandwagon.

Finally, new and more established investigators also bought the package because of promised intellectual payoff and new generations of downstream questions. Novel findings from oncogene research were not only useful for fattening publications lists for academic researchers. They were also intellectually "hot." For example, in 1983, *Nature* (Newmark, 1983:470) published an article in its "News and Views" entitled "Oncogenic Intelligence: The Rasmatazz of Cancer Genes." The article was just one of many published between 1978 and 1985 announcing exciting new findings from oncogene research. Researchers provided novel, intellectually exciting information and mined their findings for further experimental questions.

The intellectual excitement was not limited to oncogene research but extended to all molecular biological research. Almost all respondents, independent of their political views about how the new molecular biological technologies should be used, echoed this excitement. A respondent who had been conducting protein biochemical research explained the excitement in terms of a whole new level of analysis opening up to scientists:

> You can ask certain sorts of questions which you can't really answer with just the biochemical methodology. . . . Genetics essentially involves modifying what's already there, rather than simply describing what's going on. It allows you to ask much more specific questions about which components of the system are necessary to do what. Recombinant DNA technology is starting to allow one to ask those sorts of questions in animal cells, tumor cells. . . . Questions which there is as yet no other way of approaching.

Established researchers also found the possibilities for exploring new levels of analysis useful. An example was the senior investigator who had been studying the effect of radiation on transforming cells in culture. After much excitement about the oncogene theories of carcinogenesis, he sent his student to train in recombinant DNA techniques in a nearby laboratory in order to test two hypotheses: first, whether radiation played a role in mutating or transposing one or several proto-oncogenes and, second, whether radiation damage to cells made it easier for the viral oncogene to become integrated into the normal cellular genome. Thus, the graduate student gained the benefits enrolled behind the oncogene theory, and the senior investigator imported new skills and a new line of research into his laboratory. There appear then to be many benefits to be gained from pursuing oncogene research.

Incentives for Private Industry. Despite the uncertain commercial payoff from oncogene research, several large pharmaceutical companies and major research and development (R&D) companies have committed funds, researchers, and laboratories to oncogene research and recombinant DNA technologies (Koenig, 1985). These "betting" pharmaceuticals include Hoffman-La Roche Inc., Smith Kline Beckman Corporation, Merck and Co., and Abbot Laboratories. Investing R&D biotechnology companies include Genentech and Cetus and especially smaller companies aimed specifically at oncogene products including Oncogene Science Inc., Oncogen, and Centocor Oncogene Research Partners.

One respondent regarded these commitments as an effort to "get in on the ground floor." Even if a particular company is not the home of the desired new discovery that leads to a patentable diagnostic or therapeutic product, it will have established the infrastructure for early entry into the race to produce the final commercial product(s). A research director at Hoffman-La Roche stated, "If you're interested in [oncogene] products, you can't afford not to be in the race now" (Koenig, 1985:25).

Commercial biological material suppliers, however, could invest in oncogene materials only with the arrival of standardized technologies. They would not have been able to profit on high-cost, state-of-the-art technologies. Stephen Turner founded Oncor

to capitalize on the emerging diagnostic market from recent developments in cancer molecular biology. . . . There is no clear-cut link between oncogenes and clinical claims, but I'm gambling that it will happen. It was a greater risk a year ago than today. Look at *Nature;* there are four to five articles per week about oncogenes. (quoted in Johnson, 1984:18)

Turner also referred to other commitments made to this goal by Oncogen (another small biotechnology supply firm), a collaboration between Genetic Systems and Syntex, and a joint venture between Becton-Dickinson (a large, diversified biological research supply company) and Cold Spring Harbor Laboratory. In Turner's words,

> clearly this is a hot area. My business goal is not unique. . . . In cancer molecular biology, there is a need for standard reagents in highly convenient, quality-controlled assays that researchers can use to detect human and other species of oncogenes, genetic arrangements, gene amplification and gene expression. (Johnson, 1984:18)

While Turner aimed his efforts at the long-term goal of supplying clinical researchers with tools for diagnosing tumors in human patients, his immediate clients were basic cancer researchers. They used the products to manipulate genes and tumor tissue in their fundamental research in test tubes, petri dishes, and lab animals. A well-worn photocopy of an advertisement for Oncor products from the journal *Science* was taped to the wall by one graduate student's bench in an academic oncogene research laboratory.

These commitments to oncogene research on the part of private industry refer back to similar commitments of new researchers. These commercial investments provide both job opportunities and more affordable research tools for new investigators jumping on the bandwagon.

The Bandwagon's "Snowball" Effect

By 1984 the molecular biological cancer research bandwagon was a distinct phenomenon. Scientists were acting on the basis of its existence. Researchers referred to the oncogene bandwagon in conversations. More generally, modern biology was molecular biology. The bandwagon had grown to the point where it was sustained by its own momentum. That is, researchers joined the bandwagon primarily because it *was* a bandwagon, its continued growth produced by a "snowball" effect.

Actors from diverse social worlds had committed their resources to molecular biological cancer research. These commitments included: (1) very large increases in funding allocations; (2) designated positions in academic departments, research institutes, and private industrial laboratories; (3) easily accessible training and tools, including knowledge, standardized technologies, materials, and instruments; and (4) a cadre of researchers training in molecular biological skills. That is, an infrastructure of skills, funding allocations, committed researchers and teachers, positions committed to molecular biologists, biological material suppliers, and even whole companies and research institutes committed to oncogene research problems was established by 1984. This infrastructure then constrained and influenced the decisions of new investigators. It served to maintain previous commitments as well as to gain new commitments.

Molecular biological cancer research by 1984 appeared to new investigators to be the research line of choice. Scientists joined the bandwagon in order to build successful careers. For many new researchers, this decision to jump on the bandwagon to construct and solve problems on cancer in molecular biological terms was independent of whether or not the problems would yield cures for cancer. Building individual and collective careers was their foremost concern. While curing cancer would be a welcome reward, it was only one consideration among many for their decisions to jump on the bandwagon.

Discussion

The research on which this paper draws is a study of change in science. It examines how the process of theoretical or conceptual shifts is inseparable from both the local and broad scale organization of work and technical infrastructures of science. In the molecular biological cancer research bandwagon, cancer was repackaged as a disease of the cell nucleus and specifically of the DNA. Researchers in other lines of work had previously studied cancer as a disease of the cell, the immune or endocrine system, the entire organism, or the interaction between organism and environment. In the late 1970s and early 1980s, molecular biologists and tumor virologists developed a theory-method package and "marketed" it as a new and possibly more productive perspective on cancer. This new package consisted of a molecular biological *theory* of cancer and a *set of technologies* for testing and exploring the theory. They constructed the oncogene theory so that it mapped onto the intellectual problems of many different scientific social worlds. In addition, by the early 1980s, recombinant DNA technologies were standardized and thus highly transportable between social worlds. The combined advantages of the theory and technologies made the new package, and therefore the new definition of cancer, accessible and attractive to many different scientists, laboratories, organizations (including funding agencies), and lines of research.

Accessibility depends on the transportability of methods. Technologies are highly transportable when tasks and procedures are standardized, that is, conventionalized and routinized. Standardized procedures reduce the amount of tacit knowledge, discretionary decision making, or trial-and-error procedures needed to solve problems. What is done to which material for what reason or purpose and with which outcome are all built into the "black box" of transportable technologies. In the molecular biological cancer research bandwagon, molecular biologists constructed standardized tools for manipulating DNA in higher organisms. They transformed "state-of-the-art" tools into routine tools and made it possible for established researchers in other biological specialties to move them into their own labs and for new researchers to gain access easily to these tools. Another important aspect of accessibility is funding. Since funding agencies had bought the package, getting research grants to incorporate the new tools was relatively easy. This combination of routine tools and available research funds resulted in decreased articulation requirements for those who joined the bandwagon.

My point about the package of theory and methods is that the package itself is another step in the construction of prepackaged conventions for action. Scientists now manipulate a particular gene through a relatively straightforward series of steps with reference to the role that that gene plays in cancer. Oncogene researchers know not only how to manipulate the gene, but which gene to manipulate and for which purposes. They also have a framework within which to interpret the outcomes of such manipulations. Thus, scientists benefited, first, from the standardization of recombinant DNA technologies and, secondly, from the "standardization" of the package of oncogene theory and recombinant DNA technologies.

The standardized package of the oncogene theory and transportable recombinant DNA technologies together served as an *interface* among different social worlds. An interface is the means by which interaction or communication is effected at the places "where peoples meet" or different social worlds intersect. A standardized package is an interface that operates simultaneously in many different social worlds as compared to an interface that links two social worlds. It is the mechanism by which multiple intersections occur.

In science, we see many intersections between two or three disciplines or lines of research, for instance, between biology and chemistry (Gerson, 1983). Molecular biology itself is the product of the intersection of physics, chemistry, and biology. These intersections arose through long periods of detailed, repeated, and long-term negotiations among many participants and in many situations (see, for example, Clarke, 1985; and Gokalp, 1987). In oncogene research and the molecular biology of cancer, we find an intersection among multiple different lines of work that arose very quickly.

The standardized package facilitated this bandwagon's rapid development because it facilitated interaction among members of different social worlds.[4] Its conventionalized ways of carrying out tasks (or standard operating procedures) allowed people in different lines of work to adopt and incorporate them into their laboratories and ongoing enterprises more easily and quickly. That is, it facilitated the flow of resources among many different lines of work. People in one line of research could rapidly and relatively easily adopt resources from another line of research and come to a common practice.

The success of molecular biologists' and tumor virologists' marketing efforts to many different social worlds was largely due to the following: first, the theory-method package provided procedures for a relatively straightforward construction of doable problems, or what Kuhn (1962/1970) would call "normal science." Second, the experiments involved new, "sexy," recombinant DNA techniques, as compared with old, well-known routines. Third, early oncogene theorists demonstrated that, within their model, their doable problems quickly produced novel information about cancer at the molecular level. As scientists making maps of nature, they attempted to chart previously unexplored territory, that is, cancer at the molecular level of analysis. However, anyone entering uncharted territory will likely find something interesting, some new way of representing nature. Finally, then, this particular representation of cancer won so many allies because the theory-method package fit within the institutional and organizational constraints of scientific work of these multiple different social worlds.

Acknowledgments

I am grateful to L. Asato, H. S. Becker, N. P. Chico, A. E. Clarke, K. A. Doksum, T. Duster, E. M. Gerson, P. Keating, A. Rip, P. St. Lawrence, S. L. Star, A. L. Strauss, and three anonymous referees for their helpful comments on the material presented here. This paper is based in part on my Ph.D. dissertation (Fujimura, 1986b) in sociology, University of California, Berkeley. The writing of this paper was supported in part by an NIMH postdoctoral fellowship at Stanford University. Correspondence to: Department of Sociology, Harvard University, Cambridge, MA 02138.

Notes

1. For a short list of the social studies of science and technology literature in this vein, see Busch (1982), Callon (1985), Cambrosio and Keating (1988), Clarke (1987), Collins (1985), Fujimura (1987), Fujimura et al. (1987), Knorr-Cetina (1981), Latour (1987), Latour and Woolgar (1979), Law (1986), Lynch (1985), Pickering (1984), Shapin (1982), Star (1989), Star and Gerson (1986). For literature on bandwagons or crusades in science, see Panem (1984), Rip and Nederhoff (1986), and Studer and Chubin (1980).

2. Reported NIH funding data is from the Computer Retrieval of Information on Scientific Projects (CRISP) system of references to United States Public Health Service grants and contracts and to NIH intramural projects and retrieved through their keywords. I am grateful to F. M. Biggs and Seu-Lain Chen of the Division of Research Grants and N. Sue Meadows of the Office of Grants Inquiries for their assistance in this data collection.

3. The "logical" sequences of steps in recombinant DNA research discussed above are logical only insofar as a number of contemporary biologists collectively agree to represent nature in this fashion. When the organization of their work changes (for whatever reasons), their representations of nature and their "logical" experimental steps will most likely also change.

4. Whether theory-method packages play such significant roles in the development of other bandwagons is an empirical question. Other kinds of packages—for example, problem-data representations, problem-methods, methods-data representations, and other combinations of problems, methods, data representations, and theory—may serve as interfaces in other bandwagons. We also need comparative studies of bandwagons at different organizational scales: within and across lines of research, within and across disciplines, and across countries.

References

Becker, Howard S.
    1982   Art Worlds. Berkeley: University of California Press.
    1967   "Whose side are we on?" Social Problems 14:239-48.
Bendifallah, Salah and Walt Scacchi
    1987   "Understanding software maintenance work." IEEE Transactions of Software Engineering 13:311-23.
Bishop, J. Michael
    1983   "Cellular oncogenes and retroviruses." Annual Review of Biochemistry 52:301-54.
    1982   "Oncogenes." Scientific American 246:80-92.
Boffey, Philip M.
    1987   "Dr. Marks' crusade: Shaking up Sloan-Kettering for a new assault on cancer." The New York Times Magazine April 26:25-31, 60-67.
Bud, R. F.
    1978   "Strategy in American cancer research after World War II: A case study." Social Studies of Science 8:425-59.
Busch, Lawrence
    1982   "History, negotiation, and structure in agricultural research." Urban Life 11:368-84.
Cairns, John
    1978   Cancer: Science and Society. San Francisco: W. H. Freeman and Co.

Callon, Michel
    1985   "Some elements of a sociology of translation: Domestication of the scallops and the fishermen of St. Brieuc Bay." Pp. 196-233 in John Law (ed.), Power, Action and Belief, Sociological Review Monograph. Boston: Routledge and Kegan Paul.

Cambrosio, Alberto and Peter Keating
    1988   "Going monoclonal: Art, science, and magic in the day-to-day use of hybridoma technology." Social Problems 35:244-60.

Cherfas, Jeremy
    1982   Man-Made Life: An Overview of the Science, Technology and Commerce of Genetic Engineering. New York: Pantheon Books.

Chubin, Daryl E. and Kenneth E. Studer
    1978   "The politics of cancer." Theory and Society 6:55-74.

Clark, Matt
    1983   "Spotting the cancer genes." Newsweek 3 May:84.

Clark, Matt and Deborah Witherspoon
    1984   "Cancer: The enemy within." Newsweek 5 March:66-67.

Clark, Matt, Mariana Gosnell, Deborah Shapiro, and Mary Hager
    1984   "Medicine: A brave new world." Newsweek 5 March:64-70.

Clarke, Adele E.
    1985   "Emergence of the reproductive research enterprise: A sociology of biological, medical, and agricultural science in the United States, 1910-1940. Ph.D. Diss., University of California, San Francisco.
    1987   "Research materials and reproductive science in the United States, 1910-1940." Pp. 323-50 in Gerald L. Geison (ed.), Physiology in the American Context, 1850-1940. Bethesda, MD: American Physiological Society.

Collins, Harry M.
    1985   Changing Order: Replication and Induction in Scientific Practice. Beverly Hills, CA: Sage.

DeVita, Vincent T.
    1984   "The governance of science at the National Cancer Institute: A perspective on misperceptions." Pp. 1-5 in Management Operations of the National Cancer Institute that Influence the Governance of Science, National Cancer Institute Monograph 64. Bethesda, MD: U.S. Department of Health and Human Services, NIH Publication No. 84-2651.

Duster, Troy
    Forth-   Eugenics Through the Back Door. Berkeley: University of California Press.
    coming
    1987   "Cline's recombinant DNA experiment as political Rashomon." Politics and the Life Sciences 6:16-18.
    1981   "Intermediate steps between micro- and macro-integration: The case of screening for inherited disorders." Pp. 109-35 in Karin Knorr-Cetina and Aaron V. Cicourel (eds.), Advances in Social Theory and Methodology: Toward an Integration of Micro- and Macro-Sociologies. Boston: Routledge & Kegan Paul.

Fujimura, Joan H.
    1987   "Constructing doable problems in cancer research: Articulating alignment." Social Studies of Science 17:257-93.
    1986a "Problem paths: An analytical tool for studying the social construction of scientific knowledge." Paper presented to the Society for the Social Studies of Science, Pittsburgh, PA.

1986b   Bandwagons in Science: Doable Problems and Transportable Packages as Factors in the Development of the Molecular Genetic Bandwagon in Cancer Research. Ph.D. Diss., University of California, Berkeley.

Fujimura, Joan H., Susan Leigh Star, and Elihu M. Gerson
1987   "Methodes de recherche en sociologie des sciences: Travail, pragmatisme et interactionnisme symbolique (research methods in the sociology of science and technology: Work, pragmatism, and symbolic interactionism)." Cahiers de Recherche Sociologique 5:65-85

Furmanski, Philip, Jean Carol Hager, and Marvin A. Rich, eds.
1985   RNA Tumor Viruses, Oncogenes, Human Cancer and Aids: On the Frontiers of Understanding. Proceedings of the International Conference on RNA Tumor Viruses in Human Cancer, Denver, Colorado, June 10-14, 1984. Boston: Martinus Nijhoff Publishing.

Gallo, Robert C.
1986   "The first human retrovirus." Scientific American 255:88-98.

Gasser, Les
1984   "The social dynamics of routine computer use in complex organizations." Ph.D. Diss., University of California, Irvine.

Gerson, Elihu M.
1983   "Scientific work and social worlds." Knowledge 4:357-77.

Gokalp, Iskender
1987   "On the dynamics of controversies in a borderland scientific domain: The case of turbulent combustion." Social Science Information 26:551-76.

Hughes, Everett C.
1971   The Sociological Eye. Chicago: Aldine.

Johnson, Roger S.
1984   "Oncor, oncogene diagnostics venture, is 'encore' for BRL cofounder Turner." Genetic Engineering News 4 May/June:18, 33.

Kling, Rob and Elihu M. Gerson
1978   "Patterns of segmentation and intersection in the computing world." Symbolic Interaction 1:24-43.
1977   "The social dynamics of technical innovation in the computing world." Symbolic Interaction 2:132-46.

Kling, Rob and Walt Scacchi
1982   "The web of computing: Computer technology as social organization." Advances in Computers 21:1-90.

Knorr-Cetina, Karin
1981   The Manufacture of Knowledge. Oxford: Pergamon Press.

Koenig, R.
1985   "Technology: Product payoffs prove elusive after a cancer research gain." The Wall Street Journal June 28:25.

Kuhn, Thomas S.
[1962] The Structure of Scientific Revolutions. Chicago: University of Chicago Press. Reprinted 1970

Kumar, Ajit, ed.
1984   Eukaryotic Gene Expression. New York: Plenum Press.

Land, Harmut, Luis F. Parada, and Robert A. Weinberg
    1984   "Cellular oncogenes and multistep carcinogenesis." Pp. 391-406 in Philip H. Abelson (ed.), Biotechnology and Biological Frontiers. Washington, DC: American Association for the Advancement of Science.
Latour, Bruno
    1987   Science in Action: How to Follow Scientists and Engineers Through Society. Cambridge, MA: Harvard University.
Latour, Bruno and Steve Woolgar
    1979   Laboratory Life: The Social Construction of Scientific Facts. Beverly Hills, CA: Sage.
Law, John
    1986   "On the methods of long-distance control: Vessels, navigation and the Portuguese route to India." Pp. 231-60 in John Law (ed.), Power, Action and Belief. London: Routledge & Kegan Paul.
Lynch, Michael
    1985   Art and Artifact in Laboratory Science. London: Routledge & Kegan Paul.
Maniatis, T., E. F. Fritsch, and J. Sambrook
    1982   Molecular Cloning: A Laboratory Manual. Cold Spring Harbor, NY: Cold Spring Harbor Laboratory.
Marx, Jean L.
    1984   "Oncogene overview: What do oncogenes do?" Science 223:673-76.
Morrow, J. F., S. N. Cohen, A. C. Y. Chang, H. W. Boyer, H. M. Goodman, and R. B. Helling
    1974   "Replication and transcription of eucaryotic DNA in Escherichia coli." Proceedings of the National Academia of Sciences U.S.A. 71:1743-47.
Newmark, Peter
    1983   "Oncogenic intelligence: The rasmatazz of cancer genes." Nature 305:470-71.
New York Times
    1987   "Young science of cancer genes begins to yield practical applications." October 6:19.
Panem, Sandra
    1984   The Interferon Crusade. Washington, DC: The Brookings Institution.
Pickering, Andrew
    1984   Constructing Quarks: A Sociological History of Particle Physics. Chicago: University of Chicago Press.
Rather, L. J.
    1978   The Genesis of Cancer: A Study in the History of Ideas. Baltimore: Johns Hopkins University Press.
Rettig, Richard A.
    1977   Cancer Crusade: The Story of the National Cancer Act of 1971. Princeton: Princeton University.
Rip, Arie and Anton J. Nederhof
    1986   "Between dirigism and laissez-faire: Effects of implementing the science policy priority for biotechnology in the Netherlands." Research Policy 15:253-68.
Shapin, Steve
    1982   "History of science and its sociological reconstructions." History of Science 20:157-211.

Shapley, Deborah
    1983   "U.S. cancer research: Oncogenes cause cancer institute to change tack." Nature 301:5.
Shibutani, Tamotsu
    1955   "Reference groups as perspectives." American Journal of Sociology 60:522-29.
Shimkin, Michael B.
    1977   Contrary to Nature: Being an Illustrated Commentary on Some Persons and Events of Historical Importance in the Development of Knowledge Concerning Cancer. Washington, DC: U.S. Department of Health, Education, and Welfare DHEW Publication No. (NIH) 76-720.
Smith, L. M.
    1986   "The synthesis and sequence analysis of DNA." Science 232:G63.
Star, Susan Leigh
    1989   Regions of the Mind: British Brain Research, 1870-1906. Stanford: Stanford University Press.
    1985   "Scientific work and uncertainty." Social Studies of Science 15:391-427.
    1983   "Simplification in scientific work: An example from neuroscience research." Social Studies of Science 13:205-28.
Star, Susan Leigh and Elihu M. Gerson
    1986   "The management and dynamics of anomalies in scientific work." Sociological Quarterly 28:147-69.
Stokes, Terry D.
    1985   "The role of molecular biology in an immunological institute." Paper presented at the International Congress of History of Science, July 31-August 8, University of California, Berkeley.
Strauss, Anselm L.
    1988   "The articulation of project work: An organizational process." Sociological Quarterly 29.
    1978a   Negotiations: Varieties, Contexts, Processes, and Social Order. San Francisco: Jossey-Bass.
    1978b   "A social world perspective." Studies in Symbolic Interaction 1:119-28.
Strauss, Anselm, Shizuko Fagerhaugh, Barbara Suczek, and Carolyn Wiener
    1985   The Organization of Medical Work. Chicago: University of Chicago Press.
Studer, Kenneth E. and Daryl E. Chubin
    1980   The Cancer Mission: Social Contexts of Biomedical Research. London: Sage.
Tucker, Jonathan B.
    1984   "Gene machines: The second wave." High Technology 4:50-59.
Weinberg, Robert A.
    1983   "A molecular basis of cancer." Scientific American 249:126-43.
    1982   "Review: Oncogenes of human tumor cells." Pp. 135-36 in S. Prentis (ed.), Trends in Biochemical Sciences, Vol. 7. Amsterdam: Elsevier Biomedical Press BV.
Wright, Susan
    1986   "Recombinant DNA technology and its social transformation, 1972-1982." In Osiris, Second Series II:303-60.
Zeldenrust, Sjerp
    1985   "Strategic action in the laboratory: (Inter-)organizational resources and constraints in industrial and university research." Paper presented at the 10th Annual Meeting of the Society for Social Studies of Science, Rensselaer Polytechnic Institute, Troy, NY.

5

Time in the Recruiting Search Process by Headhunting Companies

KRZYSZTOF KONECKI

Commentary

Krzysztof Konecki is a Polish sociologist who has specialized in field studies of work and industrial organizations. He teaches in those areas at the University of Lodz. A year's fellowship in the United States brought him to the University of California at San Francisco and to Strauss' seminar on grounded theory (a methodology with which he was already well acquainted and had written about in Polish). In California, he did a number of intensive interviews with recruiters (so-called "head hunters") from executive recruitment firms who specialized in finding candidates for executive positions at client business companies. We have included this chapter by Dr. Konecki on this topic, written at our request for this book. It illustrates well several points, besides the usual ones, about the use of grounded theory methodology and methods.

AUTHOR'S NOTE: This research was possible thanks to the Fulbright Foundation. I would also like to thank my California hosts for their hospitality and inspiring discussions, especially Anselm Strauss, Charlene Harrington, Leonard Schatzman, Adele Clarke, and many other friends from San Francisco and at the University of California in San Francisco, Department of Social and Behavioral Sciences. Correspondence should be addressed to Krzysztof Konecki, Institute of Sociology, University of Lodz, IS, ul Rewolucji 1905r, 41/43, 90-914 Lodz, Poland. E-mail: konecki@krysia.uni.lodz.pl

When attending the research seminar, he was particularly struck by the applicability of the discussion of conditional matrix to his interview materials. His chapter is a nice example of how this procedural device can guide a researcher. Of course, it does not at all guarantee that the researcher will tightly and specifically link intervening conditions with the particular form of interaction under research focus, but Dr. Konecki skillfully and convincingly weaves these sets of conditions into his explanations. Furthermore, he relates these sets of conditions to each other. You can see this clearly because he has taken pains to show this with the particular format of presentation he has used. (In fact, note how differently he has presented his materials than the authors of other chapters.)

Strikingly illustrated in the chapter, also, is the typical interactionist focus on temporal matters, when seemingly relevant in one's data. His treatment of temporal issues is subtle and refreshingly detailed, and specifically tied to conditions at all levels of the matrix—interactional, internal to the work itself, organizational, market and complex cultural conditions.

*   *   *

Introduction

This chapter presents a reconstruction of conditions for effective work by professional recruiters. These include the internal circumstances for recruitment searching work, as well as the organizational, interactional, market and cultural conditions of this work. Reconstruction of those conditions has involved use of two grounded theory conceptions. One was that of a "conditional matrix," and the other was that of a basic "paradigm." (Both conceptions are well known to readers of this chapter, so I will not discuss them as such.) These conceptions are useful for generating a grounded theory, because they reveal connections between *working time* and *different conditions* (and their permutations). This reconstruction of conditions also has practical implications because it gives knowledge about conditions that should be taken into account when planning recruitment work, thus helping to prepare recruiters for difficult work conditions that might influence coordination of their work and their interaction with clients and potential employees.

This chapter is based on qualitative empirical research conducted in the San Francisco Bay Area. The topic of the research was the following: The process of recruitment and selection of candidates for working, as carried out by executive search companies. These companies are usually called "head-hunting firms." A total of 22 interviews were conducted—20 with headhunters from 20 firms, one interview with a candidate later employed by the client company, and one interview with a client company that had used an executive search company. These interviews were open ended. The researcher wished to get a complete description of the recruiters' work and their vision of the basic pattern of the search process itself. The researcher also wished to obtain in each of the latter interviews at least one authentic story of a recruitment search. After each conversation, the interviews were completely transcribed, and analyzed according to the methodology of grounded theory (Konecki, 1989; Strauss, 1987; Strauss & Corbin, 1990). Also included in the analysis were previously published case study descriptions of the searching process. The cases were used as data for comparative analysis. Every interview was coded by open coding,[1] and during this procedure the concepts, hypotheses, and research questions were created. I went into the field once again to get answers to those questions. That procedure was repeated 21 times. During that period, I wrote theoretical memos[2] and compared data gathered from different kinds of headhunting firms (e.g., from companies of different sizes).

As mentioned previously, the basic paradigm characterizing grounded theory research was used, involving the connecting of theoretical categories by tracing of the relations between them and the following:

- The central phenomenon studied
- The conditions (causal and intervening)
- The context
- The strategies of action
- The interactions
- The consequences

The entire procedure for doing this work of relating is called *axial coding* (Strauss & Corbin, 1990, pp. 96-115). The category name that refers to the phenomenon that was researched is "*the length of time* of the searching process." (This is a subcategory of the more general category of "trajectory of the searching process.") In this chapter, I will concentrate on the axial coding of the first process. Also, I will indicate some practical consequences (sociotechnical) of this knowledge for increasing effectiveness of recruitment research, gotten from reconstructing the search conditions.

The effectiveness of the recruit's work (a category) is here defined (not measured) through a property of the category, *"the length of time* of the searching process." The employment of a suitable candidate is here the aim of the headhunter's work and, ideally, the aim should always be achieved by professional recruiters (Backer, 1993; Brown & Martin, 1991; Dingman, 1993; Sherman & Bolander, 1992). From this point of view the work of the search companies should always be effective.

1. The Effectiveness of the Consultant Work and the Length of Time of the Search for an Appropriate Candidate

Searching for candidates to fill new job openings has a temporal character. Respondents emphasized many times the temporal aspects of a search when they named "searching for candidates" by the formula, "a research process." The word "process" (an in vivo concept) underlines the temporal character of the recruitment search. The idea of process in search companies was, probably, taken from manufacturing and industrial settings in which the production processes are planned and strategized by sequence. The planning of production is aimed at saving time during the production process. One of the recruitment consultants also compared a recruitment search to a living being: "They are like pets." The search has a beginning, a growing stage, a loitering stage, and a death when the individual either is hired or the client drops the search. Thus a recruiter moves forward in a logical sequence. His or her search is based, however, on a specific requirement because some steps can be performed simultaneously. What is important here is the phasing of this recruitment process. This phasing indicates, in turn, a broader theoretical category—namely, "the trajectory of the searching process" (this category is analyzed in Konecki, in press).

Temporality is connected also with the timing of the recruitment search. "Timing" means the *amount of time* spent by a recruit for a search (see Figure 5.1). Timing depends on (is a consequence of) the organizational conditions that induce the search company to adopt appropriate strategies for conducting the search for making the placement. Effectiveness of this search means achieving the placement of an appropriate candidate in the client firm. This is defined (not measured) through a more general condition, that is, the length of time of the searching process.

Involved in the pattern of effectiveness are the following:

1. *Conditions,* for example, organizational ones →
2. *Effectiveness* of the search (placement of the candidate—phenomenon) →
3. *Cultural context* →
4. *Strategies,* for example, time line →
5. Search *(action)* →
6. Timing *(consequence)*

The structural organizational conditions, that is, the kind of search company (a retaining one or a contingency one) and recruitment company size, can influence both the length of time of a search and the search accomplishment. The retainer firms work on an exclusive basis—only one search firm looks for candidates, and is paid for the service even before finding an appropriate candidate. Some contingency companies also try to get their searches on an exclusive basis. But there is an opposite approach by contingency companies that generally accept orders on a nonexclusive basis and are paid after the employment of a candidate by the client. Many contingency companies look for candidates to fill the same opening but only one company can win the competition and receive payment for its search.

Client firms wanting a nonexclusive search will call a few headhunter companies to maximize the probability of a swift placement ("a shotgun approach"). This then, however, has a low probability of getting money from a placement. Only the consultant who has placed a candidate receives payment. If there are four consultants in the competition, the probability of getting money is only 25% per an individual recruiter. The consultant can spend a lot of time on a search without receiving any financial reward. The time spent on the search gives, in this situation, zero results and leads to an unsuccessful search. This anticipated possible consequence of the nonexclusive search is the reason (condition) that many consultants do not accept searches on a nonexclusive basis, or else they perform these jobs poorly.

2. The Difficulty Dimension of the Searching Process and Timing

"The length of time of a search" is a different concept from the temporality. Timing is a dimension of the search, and a search can be short or long.

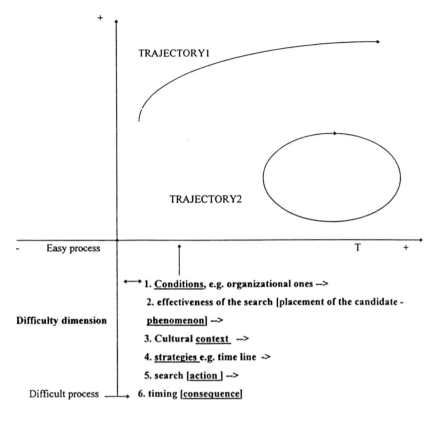

T - time
TRAJECTORY1 -   a linear schema of the search trajectory (*a priori* articulation of a
                trajectory.
TRAJECTORY2 -   a concentric ordering schema of the trajectory (factual articulation of a
                trajectory).

Figure 5.1. The Conditions and Length of the Search Trajectory; Difficulty Dimension

Temporality is a category dimensionalizing the phenomenon of the search and dividing it into sequences, phases of the search (trajectory of the search: Konecki, in press; also see Figure 5.1).

Good timing seems to be fundamental to the recruitment business. This is not different from other kinds of business: "They must recruit fast, if they do not, they go to somebody else. Timing is everything" (a client). Timing in searching for and selection of candidates is, however, a very difficult issue because of the nature of the headhunting industry. The recruiters deal mainly with human beings, so the work involves communicational and emotional aspects.

Timing is also a condition of client companies hiring the headhunters. Because the former want to hire new specialists or executives quickly, there can be stiff competition among them. These client firms hire headhunters to speed up this recruitment. Their sense of time, "being in a hurry," is transferred to a headhunting company that is also "in a hurry" to find the appropriate candidate as soon as possible.

The process of searching can be dimensionalized according to the criterion of "search difficulty" (the process can be difficult or easy). We can formulate a hypothesis that has emerged from our research: "The more difficult the searching process, the longer is the time spent on it." If so, we can note a difficulty dimension of this search for candidates.

We start from a descriptive list of conditions that influence this difficulty dimension:

1. Internal search work circumstances
   1a. The beginning of the search → difficult process
   1b. The next stages of the search → easy process
   1c. The first search for a client company → difficult process
   1d. The next searches for a client company → easy process
2. Organizational conditions
   2a. Hiring is not a priority for the client → difficult process
   2b. Hiring is a priority for the client → easy process
   2c. The client company is declining → difficult process
   2d. The client company is developing → easy process
   2e. High position of the candidate → difficult process
   2f. Lower position of the candidate → easy process
   2g. Good communication with Human Resources Department → easy process
   2h. Lack of communication with Human Resources Department → difficult process
3. Interactional conditions
   3a. Candidate, at the same time, looks for a job somewhere else; overselling practices by candidate → difficult process

3b. Candidate wants to work only in the client's company; lack of over-selling practices by candidate→easy process
4. Market conditions
   4a. Vast supply of candidates→easy process
   4b. Shortage of candidates→difficult process
5. Cultural context
   5a. Cultural context not advantageous for headhunting (as in Japan)→difficult process
   5b. Cultural context advantageous for headhunting (as in the United States)→easy process

If we multiply the aforementioned conditions based on influencing the difficulty or ease of the search (the minus and plus signs), then we get a pattern of conditions influencing the timing of the search:

$-1*-2*-3*-4*-5 \rightarrow D$, difficult search $\rightarrow$ T, poor timing of the search
or
$+1*+2*+3*+4*+5 \rightarrow D1$, easier search $\rightarrow$ T1, good timing of the search

We can then formulate a hypothesis: Under the internal searching work circumstances (see Condition 1), organizational circumstances of the client company (Condition 2), interactional conditions of a candidate and a consultant dealings (Condition 3), the market conditions (Condition 4), and the cultural context (Condition 5), can cause a search to become more or less difficult—and the degree of the difficulty (*/−) leads to good or bad timing of the search (T/T1). If all the conditions have a negative sign (−), this leads to the multiplication of the degree of difficulty of the search, and at the same time leads to poor timing.

The Explanation of the Conditions

1. The Internal Searching Work Circumstances Are Very Important for the Difficulty Dimension of any Recruitment Search. The first week of the search is the most difficult. It is associated with the strategizing stage, when a job specification and a candidate's profile must be accurately described. Some consultants say that at this time the success of a search is really decided. If the job specification and desired person's profile are described adequately, then the next stages of the search can be easily performed. There is, then, this responsibility at the beginning of the search—a consultant must learn a lot about the client company and the position that it is offering to a prospective candidate.

The first search done for a client firm is the most difficult. Moreover, if the first search is associated with the first week of the search, the level of difficulty for the researcher is multiplied. The client company is completely unknown and considerable effort and time is needed to learn about the position being offered, as well as the demands of the hiring manager and the company culture. The next searches for the same client company are easier and take less time. This is because the consultant already has learned a lot about the client. He or she can also refuse an order from a client who has proven to be uncooperative during a previous search. The good timing of future searches is then taken into consideration when making a decision to accept another job search for this particular client.

2. A Search Can be Prolonged or Delayed Because of the Following Organizational Conditions

A. The hiring manager travels and is not available for an interview with the candidate.

B. The client does not see the interview as a priority.

According to one recruiter, when the client receives a first candidate to interview, the search usually slows down. The client may lose motivation. Sometimes, too, it is difficult to get the client to meet the candidate for his or her interview. The recruiter's strategy then is to persuade the client to do the interview. If done, the search can be finished earlier and time is saved.

C. Internal communication problems in the client's company often occur, especially between the hiring manager and the Human Resources Department.

The recruiter's strategy is to encourage communication and to speed up the flow of communication between them.

The search can also be delayed because of poor communication between a recruiter and the Human Resources Department. The departmental managers can only give about 20% of their time to recruitment and to cooperation with the recruiter or hiring manager. This department's estimations of timing and temporal resources are different than the recruiter's. They concentrate more on other departmental functions, for recruitment is only part of their work. The opposite situation occurs with a recruiter who concentrates only on recruitment, and so the timing of a search is his priority. This recruiter's strategy in dealing with those managers effectively is to maintain good relations with their departments, and to communicate with them as a given search evolves.

> D. Another organizational condition bearing on the difficulty dimension is the financial standing of the client's company.

It is very difficult to recruit somebody for a company that is known to be on the decline. In such a situation it is difficult to attract candidates to the client company. It is easier to attract candidates to one that is visibly growing and developing.

> E. Another organizational condition can be the high or low organizational position of the candidate.

Those at the highest positions are very busy and very rarely available to the recruiter. This can create a problem with timing—for example, being able to arrange time for an interview with a client company.

> F. Another organization condition can be the different time expectations of the client and the recruiter.

For instance, the client and the recruiter see the starting point of the search differently—"The client starts the search too late; even at the beginning of the search he is already a month behind. They don't start early enough. It takes longer to get approval. When the recruiter starts, they say 'We have already wasted 2 months, when are you going to do something?' [laughter] So they are working to a different time schedule."

3. Interactional Conditions

A consultant also tries to keep the candidate interested in the potential job during the search. The consultant wants to sell his candidate's qualifications. Sometimes a candidate makes the search difficult because he or she wants to oversell himself or herself—sometimes the recruiter must work to differentiate the candidate's self-evaluation practices from real qualifications. These interactional conditions also influence the timing of a search and can delay it.

It is often difficult to maintain the interest of a candidate in the search ("to keep the temperature of the candidate hot"), perhaps because the interview with the client has been postponed and the candidate may then think the client is not very interested in him or her. At the same time, the candidate may have other interviews lined up with other companies. The consultant tries, therefore, to persuade the client to do an interview immediately. Tactics for persuading the client can include the recruiter calling the client and urging an interview, then telling a story about the candidate's interviews with other companies. Sometimes the recruiting consultant will lie to push the client toward doing an interview quickly with the candidate.

Sometimes a candidate arranges an interview with a company other than the one proposed by the recruiter. Thus, the candidate maximizes his or her chances of getting a job, but at the same time minimizes the chances of the recruiter's accomplishment and lessens the recruiter's temporal efficiency. These actions by the candidate are conditions of a difficult search for the recruiter and casual conditions of a delay.

There are also other actors who participate in the searching game: the family of the candidate. It is very important in the searching process to include the family of the candidate. If, for example, a wife opposes her husband's moving, then the recruiter's work will not be successful. The candidate will have an opponent at home and this can be destructive the recruiter's work (Berger, 1990). Therefore, including the family in a search process is a condition of a successful or unsuccessful search. (This is important both in Japan and in the United States, so the condition seems to be transcultural.) If the wife is opposed to her husband's changing his job then the consultant has to spend a lot of time persuading her to agree to the move: "But his wife . . . was adamantly opposed, because she thought the new business might fail. It took me 11 months, including making full financial presentations to her on behalf of the new company, to convince her that the business would succeed" (example from Japan in Berger, 1990, p. 59). "They spent several days, they interviewed, they showed them (the family) houses. It was a big effort. And finally they made the offer" (an American executive recruiter). Even when the consultant and a client company make an effort to persuade the wife of a candidate to a move, she can refuse or change her mind after some time, and so a search or placement can fail.

4. The Vast Supply of Candidates in the Labor Market Makes the Search Easier for a Recruiter

This happens after the acquisition of large companies or their downsizing. There is a higher probability of choosing the right candidate for a position if a large number of candidates are available for screening. A shortage of candidates lessens the probability of finding the right candidate although it does not exclude matching an appropriate person to the position.

5. Cultural Context

From a cultural point of view, we can speculate that a value underlying the "assumption of a quick search" is the emphasis on time/timing—in the United States it is an important part of the culture. The phrase "time is money" should be transformed to "being fast is the value in itself." Money can be a consequence of fast work, but not necessarily. This assumption as a condition would influence all kinds of recruitment strategies. It would then be an intervening condition for recruitment actions.

Yet it is very difficult to specifically trace the cultural conditions that influence the temporal routines and procedures of work in U.S. companies. It is difficult to find research tools that can be used to connect the value of time to everyday life activities in a U.S. cultural context. It is more reasonable from an empirical point of view to look at the direct conditions that are connected with the timing of work, and that provide support in the data themselves. We can, of course, use cross-cultural comparisons to explain some differences in approach to time.

Japan, as usual, provides excellent comparative data (Konecki, 1994). For example, Western financial houses in Tokyo must accept the reality that searches for executives take 25% to 50% longer than in the West. The problem in Japan is not primarily in identifying suitable candidates, but in arranging meetings within the very long workday in Tokyo. The presentation of consultants to candidates also consumes a lot of time. The consultants need to explain the character of their work. Moreover, there appears to be a problem of trust between the recruiter and candidates. Trust is part of the credibility dimension. The Japanese cultural context influences the work that must be done on building trust and introducing it into relationships and achieving credibility. The work on trust then influences the timing of the search.

culture as a condition → work on trust → length of a search process

Moreover, the problem of timing is exacerbated by Western employers in Japan insisting on good English-language capability.

Veterans of headhunting, however, say that convincing Japanese executives to switch jobs usually has as much to do with opportunity, psychology, and timing as it does with money. Most managers who are recruited are in a state of disequilibrium. They might have been unhappy in their work, or have returned from overseas and no longer fit in with their Japanese colleagues at work, or perhaps they are in a business section that is being phased out. Even with the right psychological factors in place, convincing an experienced Japanese worker to make the big switch remains a time-consuming task (Berger, 1990, p. 59).

The everyday work of headhunters and their time schedules are also influenced by the Japanese cultural context. The long working hours mean that a recruiter can call a candidate only during the weekend. Usually a recruiter calls at 10:00 a.m. on Sunday because the candidate then is likely to be relaxed. Their meetings together also have a clandestine flavor. Secrecy is essential for any Japanese candidate who is still working; sometimes managers in Japanese companies can intercept mail to an executive who is suspected of wanting to leave the company (Berger, 1990, p. 59).

"Time is money," so recruitment in Japan can be costly for clients. The search firms that work there insist on payment according to the time and difficulty (dimension) of assignment, rather than on the basis of one third remuneration of the successful candidate—a system favored in the United States and, to a lesser extent, in Britain (Jones, 1988, p. 25; see also Berger, 1990). So the perception of time also becomes a condition influencing the structural factors of the recruitment business as, for example, is the payment for the search. Thus, the culture is an intervening condition that influences the work of recruiters, in this case influencing the length of the search process.

Some Theoretical Conclusions

The effectiveness of the search process has many conditions. We have reconstructed through the research the following conditions:

- Internal search work circumstances
- Organization conditions
- Interactional conditions

- Market conditions
- Cultural conditions

The conditions influence the degree of difficulty of the search positively or negatively, and consequently the length of a search process. There are several possibly different permutations of the aforementioned conditions. The headhunters when articulating their work[3] must take into account the conditions and prepare strategies to deal with them. A priori and fully worked out articulation of work is impossible because of the possibility of emerging unpredictable conditions of work. A suitable response to an emerging condition is, however, part of the permanent articulation of work. Adjusting to new and emerging conditions of actions would be impossible without permanent coordination of actions and lines of work by candidates, clients, and recruiters. Knowledge about the conditions may improve the effectiveness of work and actions of all participants in this process.

The methodology of grounded theory is therefore a very useful tool for the reconstruction of conditions and combinations of the conditions of a category. Knowledge of the conditions that influence the length of time of work is a first step toward an effective articulation of this recruitment work.

Notes

1. Open coding is a procedure by which empirical data are conceptualized. A transcribed text can be analyzed in this way, through examining minutely every line, sentence, or paragraph. The conceptual labels are analyzed and compared and subsequently a list of conceptual categories is created (Strauss & Corbin, 1990, pp. 61-74).

2. Theoretical memos refer to descriptions of important categories of generated theory, their properties, dimensions, relations between categories, and their conditions. This chapter is one of the many versions of some of my theoretical memos describing the temporal dimension of recruiters' work.

3. What is "articulation?" The several or many participants in an interactional course necessitate the coordination of their respective actions. Articulation is thus instrumental in the temporal ordering of social reality. It includes interactional processes of negotiation, persuasion, manipulation, teaching, the threat of coercion, and perhaps actual coercion (Strauss, 1993, pp. 40-41). "Articulation stands for the coordination of lines of work. This is accomplished by means of interactional processes of working out and carrying through of work-related arrangements" (Strauss, 1993, p. 87).

References

Backer, P. (1993). Space, time, space-time, and society. *Sociological Inquiry, 63,* 406-424.

Berger, M. (1990). The gentle art of headhunting. *International Management, 57,* 59.

Brown, L., & Martin, D. (1991). What to expect from an executive search firm. *HR Magazine, 36,* 56-58.

Dingman, H. (1993). The right fit executive search by retained recruiters. *Cornell Hotel and Administration Quarterly, 34,* 26-31.

Jones, S. (1988). Headhunting in financial services: London, New York, and Tokyo compared. *Multinational Business, 4,* 14-26.

Konecki, K. (1989). The methodology of grounded theory in the research of the situation of work. *Polish Sociological Bulletin, 2,* 59-74.

Konecki, K. (1994). *The organizational culture of Japanese industrial enterprises* (in Polish). Lodz, Poland: Lodz University Publications.

Konecki, K. (in press). Temporal aspects of the process of searching for candidates to work (in Polish). *Culture and Society.*

Sherman, A., & Bolander, G. (1992). *Managing human resources.* Cincinnati, OH: South-Western Publishing, College Division.

Strauss, A. (1987). *Qualitative analysis for social scientists.* New York: Cambridge University Press.

Strauss, A. (1993). *Continual permutations of action.* New York: Aldine de Gruyter.

Strauss, A., & Corbin, J. (1990). *Basics of qualitative research.* Newbury Park, CA: Sage.

6

The Line in the Sand

Definitional Dialogues in Abusive Relationships

LORA BEX LEMPERT

Commentary

This chapter, about "definitional dialogues in abusive (husband to wife) relationships," was written by Lora Lempert shortly after finishing a doctoral dissertation about sexual abuse. The history of her research is pertinent to understanding her chapter. She had worked as a volunteer with a self-help group for sexually abused women, finally deciding to do research about their relationships with abusive husbands. So by the time she read the accumulated social science literature on this phenomenon, she was already steeped in her own experiences and research, with relatively well-formed, if not yet systematically conceptualized, ideas about some aspects of sexual harassment. Her chapter can be usefully read as primarily an argument (based on those experiences and research) directed against prevalent masculine-oriented interpretations of the harassment phenomenon. This argument, although partly appreciative of the work of her opponents, is directed not only to those other particular researchers, but to the special audience represented by interactionist sociologists who regularly read the annual publication, *Studies in Symbolic Interaction*. Interestingly, its long-time editor, Norman Denzin, a well-known and esteemed interactionist, and very influential among the harassment researchers for an early article on the topic, is her principal opponent in her attack on the specialist literature.

The format of her chapter quickly signals the argument. After a brief section in which it is suggested that "women's changing and evolving definitions of the situation (of harassment and violence) are the necessary conditions for their simultaneous and subsequent transformations of self," the chapter moves to a section titled The Abused Women's Self. This directly takes up specialist research and its deficient emphases and assumptions that simplify the harassment situation; fails to see that the women are not entirely victims but also active agents in these complex situations; and that those emphases and assumptions insure "the conditions, contexts, and consequences of (the women's) actions are further removed from consideration." On the other hand, Dr. Lempert is not claiming the literature is all wrong, but only that her work aims at complementing and extending that writing.

Given the argumentative intent, her discussion of methods and methodology is but two brief paragraphs, moving quickly to a precis of what will be her analytic presentation. The heart of this consists of the "definitional dialogues" and self-definitions of the women: The nature of these is spelled out in detail, with supporting and exemplifying quotations from the interviews, but also with linkages back to disciplinary literature about harassment. The final section gives a focused but extended summary of her argument as based on her research materials.

The last paragraph sums up the argument: "In seeking to understand the complexity of women's lived experiences of intimate, interpersonal violence, it is necessary to place women at the center of the analysis. Gender neutral theoretical formulations of abuse fail to account for the simultaneity of love and violence and the simultaneity of agency and victimization that make women's definitions of their violent situations understandable." In this research, grounded theory methods and general "methodology that stresses discovery and theory development" (as learned in our research seminar) was used, although the conceptualization is less elaborately developed than in Dr. Lempert's thesis. Here the conceptualization functions primarily to generate and support her theoretical argument.

*   *   *

Introduction

Sociologists have long been aware that one person can greatly affect the definition of the situation for another (Mead, 1934; Waller, 1970). In cases of intimate, interpersonal violence directed by men against their female partners, definitions of the situation are influenced by structural inequalities of power and control. The macro politics of the social control of women through violence and threats of violence (Dobash and Dobash, 1992) are reflected on the interactional level. Men generally have more power than women and can frequently enforce their definitions. In violent relationships, men's views can (and do) become hegemonic. In a micro interaction where an individual man is harming or threatening an individual woman, it is the woman's definition of the situation, rather than the "objective" characteristics of "reality" that is the critical factor in understanding her actions and responses within the context of the relationship.

My analysis of abused women's interview narratives suggests that women's changing and evolving definitions of the situation are the necessary conditions for their simultaneous and subsequent transformations of self. Their constructive processes originate in definitional dialogues with self, with partners, and with outsiders. Under the impact of definitional struggles and the cumulative effects of violence, the abused women in this study constructed new meanings for their experiences and transformed their perceptions of self. I analyze the initiation of these processes by examining definitional dialogues, or ongoing negotiations, which according to the women's accounts occurred almost exclusively between the women and the abusing males and, simultaneously, within the women themselves. The definitional dialogues that are part of this research are located in both the social-structural and the cultural dynamics of the society, as well as in the social-organizational and interpersonal dynamics of the family (Tifft, 1993). They are the outcomes of the social organization of domestic arrangements in the homes of abused women and in the more public arenas of contemporary life.

The paradox between women's agency and women's victimization is salient in this analysis for these "victims" are also active agents defining, interpreting, and to a limited extent, negotiating with their partners. As "victims" they are not entirely passive and as "agents" they are not co-acting equals in the interactions. Their participation in definitional dialogues highlights the overt and covert tensions existent in male/female interactions throughout our society.

In analyzing these constructions, I run the risk of ascribing a false linearity to dynamic processes. It must, therefore, be emphasized that the processes are circular, simultaneous, and overlapping. They are part of ongoing interactions and are, therefore, affected by prior incidents and affecting of subsequent interactions. However, this does not necessarily mean that the women could chart what was happening to them while they were in the chaos of the relationships.

The Abused Women's Self

Focused sociological attention on the social problem of "wife abuse" began only two decades ago, yet a considerable volume of theory has already been generated.[1] With the following exceptions, little analytical attention has been paid to abused women's experiences of self in violent relationships.

In a review of phenomenological, sociological writings concerned with domestic violence, Denzin (1984) argues that emotionality and the self form the core of domestic violence interactions. He posits violence as occurring within interactional frameworks of super and subordinate relationships, where the interactional order mirrors the economic, cultural, social, legal, and ideological contradictions and tensions of the broader society. Denzin (1984), and Cho (1991) and Tifft (1993), in expansions of his argument, further suggest that negative structures of experience from domestic violence episodes become embedded in ongoing interactional structures. Eventually a fairly stable structure of negative symbolic interaction locks families into a "circuit of violent selfness" that attaches and connects each subject to a "web of violence" that is chainlike in its hold on them. Denzin's compelling formulation has significantly influenced sociological theorizing about wife abuse, yet this formulation and its expansions are incomplete in that they are gender neutral and assume that each family member exists autonomously within the life of the family. My research indicates that Denzin's gender neutrality seriously flaws his argument (see Discussion).

Ferraro and Johnson (1983), Johnson and Ferraro (1984), Mills (1985; with Kleinman, 1988), and Chang (1989) have also explored the impact of the lived experiences of violence on abused women's senses of self. Ferraro and Johnson's (1983, Johnson and Ferraro, 1984) work highlights the phenomenon of surrender, as well as breaking out of bad faith (Denzin, 1984) and double bind (Cho, 1991), as it examines the victimized self of the abused women. The new victimized self is presented as a positive identity assumed by abused women as they redefine themselves in their violent relationships. While significant in its analytical insights, this analysis nonetheless contains some problematic assumptions. First is a presumption that women in abusive relationships want to leave their partners, a supposition that is not consistently supported in research since many abused women choose to return to their abusers after leaving and after shelter stays. Second, there is an assumption that leaving the relationship is the correct course of action.

Mills (1985) and Mills and Kleinman (1988) adopt an interactionist perspective in their analyses of assaults on abused women's senses of self. Mills (1985) examines the changes that abused women experience as they deal with their violent partners and hypothesizes victimization as a gradual process. According to Mills, although men's demands on their partners vary, the goal is always control. Women respond to these demands by developing minimizing strategies that create identities for themselves consonant with socio-cultural expectations.

Mills and Kleinman (1988) explore the variety of ways that shelter residents report their thoughts and feelings. In addition to describing the experiences, the researchers identify two means through which abused women suspended reflexivity, that is, numbness and spontaneous action. They hypothesize that in the context of the seeming inevitability of unhappy marriages, women become numb. Inevitability is also identified as the context within which spontaneous activity, like the murder of an abusive partner, occurs.

Chang (1989) posits social isolation both in and out of the shelter as the critical factor that explains why some women shelter residents do not become "self-savers" and do return to their abusing partners. Chang (1989) makes many of the assumptions already detailed in this section, that is, that the relationships can be reduced to the acts of violence, that the correct interpretation of intimate violence is a feminist interpretation, that the proper course of action for abused women is exiting the relationships, and that women who do not choose to leave need some sort of re-education.

The assumptions in all these studies reflect a tension in the implicit, and unacknowledged, alliance between politics and scholarship that results in the imposition of external definitions on women's interactions. This epistemological underlay reduces the complexities of abusive relationships to incidents of violence, thus rendering women's actions in violent relationships invisible. Women become victims without agency and the conditions, contexts, and consequences of their actions are further removed from consideration.

How abused women negotiate constructions of knowledge of self, situation, and violence within the complexity of these relationships constitutes the fundamental focus of my analysis. Previous analyses of abused women's struggles to construct/reconstruct, maintain, alter, and/or develop senses of self (Denzin, 1984; Ferraro and Johnson, 1983; Johnson and Ferraro, 1984; Mills, 1985; Mills and Kleinman, 1988; Chang, 1989; Cho, 1991; Tifft, 1993) warrant further study. Analysis of the simultaneity of love and violence and the simultaneity of victimization and agency, which form the contextual frames of the interactions, is necessary to shed light on the organization and display of violence in intimate, interpersonal relationships. This research thus complements and extends the survey and interview observations of previous researchers on the lived experiences of abused women.

Methodology

This analysis is grounded in in-depth interview data from 32 self-selected women participating in an outreach support group (an ancillary service to a battered women's shelter), who reported experiencing repeated interpersonal violence of a physical, psychological, and/or emotional nature at the hands of their intimate male partners. I asked these abused women to tell the stories of their relationships. I then analyzed their responses utilizing grounded theory methodology which stresses discovery and theory development (Glaser and Strauss, 1967; Glaser, 1978; Strauss, 1987; Strauss and Corbin, 1990).

The interviews ranged in duration from one to four and a half hours. Of the 32 participants, nine were women of color. Most participants had some college education, and they ranged in age from 21 to 57 years old.

This presentation is an analysis of definitional dialogues, centering around control of the definitions of the situations and, consequently, of the women and the violence, recounted by all of the women in the study. Almost all of the respondents indicated that these definitional struggles initially occurred in the absence of significant others, that is, generally there were no witnesses. In presenting these negotiations analytically, I first delineate those definitional processes that occurred across the violent interactions, focusing on the women's responses to the men's strategies for gaining definitional hegemony. I then turn to a discussion of the women's internal dialogues as they occurred simultaneously, overlapping with and greatly affected by the negotiations with their partners. The analysis continues with the refining process of defining the self in the situation. I conclude with a section defining the violence, although the definitional dialectics around violence also inhered in the previously presented analyses.

Definitional Dialogues

Hegemony

According to the women's accounts of their abusive relationships, before any physical violence occurred, their abusive partners sought definitional hegemony over their mutually interactive situations. The men attempted to impose their definitions of the very nature of the women's worlds by controlling the external definitions of their relational situations and by deconstructing the identities of the participants. This respondent's account of her partner's reaction to disagreement was typical of the incidents related:

> Well, he would tell me it's my fault, it's my fault, it's my fault, 'cause I make things bigger than they are and, I have no control (laughs), you know. (Respondent 14)

The repetitive use of "it's my fault" in this recounting is indicative of the pervasive effect of the man's definitional hegemony over time, of the effects of negative symbolic interaction (Denzin, 1984; Cho, 1991; Tifft, 1993). The account is a retrospective reconstruction of events in the relationship. For this respondent time has telescoped; events have lost their unique characteristics and collapsed into one another. The repetition of "fault" implicitly suggested an attribution of blame for problems in the relationship that reach beyond the disagreement. As related, the man ascribed the "fault" to stereotypically emotional, feminine responses, such as making things "bigger than they are" or having "no control." In short, fault lies in not accepting his definition of the situation.

Respondents report their abusive partners used words to construct their realities at deep levels. The words used influenced the women's identities and defined their life situations: "stupid bitch," "selfish fucking asshole," "career woman hag," "cunt," and so on. For the women, these terms of abuse became more than just features of their lives with these men: They began to constitute the definitional frames of their worlds. Publicly most of the women acquiesced to these definitions in a "fiction of intimacy" (Tifft, 1993), but privately they resisted. The women were torn. With ambiguity as a criterion for accusation, the women were never sure that the men's definitions were not correct.

These abused women maintained a certain skepticism but, as a consequence of the ambiguity, they were often unable to act on it. The men's definitions deconstructed and eroded the women's existential presence (Tifft, 1993) in part because the definitions were not consonant with the ways that the women experienced self. The women struggled with the existential dilemma that Denzin (1984) has represented as a distinction between an abused woman's surface self, that which is revealed through external expression, and a deeper self involving their own senses of moral worth.

Although the women resisted the derogatory definitions, they wondered why the men thought that they were true. Because the men were significant others in their lives, the women accorded legitimacy to the men's perceptions of them. Consequently, they altered their actions, or abandoned potential actions, in attempts to alter the definitions, as this respondent made clear:

> I think I changed my whole lifestyle to accommodate—centered around his feelings. When he started accusing me of this one and that one and going to bed with this man and that man, in order to combat all of that, I just started, I was real active, I was real active in a lot of volunteer work and things . . . and now a lot of people who used to call me don't call. . . . And I want to start going back to the gym and things like that, and I'm not doing that for fear that he might say, accuse me of looking for guys at the gym. He was accusing me of going with someone in the office, I mean of actually having sex. He would accuse me of having sexual intercourse with somebody while I was talking to him on the telephone. . . . It's not only that [he] accused me of being with men, he said, "well, maybe you like women," you know, I mean (sigh) . . . I guess I could have made it to my classes, but it was that it would be harder to listen to him accuse me of being someplace else doing something else than it would be to just go and be with him and maybe this is the right relationship, this is what I was thinking at first and it's okay and da da da da da. . . . (Respondent 25)

Denzin (1984) posits sexual jealousy as a stage of negative symbolic interaction in which the marital partners suspect one another of infidelity.

These suspicions are presumed to result in mutual hatred and mutual hostility. In contrast, rather than mutuality most of the women in this study related accusations of *their* infidelity as an ongoing feature of the definitional dialogues. Most also denied any basis for the accusations. Nonetheless, they monitored those actions that could be constructed as contributing to the characterizations.

Infidelity was a particularly pervasive accusation that had diverse ramifications for the men's assertions of power and control, that is, whether the women were characterized as the "whores" or "madonnas" of dichotomous gender divisions. Imputations of infidelity were part of the definitional dialogues around the right to own and control the women's sexuality, as well as many of their activities. The abuser's accusations reflected their culturally assumed claims as male partners to rights of sexual privilege. By reducing the women to sexual objects, or by making their sexuality an important focal point, the abusive men rendered every social space a potential arena for sexuality, including gyms, supermarkets, job sites, and so on. Where there was recognition that women's primary power leverage in the relationship was in their choices to stay or leave, infidelity could also be seen by the men as an exit enabler. Women were accused of searching for *a* man "to take them away" from *this* man. Implicit in this accusation was the assumption that women would be unable to act as active agents on their own behalf without assistance from men.

Abusing men were reported to have based their accusations of women's incompetence, ineptitude, and inadequacy on their partners' executions of stereotypic feminine roles. The men's definitional dialogues did not, for the most part, focus on what the women were expected to do as wives, mothers, and/or as sex partners; on that there was essential agreement. Rather, the focus was on the women's actual performances in each of these areas. These accusations were specific gender reductions that impacted negatively on the women's own perceptions of their competency in enacting social roles. They were attempts to nullify the women's own definitions of self as women, deconstructing their senses of self and reality, as this respondent, an interior designer, articulated:

During that last year too I really tried to make it work. It was important to him that I cook dinner. So I made sure that I cooked dinner for him every evening. He'd come, he'd eat, he'd go back to the office which was, ah, two blocks away. So I really tried. I thought, "Well it's me. I'm not pleasing him." So I tried to really be a good wife. I won't take as many classes. I'll really concentrate on making the marriage work. I'll keep the house really clean and I'll do his laundry and I'll cook him his meals and I'll do everything to make him happy so that he won't be unhappy anymore. And his problem will go away. And ha ha, you know, I mean it doesn't matter what you've done. They're still going to find something to explode about. . . . What I've realized since then is how eroded my self is and my self was. I didn't get married until I was 36. I've always been independent. How did I get so crumpled over this 5 year period? By intimidating. Intimidating me with all 6'6" of him. Screaming at me. Yelling at me. Screaming at the top of his lungs two inches from my face is something that he regularly did. Calling me names saying that he had no problems like this with his first wife. That he, you know, it was, it was all my fault. Ah, and then the physical abuse and, ah, and, and, and. . . . By the time the whole thing ended, I just felt like a rag. I didn't feel attractive at all. I felt—oh, I did not. I was not attractive, I was, you know, I just felt totally worthless. I felt totally worthless. How could I possibly get out of this marriage, I was worthless. How could I have any kind of life outside of him now? (Respondent 23)

Essentially, the accusations were based in claims that the women were inadequate in meeting the stereotypic "madonna" gender expectations. In response, the women monitored all actions that could be construed as contributing to the "whore" definitions, since "whore" ran counter to cultural expectations of good wife, mother, and sex partner. By modifying their actions, they contributed to and supported the men's definitions of them and, consequently, participated in creating their own interactional environments (Tifft, 1993).

In the process of modifying their actions to placate their partners, the selves of the abused women were also modified. Their actions became circumscribed by the abusing males' definitions and, consequently, the women experienced changes in self-regard. By altering their actions in attempts to alter men's definitions of them, their own understandings of self, their interpretive frames (Denzin, 1984) were transformed.

Because a sense of self is embedded in a context of interactions with others, if the abusers are seen as only one of many significant people in the women's lives, while their definitions would be important, they would be subject to comparison. If, however, the abusive males are the most, or only, significant people in their lives on a routine basis, then the men may have monopoly input in the construction of the women's situations and self. As an abusive male attempts to impose his will on his partner's subjectivity, he initiates a process to annihilate her consciousness and being in the world (Denzin, 1984). Continuous struggles are waged over these conflicting definitions between the women's constructions of self and the men's deconstructions of them.

Internal Dialogues

While involved in these definitional dialogues with their abusive partners, the women were simultaneously involved in internal dialogues. They reported continuously trying to figure out what was going on in the relationships without input from outsiders and using only their own definitional frames as guides. When untoward incidents occurred, these women were initially uncertain that violence had, in fact, taken place. In their retrospective accountings, the women identified these early episodes as violent and/or abusive, but they were not able to do so at the time of the incident. Even for those women with previous histories of violence, their definitional frames did not account for situationally ambiguous physical, psychological, or emotionally violent acts from intimate partners. The ambiguity begged for interpretation. Through their own internal dialogues, the women reconstructed the acts within their operative frames of meaning. This respondent's story vividly exemplifies this reconstructive effort:

> Before we got married, we bought a singing canary. And I trained him, brought him from being a wild bird to one that would jump off his perch and come sing for me, or when I was in the kitchen we would walk around the kitchen and cook together . . . and—before we got married, [he] got mad at him and killed him, just threw him across the room and broke his neck. And, uh, so there were signs— that was my baby—and, uh (pause 7 seconds) (tearful) I tried to deal with it—I, uh, spent a week in the hospital for—kind of cuckoo, after that happened. I don't know if it was a combination of PMS or, you know, (very tearful) the loss over that canary. 'Cause I rationalized it, "God, you love this human being. The human being has to take precedence over a bird." So I still ended up marrying my husband. (Respondent 11)

There was no ambiguity about the act itself. Nonetheless, this woman did not hold her partner accountable for the physical violence done to the canary or for the emotional trauma that she suffered. She did not define the act as violent. Instead, she focused on explaining her response to his actions *as though her response was the problem.* Mead (1934) and Stone and Farberman (1970) long ago posited that forged meaning was not rooted in the act, but rather in the response to it. In this case, the meaning is rooted in the interpretation that the respondent originally assigned to the act as violence. She was in dialogue with herself over the meaning of the event and her response to it. As a consequence of her original interpretation of his actions, she spent a week in the hospital "kind of cuckoo." Nonetheless, she began the reconstruction of *her response* as PMS or grief and she weighed her love for the man against her love for the bird. In that equation, it is understandable that she concluded that the man was more important. She had, however, transformed the problem of his violence into the problem of her response. She ended by blaming herself. As long as women can be convinced, or can convince themselves, that they are responsible for the precipitation of the violence, then abusive males are successful in controlling the definitions of the situations (Tifft, 1993).

Defining the Self in the Situation

Within this context of control and negotiated definitions of self, situation, and reality, episodes occurred in which the women were the targets of physical violence. The women reported that after such episodes, the abusers acted differently toward them. Sometimes the women could not say exactly how the men were different until more episodes that the women defined as violent had occurred. But the women were also different persons after the episodes: they had experienced changes in self-regard. If as Denzin (1984) and Tifft (1993) suggest the women's interpretive frames are structures of definitions and feelings that reflect their current states of mind concerning self and location in the world, then intimate, interpersonal violence results in a radical restructuring of the frame particularly as it relates to self and other.

Spin Cycle

When physical violence occurred, the women initially questioned themselves. They did not know how to characterize the actions. They were alone with the experiences, wrestling with what was not communicable—the meanings of the events to self. There was usually a lacunae between the events and their understandings of them. Most often, the women were aware of the gap. The definitional processes had triggered changes in their feelings and thoughts about who they were. The deconstructions of their worlds—of domestic objects, of physical and emotional experience, of intimate reality—left them

in the grip of their partners' violence (Tifft, 1993). This respondent recounts
these feelings:

> But, I mean, all of a sudden, then, we had to leave. That's how he is. All of a sudden,
> we're going. All of a sudden, we're leaving. All of a sudden, we're doing this, we're
> doing that—and you wonder why. Why? I never asked him why. Why didn't I ever
> ask him why? Why didn't he ever ask me, "Well, shall we go now?" We just went
> . . . I wasn't me. I was somebody else. He molded someone else, and that wasn't
> me. That wasn't me. And I see it now. It's so obvious. I mean, anyone in their right
> mind wouldn't have stayed over there [Europe], when that man was in jail. I mean,
> he was a thief and a liar and a drug pusher. And I still stayed there? I'm a good
> person. I mean, I was raised a good Catholic girl, I never did any stuff like that. Or
> stole, you know. But, he'd just, "Oh, everything will be all right. Nothing's going
> to happen." It was like he was Houdini or something. I was mesmerized . . . I was
> basically still the same person, but (pause 5 seconds) he made the person inside of
> me disappear, you know. Real deep inside of me. And brought, maybe, another side
> of me out. That didn't want to see things. That little girl side where, you know, you
> trust everybody. (Respondent 9)

In conventional interactions, the actions of the participants are understood as
flowing from the definition of the situation and from conventional actions
embedded in routine realities. Most aspects of interaction are taken for
granted. These assumptions were the routine schema within which abused
women began interpreting the abuse. But abuse, whether it is physical,
psychological, and/or emotional, is not a conventional interaction. Abuse is
problematic. It dramatically ruptures the taken for granted flow of interaction.

Conventional explanations for the violence are inadequate. If the abused
women reject their old definitional frames, which include their ideologies of
love and family, then they become alienated. They lose their way in the world
and doubt their knowledge of self so they must create or invent new explanations.

The ambiguities of the situations force them to ask questions of self. What
do his actions mean? Why did he do it? What was the intent of the violence?
Was it precipitated by something I said or did? To answer these questions, I
draw on Strauss' (1969) discussion of assigning situational identities to self
and other. Assigning situational identities required that the women make
judgments about men's motives. Imputing motives was a subtle combining of
"cause for" and "meaning of" action. Imputation of motives was necessary
for the women to take action. Assigning reasons for the men's ambiguous
actions was essentially a way of saying what these actions meant from the
women's perspectives. They defined their situations in terms and on the basis

of the assumptions familiar to them and so allowed for responses to the ambiguous acts other than acceptance, confusion, or paralysis.

The women, who remained in the relationships, continued to construct these explanations in internal dialogues as they did not report asking for, or receiving, assistance with the interpretations from persons outside the relationships. Their not telling can be viewed analytically as a deliberate social act set within abused women's definitions of their situations. Implicit in not telling is an interpretation of the violence as a violation of conventional social intercourse. Since ambiguities existed around both the violence and its precipitating factors, the women were vulnerable to the abusers' derogatory definitions. They had accepted without question the cultural ideologies of love and family that constructed the wife as responsible for well being in the private sphere of the home. So they reported blaming themselves *and* expecting others to blame them for the problematic nature of their intimate relationships. Consequently, they chose not to reveal the violence. This respondent articulated such feelings:

> So I was ashamed of what had happened. I was ashamed that it was even going on. I wanted to pretend that it hadn't happened. I wanted to forget that it had ever happened. It was a mistake. He promised it was never going to happen again. It was just one of those things that happen in a marriage that was never going to happen again. And therefore it was just, you know, not talked about . . . I felt that I was hiding. I felt like I was kind of hiding in a sense from those guys [her friends]. I didn't want to call them and tell them how horrible everything was. And what was really going on. I think I was ashamed of my staying in it and ashamed that it was going on at all in my life. This is something that doesn't happen. Happens to other people. And those people are people you never associate with of course because they are drug addicts and the total down and out losers. (Respondent 23)

The motives that the women were able to impute for the violence did not accord with what the abusers said they had done. The definitions were again ambiguous and problematic. Obviously, motives other than those ascribed by the women existed for the men. The women wanted to learn what they were. When an action is ambiguous, it elicits interpretation. The interpretation then defines the definer's courses of action. The abused women tried to identify the men's motivations, their definitions and interpretations, in order to cope with them. When the men's actions were abusive, the women searched for cues in the relationships that could help them interpret the motives for the events. In this quasi-investigative process, they tried to discriminate among relevant events, things, and persons, including self. They attempted to identify self in relation to the men. To make interpretations, they tried to understand their actions and their own motivations in the situation.

Responses and Self Blame

Action responses depended on the women's assessments of the violence and on their definitions of the situations. Situationally these women could sometimes, by using calculated responses, steer the men's actions away from abuse or they could escalate the occasions into violence. If the women responded in the manners desired by the men, if they conformed to the men's expectations, violence could sometimes be deferred or delayed for awhile or it could be lessened in severity. It was important that the response be in *the men's* terms, what *they* wanted. If not, the men became more punitive. And the men could destabilize at any time. Most often, for the women these negotiation cycles ended in feelings of complicity, self-questioning, and self-blame.

Abuse was rarely confined to a single episode. It continued and escalated in the severity of its consequences. It was interactionally constituted. When the abuser asserted hegemony over the power to define, his understandings formed preemptive definitions in the face of new and differing situations. As the women and their abusers continued to negotiate the definitions of violence within their previously existing frameworks, definitions became even more unstable and inconsistent. The men denied the violence and attributed blame to the women. The women subjectively accepted the blame. Self blame began to permeate their lives.

As women accepted responsibility, provided explanations, and/or denied the violence, they participated in a fiction that secured a permanent place for violence in the relationship (Denzin, 1984).

Defining the Violence

Definitional dialogues occur within a framework of cultural gender-based, hierarchical expectations, a system of ideologies and propaganda that legitimates relationships of mastery and control (Tifft, 1993). Kelly (1988) identified a continuum of sexual violence, a series of events that merge into one another and are connected by the basic characteristic that physical, verbal, and sexual assault and coercion are employed by men against women. Whether or not an action is defined as violent or abusive, the terms "violent," "abusive," and "battered" were negotiated by the abusive men and the abused women often in terms of severity, NOT legitimacy. Many women implicitly accepted the assumption that there were conditions under which their partners could control them through the use of force. This respondent, still in the relationship, explained the distinction drawn by her partner:

> It's not that I'm doing this because I like to get pushed around. And he thinks that he's OK. He thinks that he's not that bad. He's finally admitted that he's a batterer, but he's not a bad batterer, only because he hasn't put me in the hospital. And he's in this group with these guys who have put their wives in the hospital. (Respondent 25)

This couple negotiated the boundaries of battery. The man admitted his behavior but qualified it through negotiation, that is, "he's not a bad batterer." He had assaulted her, but not seriously enough to require hospitalization. One consequence of these "severity" negotiations was that the respondents came to feel grateful that the abuse that they experienced was not more profound. They came to understand the men's physical violence potential: "I could kill you if I wanted to" (Respondent 15). They were grateful to be alive. They knew what Walker (1989) contends, that is, death always lurks as a potential in violent relationships.

Definitions of abuse did not appear full blown to the couples. They emerged slowly from other definitional interactions. Violence developed in the control that the men exerted over the women. In her discussion of abused Korean women, Cho (1991) argued that the husband and wife become defined to each other and to the abuse. The system of abuse that develops takes hold of both and maintains the abusive interactions. Cho's provocative construction is, I believe, too determined. It denies the women's agency, as supported in this research, in attempting to modify and change the abusive patterns.

The definitional dialogues of abuse, in which the women engaged, were part of the ongoing struggles over definitional autonomy within the evolving relationships. When the men asserted definitional hegemony and the assertions were accepted, or at least not questioned overtly, these then became the preemptive definitions in new situations. These definitions then became a significant part of the everyday world of the women's lives. The women began to internalize the men's definitions and in due course they transformed their own meanings through their inner dialogues. As one respondent said, in characterizing her relationship with a man who she reported had emotionally abused her, physically attacked her property, threatened her with violence, and sexually abused both her children:

> It was violent, but it wasn't. It was abusive, but it wasn't, I mean, he never connected with me. It wasn't knock down drag out stuff. (Respondent 6)

This respondent's remarks provide clear illustration of the violence continuum (Kelly, 1988) and its definitional ambiguities. For this respondent, as for others, one condition for defining an action as violent was its severity, its "knock down drag out" quality. Presumably, assaults that fall short of that were not defined as violent. Hence her equivocations, "it was violent, but it wasn't." Interpretations of violence were subject to a wide range of variation. Violence between these intimate partners occurred on a continuum with markers that were constantly being negotiated.

Implicit in women's accounts of interactionally derived definitions of violence was the need for physical evidence, or proof, that the violence occurred. Under the impact of the day to day denials of their definitional frameworks, many women lost confidence in their abilities to define their own realities. This respondent, a 39-year-old physiologist, related a typical experience:

> I was sitting on a chair after dinner and he just came up and hit me. There wasn't an argument. There wasn't a why didn't you do this. I can't remember anything that happened before. And then one week later, the same evening, the same chair, he just hit me again. And the first time, there wasn't any bruising so I kind of thought maybe I was imagining what he did. (Respondent 2)

In the absence of conclusive physical evidence, even personal experience of physical assault can be discounted or redefined.

Discussion

Competing definitions of self, situation, and violence in abusive relationships form the matrices of conditions that affect the intensity of the violent interactions. Love and violence coexist, forming the contexts within which the paradox of women's agency and victimization are enacted.

Because Denzin's theoretical formulations about the self of abused women and the nature of intimate, interpersonal violence have been so influential in the work of subsequent researchers (Stets, 1987; Cho, 1991; Tifft, 1993), I address his work now in light of the analysis presented in this paper. While supporting many of Denzin's theoretical constructs of a structure of negative symbolic interaction in domestic violence, this research also challenges some of those formulations. Specifically, the gender neutrality of Denzin's arguments (and their extensions Cho, 1991; Tifft, 1993) as it renders invisible the simultaneity of love and violence as well as the contradictory duality of women's agency and victimization.

Denzin (1984; and Cho, 1991; Tifft, 1993) refers to a "family of violence," that is, a household where interpersonal violence has become a regular feature of daily interactions. Sociologists know that language is an active force shaping the discourse of social problems, consequent use of "family of violence" is a dangerous misnomer. It centers the violence within the group, removing responsibility from the abusing male, implying that the family members are co-acting equals engaged in violence against one another. This analytic gender neutrality results in a leveling effect that collapses both the distinctions and dimensions of gender and power that are fundamental to an understanding of wife abuse. "Family of violence" distorts and depoliticizes the particular, and gendered, experiences of women whose lives are dominated by intimate, interpersonal abuse. The household with a violent husband and/or father exists in a context of violence, or a "field of violence" (Denzin, 1984), that holds the family hostage to his emotional capture (Cuthbertson and Johnson, 1992).

Violence is situated interaction. Family members are most assuredly tainted by the violence. But they do not become a network of "violent, interacting individuals" (Denzin, 1984; Cho, 1991; Tifft, 1993). Most women in this study, for example, resisted acting or reacting violently. They held different definitions of themselves, as this respondent articulated:

> When I yell back or become violent, then I've become as violent as he has, and that's kind of the lowest of the low. (Respondent 31)

Further, to understand intimate, interpersonal violence, it is necessary to understand the simultaneity of love and violence in these relationships.

Violence may indeed be the field of experience within which daily interactions occur, but it is not the only field. Violent interpersonal relationships, like all others, are very complex. Abusive men can also be "warm, loving, nurturing" and so on (Lempert, 1992). As the violence escalates in frequency and severity, periods of calm become foreshortened and the salient field of experience may become the violent one. But this process is gradual and processual and becomes daily only after other fields have been eliminated.

Denzin (1984; Cho, 1991; Tifft, 1993) suggests that the negative structures of experience develop from the violence embedded in negative symbolic interaction. These negative structures then lock the family into a "circuit of violent selfness." As this paper argues, it is the abusing male who is locked into "selfness," possibly through emotional capture (Cuthbertson and Johnson, 1992). Other family members are participant in the circuit through reaction/response, but again not as co-acting equals. The women in this study were continuously struggling to hold onto a definition of self that was under assault.

Whether termed schismogenesis or negative symbolic interaction (Denzin, 1984), the analysis focuses on the conflict of two interacting units. But the interacting units, husband and wife, are not equally situated within the relationship culturally or socially. Wife abuse, perhaps even more than rape, is a low risk, high reward crime (Scully, 1990). Violent men use the pervasive nature of social violence and women's subordination in society to assume rights and privileges of ownership to individual women in intimate interactions. Men know how to act violently. Violence is a socially acceptable, culturally prescribed form of male conduct. Violence and threats of violence are mechanisms for the social control of women (and others).

Denzin (1984; Cho, 1991; Tifft, 1993) argues that emotional and physical force are used to recapture what abusive men lost through violence, that is, the relationship. But intimate, interpersonal violence has a beginning. Before there is relationship loss, there must be a relationship. At least the initial episodes of violence would not seem to be aimed at recapture for at that point the relationships are intact. This research suggests that the violence is indeed a response to loss, but particularly to the real or perceived *loss of control* over the woman. Violence is a strategy not only to regain lost control, but also to gain something more. In a world of social interaction where women are subordinate to men, the abusing males want women to "belong" to them, to respond to their assertions of power. When women assert themselves as separate entities violence is used to bring them back into line.

If as Denzin (1984) suggests, wife beating is characterized by interaction at (vs. interaction with), then it is not regaining the lost relationship that precipitates violence. It is the woman's perceived or actual threat to the man's authority and control that precipitates her degradation through violence. His violence is a response to his real and/or presumed loss of power and control. As this research demonstrates, violence assures acquiescence, if not agreement, to an abusive male. One of the problems of studies of abused women is the invisibility of those women who remain in violent relationships and who do not come to public attention. We don't know if their wills are broken or if they stop struggling.

Occasionally, this invisibility is shattered as it was in the notorious 1989 Steinberg-Nussbaum case. Until Joel Steinberg's trial for the murder of his seven-year-old daughter Lisa, despite systematic battering (nose without cartilage, vacant eyes, gangrenous leg, etc.) his wife, Hedda Nussbaum, had not sought, nor had she received, assistance. Hedda Nussbaum did not assist her daughter as she lay dying on the bathroom floor because she had abdicated all personal responsibility during her twelve-year marriage to Joel Steinberg. Her sense of self as separate from him no longer operated.

Several stages of negative symbolic interaction that attach to the family should perhaps be modified in light of the salience of gender. The pleasurable effects of the violence (Denzin, 1984; Cho, 1991; Tifft, 1993) for example, are ascribed motives (Strauss, 1969). The effects characterized as "seductively intoxicating" (Denzin, 1984) are certainly not so for the women or other family members receiving the blows, kicks, punches, and so on. The gendered nature of this stage of negative symbolic interaction is supported in the work of Scully (1990) who studied convicted rapists. Scully found that in contrast to the well-documented severity of the immediate impact, and in some cases, long-term trauma experienced by women victims of rape, the immediate emotional impact on the rapists was slight. In fact, a number of her respondents volunteered that raping had a positive impact on their feelings:

> After rape, I always felt like I had just conquered something, like I had just ridden the bull at Gilley's. (Scully 1990, p. 158)

The negative symbolic interaction stage of "mutual hostility" and "mutual hatred" posited by Denzin was not supported in this research. Women in this study reported "loving" their partners and hating the behavior. They didn't hate the men, especially initially; they hated the violence and they denied its intentionality. Both the relationships and the women held fast to the simultaneity of love and violence. Hatred and hostility were luxurious feelings for abused women that could not be acknowledged until the women were safely out of the relationships. Any evidence of "selfness" or mutuality in hostility could precipitate a violent encounter.

The distinctions between the types of violence also result in reducing the salience of gender in these relationships. *All* violence is violent. It may be moderated by degree, severity, or intentionality but it *all* has physical and emotional effects. The moderating feature is not the rationalization/justification, but the perceived intentionality of the violence. "Real violence" (Denzin, 1984; Cho, 1991; Tifft, 1993) is not more real than "playful violence," it is simply constructed differently.

> After that it was like a regular thing—it just started getting more and more regular—This couple moved in [to the other side of a duplex] . . . but they would come over and sit around and talk and stuff and it got to be kind of a joke that Mark would say "Oh, yeah, well you know it's Sunday. I beat her up on Sunday." Cause that's, he always did on Sundays—he'd do it other days too but it—like there was never a Sunday that went by the whole time we were married possibly that he didn't like beat me up or just go crazy and start screaming and yelling and threatening, and I sat there and I remember, you know, and I kind of joked about it, you know, and these people were sitting there and they were oh, they thought we were kidding, but. . . . (Respondent 19)

False distinctions about intentional violence contribute to women's emotional capture (Cuthbertson and Johnson, 1992) by creating socially acceptable generalizations about violence. These generalizations are influenced by the macro and micro tendencies to characterize violence as "other" than violence, that is, play, paradox, and so on. Behavioral patterns unnamed as violence aid in the "forming, entrenchment, and reinforcement of composite patterns" that are essentially captured in these false distinctions (Cuthbertson and Johnson, 1992).

In seeking to understand the complexity of women's lived experiences of intimate, interpersonal violence, it is necessary to place women at the center of the analysis. Gender neutral theoretical formulations of abuse fail to account for the simultaneity of love and violence and the simultaneity of agency and victimization that make women's definitions of their violent situations understandable.

Note

1. Although sociological attention to issues of wife abuse is of relatively recent initiation, beginning as it did in the 1970s, a considerable volume of theoretical literature has already been generated. Theoretical constructs of the problem include psychosocial theories explaining why battered women become victims (Walker, 1979, 1989); the culture of violence theory identifying the manifestations of "domestic violence" learned in the family and legitimated by a violent society (Straus, Gelles, and Steinmetz, 1980; Straus and Gelles 1986; Gelles and Straus, 1979; Gelles, 1976, 1977; Steinmetz, 1977; Shupe et al., 1987); social learning theory positing violent social learning within the family (Pagelow, 1981); general systems theory suggesting that violence is the outcome of complex and mutually causal social interactions within the family system (Giles-Sims, 1983); feminist theory relating wife abuse to the power relations between men and women that lie at the center of social interactions in this society (Kurz, 1989; Yllö, 1988; Loseke, 1987; Stanko, 1985; Bograd, 1984; Bowker, 1983; Schechter, 1982; Dobash and Dobash, 1979; Martin, 1976); and symbolic interactionism interpreting how meanings are constructed in violent interactions (Stets, 1987; Denzin, 1984). Of these theoretical constructs, only feminist researchers seek to put abused women at the center of analysis.

Despite research on the historical, social, and economic bases of women's subordination that examines how hierarchical arrangements in male/female relationships are routinely established and maintained (Belenky et al., 1986; Kelly, 1988; Riessman, 1990; West and Zimmerman, 1987), only Stets (1987) has addressed these problems as they affect control in abusive relationships. There is little sustained research about abusive relationships which starkly reflects the replication of macro level hierarchical ordering on micro level interactions.

References

Belenky, M. F., B. M. Clinchy, N. R. Goldberger, and J. M. Tarule. 1986. *Women's Ways of Knowing.* New York: Basic Books.

Bograd, M. 1984. "Family Systems Approaches to Wife Battering: A Feminist Critique." *American Journal of Orthopsychiatry* 54 (4):558-568.

Bowker, L. H. 1983. *Beating Wife-Beating.* Lexington, MA: Lexington Books.

Chang, D. B. K. 1989. "An Abused Spouse's Self-Saving Process: A Theory of Identity Transformation." *Sociological Perspectives* 32 (4):535-550.

Cho, J. 1991. "Resentiment of the Battered Wives: The Case of Korea." *Studies in Symbolic Interaction* 12:149-181.

Cuthbertson, B. A. and J. M. Johnson. 1992. "Exquisite Emotional Sensitivity and Capture." *Studies in Symbolic Interaction* 13:155-166.

Denzin, N. K. 1984. "Toward a Phenomenology of Domestic, Family Violence." *American Journal of Sociology* 90 (3):483-513.

Dobash, R. E. and R. P. Dobash. 1979. *Violence Against Wives.* New York: Free Press.

Dobash, R. E. and R. P. Dobash. 1992. *Women, Violence and Social Change.* London: Routledge.

Ferraro, K. J. and J. M. Johnson. 1983. "How Women Experience Battering: The Process of Victimization." *Social Problems* 30 (3):325-339.

Gelles, R. J. 1976. "Abused Wives: Why Do They Stay." *Journal of Marriage and the Family* 38:659-668.

Gelles, R. J. 1977. "Power, Sex, and Violence: The Case of Marital Rape." *The Family Coordinator,* pp. 339-347.

Gelles, R. J. and M. A. Straus. 1979. "Violence in the American Family." *Journal of Social Issues* 35 (2):15-39.

Giles-Sims, J. 1983. *Wife Battering: A Systems Theory Approach.* New York: Guilford.

Glaser, B. G. 1978. *Theoretical Sensitivity.* Mill Valley, CA: Sociology Press.

Glaser, B. G. and A. L. Strauss. 1967. *The Discovery of Grounded Theory.* New York: Aldine de Gruyter.

Johnson, J. M. and K. J. Ferraro. 1984. "The Victimized Self: The Case of Battered Women." Pp. 119-113 in *The Existential Self in Society,* edited by J. Kotarba and A. Fontana. Chicago: University of Chicago Press.

Kelly, L. 1988. "How Women Define Their Experiences of Violence." Pp. 114-132 in *Feminist Perspectives on Wife Abuse,* edited by K. Yllö and M. Bograd. Newbury Park: Sage.

Kurz, D. 1989. "Social Science Perspectives on Wife Abuse: Current Debates and Future Directions." *Gender & Society* 3 (4):489-505.

Lempert, L. B. 1992. "The Crucible: Violence, Help-Seeking, and Abused Women's Transformations of Self." Unpublished Dissertation. University of California, San Francisco.

Loseke, D. R. 1987. "Lived Realities and the Construction of Social Problems: The Case of Wife Abuse." *Symbolic Interaction* 10 (2):229-243.

Martin, D. 1976. *Battered Wives.* New York: Pocket Books.

Mead, G. H. 1934. *Mind, Self, and Society.* Chicago: University of Chicago Press.

Mills, T. 1985. "The Assault on the Self: Stages in Coping With Battering Husbands." *Qualitative Sociology* 8 (2):103-123.

Mills, T. and S. Kleinman. 1988. "Emotions, Reflexivity, and Action: An Interactionist Analysis." *Social Forces* 66 (4):1009-1027.

Pagelow, M. D. 1981. *Woman-Battering: Victims and Their Experiences.* Beverly Hills: Sage.

Riessman, C. K. 1990. *Divorce Talk.* New Brunswick, NJ: Rutgers University Press.

Schechter, S. 1982. *Women and Male Violence.* Boston: South End Press.

Scully, D. 1990. *Understanding Sexual Violence: A Study of Convicted Rapists.* Boston: Unwin Hyman.

Shupe, A., W. A. Stacey, and L. R. Hazelwood. 1987. *Violent Men, Violent Couples.* Lexington, MA: D. C. Heath.

Stanko, E. A. 1985. *Intimate Intrusions.* London: Routledge & Kegan Paul.

Steinmetz, S. K. 1977. *The Cycle of Violence: Assertive, Aggressive, and Abusive Family Interactions.* New York: Praeger.

Stets, J. E. 1987. "A Symbolic Interactionist Approach to Domestic Violence." Unpublished dissertation. Indiana University.

Stone, G. P. and H. A. Farberman. 1970. "The Definition of the Situation." Pp. 147-155 in *Social Psychology Through Symbolic Interaction.* Waltham, MA: Ginn-Blaisdell.

Strauss, A. L. 1969. *Mirrors and Masks.* San Francisco: Sociology Press.

Strauss, A. L. 1987. *Qualitative Analysis for Social Scientists.* Cambridge: Cambridge University Press.

Strauss, A. and J. Corbin. 1990. *Basics of Qualitative Research.* Newbury Park: Sage.

Straus, M. A. and R. J. Gelles. 1986. "Societal Change and Change in Family Violence From 1975 to 1985 as Revealed by Two National Surveys." *Journal of Marriage and the Family* 48:465-479.

Straus, M. A., R. J. Gelles, and S. Steinmetz. 1980. *Behind Closed Doors.* Garden City, NY: Doubleday.

Tifft, L. L. 1993. *Battering of Women.* Boulder: Westview.

Walker, L. E. 1979. *The Battered Woman.* New York: Harper & Row.

Walker, L. E. 1989. *Terrifying Love.* New York: Harper & Row.

Waller, W. 1970. The Definition of the Situation. Pp. 162-174 in *Social Psychology Through Symbolic Interaction.* Waltham, MA: Ginn-Blaisdell.

West, C., and D. H. Zimmerman. 1987. "Doing Gender." *Gender & Society* 1 (2):125-151.

Yllö, K. 1988. "Political and Methodological Debates in Wife Abuse Research." Pp. 28-50 in *Feminist Perspectives on Wife Abuse,* edited by K. Yllö and M. Bograd. Newbury Park: Sage.

7

Temporality and Identity Loss Due to Alzheimer's Disease

CELIA J. ORONA

Commentary

Celia Orona, a sociologist, wrote this at the request of the editor of a special edition of *Social Science and Medicine*. It was part of a group of articles designed to illustrate the potential value of qualitative methods for the study of health issues. Hence its special format: first, sections spelling out her use of grounded theory methodology and methods, then a relating of that to the substantive materials and theoretical outcomes of her research. The article, a very effective and clearly organized one, was drawn from a doctoral study of Alzheimer caregivers. It provides us with an extraordinarily nice example of a young researcher, highly intelligent, compassionate but exceptionally analytic, who although only recently trained in grounded theory understands it thoroughly. She was both able to use it constructively in her research and be articulate, here, in describing her experiences when using it.

Recently we reread the article (it was published in 1990) after we had just written a chapter titled "Teaching and Learning Grounded Theory" for the revised edition of *Basics of Qualitative Research,* and found that Dr. Orona's article was virtually a textbook exemplification of the appropriate use of grounded theory procedures, as well as showing an accurate understanding and deep appreciation of the basic methodology itself.

You will find various topics well described. Among them are the following. (a) Beginning not with a research problem but an interest in a substantive area (or in Everett Hughes' phrasing, "A good sociologist can make good sociology out of anything"). Also the experience of being a participant observer and even a worker "in the field" itself (a frequent occurrence for people trained in the interactionist tradition). (b) Supplementing this field experience and observation with substantive literature and studies about Alzheimer's disease, an immersion so to speak in the substantive materials. (c) All of this raising possible questions for the researcher. (d) Forming a wrong hypothesis because of a commonly held bias about popular attitudes toward nursing homes, and then beginning to doubt it, and really doubting it after the first interviews and coding them. (e) The coding suggests other possibilities, especially the great significance of "identity loss." Note also the role of Dr. Orona's empathy with the caretakers and her imagination of their responses. (f) Her line-by-line coding, leading to new interview questions and memos about identity loss and temporality. (g) Her formulating then of four subcategories of identity loss, and the decision (or suspicion) that this should be her core category. (h) The author's living and thinking in a kind of everyday immersion in her research. (i) Her understanding of the influence of intuitions and creativity, as well as the nonlinear nature of her research process and the vital nature of an interplay between herself as a researcher and her data. (j) Her appreciating the relationship between line-by-line coding and abstraction. (k) Her discussing several functions of memos and diagrams. (l) Thinking through the relationships between identity loss and temporality. (m) Noting the nature of indicators and finding them. (n) Using one illustrative diagram both functionally and as a device for explaining an aspect of her analysis to readers. (o) Note, too, her using of quotations in different ways: For instance, as examples of her theoretical commentary, as items for making her commentary more convincing, as representing various voices or perspectives of the caregivers. (16) And finally, offering some implications of her study for policy making concerning Alzheimer caregivers. Moreover, although not discussing them explicitly, the author understands and makes systematic comparisons and uses theoretical sampling. The entire chapter constitutes an integrated theoretical analysis.

*   *   *

Identity Construction in Everyday Living

Defined as an irreversible and degenerative disease of the brain, dementia of the Alzheimer's type (DAT) leads to personality change, loss of memory and cognition, physical disability, and eventual death [1-4]. It is estimated that 80% of those with Alzheimer's disease are cared for in a family setting. Typically, one person in the family constellation assumes the moral responsibility of providing care. Indeed, the family as a supportive network for most types of home care has been established [5].

Early studies on the impact of entering the caregiver role focused on the consequences to the caregiver [6-10]. These studies reveal several patterns:

- Over time, providing care for a disabled family member results in a drain on resources;
- Burden of care can be designated as having both a subjective and objective dimension; and
- Subjective burden continues to be experienced by the caregiver long after placement of the Alzheimer's person into long-term nursing facility.

This paper addresses one specific aspect of the caregiving experience: *temporality* in the context of providing care for a person with Alzheimer's disease as identity loss in that person is experienced. Thus, while the focus is on the subjective experience, the underlying theme is identity loss. In addition, the paper will describe several aspects of a qualitative approach to research as they pertain to the process of grounding the concepts in the data.

Part one of the paper will focus on the process of qualitative research as I experienced it. It is important to note that temporality is but one conceptual "slice" of a larger research project conducted for a doctoral dissertation. Thus, I will describe the early false starts of the research and relate how grounded theory helped me focus on the dissertation topic. Part two is the explication of one dimension of the findings—temporality. As such, the analysis and its conceptualizations focus on temporal aspects of dealing with identity loss in a person with Alzheimer's disease.

The Process: Grounded Theory

In 1985, at the end of my first year into the doctoral program, I had the opportunity to participate as a team member of an Adult Day Health Center for physically and mentally impaired elderly.[1] The elderly participants attended twice weekly and most were transported in a van. Because I had no idea at that time what my dissertation topic would be (except that it would focus on issues of the elderly), I felt the experience would be helpful.

As the sociologist of the team, my task was to help the staff with activities such as feeding participants, moving those in wheel chairs, leading exercises and games, etc. However, in general, I was free to "hang out," engaging in the participant-observation approach in the tradition of the Chicago School. My plan was simply to observe the interactions between the staff and the participants as well as the interactions between the participants. Beyond that, I had no idea what the experience would yield.

Because the program was new to me, I found the first few days somewhat confusing. Besides the participants, there were professional staff members, consulting health professionals, and volunteers. However, it was not long before I was approached by a short, stout woman who introduced herself as "Rose," one of the volunteers. She wondered if I knew where the supplies were kept and if I had met the participants. She took me in hand and assured me that should I have any questions, I need not hesitate in asking for her assistance. After all it was her job to "know where everything was."

Later, when the director of the program asked if I needed anything, I responded that Rose had already taken me aside to give me information. I looked toward the far end of the room where Rose was wiping the tables down. To my surprise, I learned from the Director that Rose was no volunteer; she was a participant. In fact, this woman who had so kindly taken me under her wing was a participant suffering from Alzheimer's disease.

What was this disease called Alzheimer's? And who was this woman who looked much as anyone on the street looked, who carried on what seemed to be a logical conversation with me? Her name was "Rose M____" and she was in her mid sixties. She lived at home with her adult children. A matronly woman who raised a large family, she was in the mid stages of Alzheimer's and in the 6 weeks that I worked at the Adult Day Health Center, I witnessed her decline with alarm.

Shortly after that incident, I found that there were other participants who most likely had Alzheimer's disease. They posed for me a most perplexing challenge: to understand what it was like for the families of Alzheimer's victims who cared for them day in, day out, often without respite except for the 2 days at the center.

Each day, I talked to Rose and the others, helped feed them, distracted them, played Bingo with them, watched that they did not hurt one another or themselves, or wander away from the center. Each day, I left the center exhausted. I would ask myself: "What must it be like for the families who know that this situation can only worsen and from which there is but one escape—institutionalization?"

My dreams during this summer were dark. Although I do not recall any of those dreams specifically (never thinking that I might want to use them as "data"), I do recall that they were similar to a dream I had when I was working with wives of stroke victims. In the dream which I recorded at the time, I was in bed and the light from the moon and stars faded until there was blackness. In spite of the blackness, however, I knew there was a large black bird perched at the foot of my bed watching me as I slept. In that dream, I could not tell if the bird was a demon or a friend. Such was the tenor of my summer.

I began to talk to the director about Alzheimer's disease and sought out literature in our library. What I learned was indeed disheartening: progressive degeneration of the brain, loss of memory and cognition, almost certain institutionalization. Each day, I was drawn more and more to those participants who were labeled as having Alzheimer's disease and each day, new questions emerged for me. How did the caregiving relatives cope after working all day to come home and care for their loved ones? Did they spend the evenings "conversing" with the Alzheimer's person? How did they manage to make the decision to institutionalize their loved ones? How did they dress them? Was this an inherited disease?

By the end of the 6 weeks, working on a daily basis with the participants at the center as well as researching the topic in the libraries, I was ready for a vacation. Troubled, fatigued, yet also intrigued, I knew I had a topic for my dissertation. The question was how to narrow it down.

Initially, I had thought that surely one aspect of the caregiving experience would be the pain and anguish when the time came to place the loved one in a long-term care facility. Would there be other such momentous decisions?

How did relatives define "profound decisions"? In a small pilot study, I began by examining the process of decision making for those informal caregivers of Alzheimer's persons. I prepared a face sheet and a list of broad questions which included, for example, "What are some of the more difficult decisions you have had to make in the care of _____?" and "Who else takes part in the decision-making process?"

Once having put together a proposal for a pilot project, I was able to locate on my own five relatives who had once cared for (or were caring for at that time) a person with Alzheimer's disease. The interviews lasted from 1.5 to 4 hours. Each interview was conducted in the home of, or a place of convenience for, the respondent.

Interestingly, the following description is representative of the "flavor" of responses I got to what I thought was a critical question. From my notes, I recall that I was sitting in a nicely furnished living room with comfortable furniture, where a stereo system with shelves of long-playing records was evident. "Karla's" home was in a pleasant, upper middle-class neighborhood. Yet, I could hear in her voice and see in her body the tiredness which had accumulated from the many years of caring for her husband, Michael. When I asked, "What was the process of coming to the decision to place your husband in a nursing home?" she leaned forward:

Decision? Decision? There was no decision. When it came time, I had no choice. It's like falling in love, no one has to tell you. You know.

For Karla, when the time came, she knew. She described the fatigue, the physical hardship on her; the drain on all her resources, including emotional. She endured the pain of knowing her "partner" of some 40-odd years was gone. During the last stage of the disease, Michael had trouble swallowing. This necessitated emergency trips to the hospital. One trip, however, became significant.

That day as she drove home alone, she looked forward to a house where she could eat a meal while it was still hot, sleep through the night and not have to care for a person who had become a stranger to her; where she did not have to feed and dress a hulking man who fought her every step of the way, who was not even able to stay balanced on the dining room chair. The significance of this drive was that she knew the time had come.

As she described that drive home, I could see in my mind's eye how her home must have looked to her as she reached that realization. However, what

I was struck by as I listened to her were my own feelings. I sensed somehow that I had heard another theme. Much as a person working absentmindedly hears an unusual sound in the background and becomes alert, I left her home with that kind of uneasy, perplexed feeling.

I wrote up my notes and listened to the tapes once again. The next two interviews followed quickly with much the same process. All interviews were transcribed and I began my first step: coding.

I began the line-by-line coding as outlined in the grounded theory literature [11-14]. I quickly coded them, writing my notes and impressions on the side margins I had purposely left. Categories emerged. However, the one I had most expected (the profoundness of placement of the Alzheimer's person) was not there with the richness I had anticipated. The issue of decision making was not so very paramount in these particular interviews.

It is the strength of the grounded theory approach, especially as it is informed by the interactionist philosophy, that conceptualizations are grounded in the empirical world. Thus, although I had entered the project with an interest in the decision-making process, I found myself drawn to, and surprised by, categories that had nothing to do with decisions, profound or otherwise. In fact, as I read and reread the interviews, I could literally "see" what the disquietude I had felt in the early interviews was all about.

Each of the first three persons I interviewed made essentially the same exact comment: By the time of the placement, the person they had once known as husband, mother or wife, was "gone." They were institutionalizing "strangers." The person who they had once known had changed to the point of being dead. Karla said it most succinctly, "Michael died a long time ago."

This, then, was the underlying theme I kept hearing in the background. When I asked at what point the other person had changed to be called "different," "gone," each had said: "I don't know but I know he's not the same person!" Identity loss was the central theme in the data.

More interviews followed; however, my focus shifted from decision making to identity loss as perceived by the respondents. Key questions, for example, were "Tell me about your _____ before onset of the disease; what was she/he like?" "What were the first changes you noticed?" Identity loss in a dyadic relationship, within the context of Alzheimer's disease, remained the focus throughout the research project.

In the beginning, I literally sat for days on end with the transcribed interviews spread out before me, absorbing them into my consciousness and letting them "float" about. I wrote memos on whatever struck my fancy or as one professor called them, my "flights of fancy." These memos included premises about how identity is perceived, what constitutes identity to the average person. I wondered why, if the person was declared "gone" did the relatives hang on to the caregiving experience for so long?

I wrote, sometimes several pages, sometimes only paragraphs, but always following the grounded theory approach. That is, I wrote as the thoughts came to me with no need to be orderly or linear. The only mandate was to write what was emerging from the data [14]. I did not try to make sense of anything yet. Instead, I let the data "talk to me."

Everywhere in my office there were notes of all shapes and sizes until finally, I piled them all in one corner of my desk. Then, there came a point when I felt that a "reading" must take place. For several days, I sat wading through the notes and placing them into what I felt were the major categories, which by then, had been abstracted to a higher level. Thus, "silent partner," "helper," and "neighbors" had been abstracted to the level of *social relations.* "Memory," "clock," and "rituals" were all placed in the category of *temporality.*

Slowly, four major themes emerged around the identity loss process: social relations, reciprocity, moral obligation, and temporality. Identity loss in a member of a dyad as perceived by the other member became the core category with the four themes constituting the key dimensions of the dissertation. Notations which were not relevant I set aside but did not discard.

I continued with the typical formulation of any research project: reading the literature on Alzheimer's disease and identity, talking to health professionals in the field, and to those professors I had hoped to have on my committee. I continued with more interviews. I continued with the open coding and wrote memos. But most of all, I walked; I sat; I daydreamed.

I found that the slightest imagery could conjure up ruminations about the theme of identity and/or temporality. For example, while driving on a coastal highway, I was struck by the sign cautioning "Drive carefully, shifting sands." The sign was clear: The sands blew off the dunes onto the highway, making the delineation of the highway and the beach difficult to see. In much the same way, I felt that the delineated identity of the Alzheimer's person was losing its "identifiable edges" or boundaries. Although I wanted to use this metaphor in the analysis, ultimately, I dropped it. What is more important here is that for a while having this imagery helped me understand the process experienced by the caregiving relatives and that I used this imagery to write a memo.

I believe the beauty and strength of the grounded theory approach is that it is *not* linear. Instead, the approach allows for the emergence of concepts out of the data—in a schema that allows for introspection, intuition, ruminating as well as analysis in the "traditional" mode. Indeed, qualitative research, especially in the grounded theory tradition, is not for those who need tight structure with little ambiguity. Strauss says it nicely when he states that "Several structural conditions *mitigate against* a neat codification of methodological rules for social research" (emphasis added) [14].

I found the approach more amorphous yet personal in that I was able to use my intuitions and creativity to help me discover and uncover what was conceptually happening in the empirical world. As I have mentioned several times, the process is not a linear one nor did it begin with any clarity. Thus, I cannot say that at step one, I coded and then, step two, I wrote memos and then, I began the analysis. Often, I went from one technique to another and back again. Rather than describe the process of qualitative research, at this point, I will describe how I used some of the techniques to my own advantage.

Coding. This technique is used with the written interviews or notes in which, line by line, the researcher conceptualizes the data. For those familiar with the grounded theory method, coding each line is the guts of the approach. Though it can sometimes be exciting especially in the moments of discovery, coding is tedious and takes time. Yet, it is critical.

I did line-by-line coding, first quickly to get impressions and then, once again but this time slowly to test my impressions and to raise each impression to a higher conceptual level. Ideally, coding is done in such a way that the data is raised to a conceptual level immediately. However, I found that if I worked quickly, without too much ruminating, I could come to some "first impressions." This seemed to be an important first step *for me.*

I then went back and more slowly reread the interviews to see if my "impressions" fit and to conceptualize the data. For example, from the early interviews, I made notations in the margins on the following statements from different interviews:

It was the *time of the year* when nobody goes in the yard anyway . . .

At the beginning . . .

It got much worse *later on.*

Who had *ever heard* of Alzheimer's *eleven years ago.*

More and more, he was leaning on me.

Before she would never be like that.

She *used to* love coffee.

Even on *free* days, you're always *up against the clock.*

I found that all my notations on these statements were somehow related to time and so, when I went back to the second coding, I relabeled them all "temporality," writing a memo to myself about the *subjective* and *objective* elements of caregiving for someone. By this time, I found that color coding was helpful. This was especially true after several runs when I began to see definite conceptual categories' emerging such as "identity" and "temporality."

Memos. Technically, the function of memos is to aid in the formulation of a grounded theory. However, *how* that end is achieved is left to the imagination of the researcher for as Strauss says "he or she is engaged in continual internal dialogue" [14]. Thus, I found that memo writing was used in several ways in various phases of the research.

First, memos were used to free associate, to enter the world of "blue skying," writing whatever thoughts I became aware of as I read the interviews or was working on anything at all. I wrote until I felt depleted on the subject or until I found myself repeating statements or veering from the topic. I allowed myself the freedom to say whatever I wanted, in whatever form seemed to flow. I did not attempt to be grammatically correct or to force myself to find sociological terms to describe what I was thinking. That, I felt, would come later. Instead, I went with an idea without monitoring or making judgments about it.

Second, I used memos for the purposes of unblocking. Often, especially during the analysis when I felt I could not quite describe in words what I felt was occurring in the data, I would begin to "write" to someone. The "letter" would begin by describing my problem, how I felt stuck and how I felt sure there was "something" there. I asked questions of that person (often one of my professors), and had that person "ask" me questions. The "dialogue" would frequently clarify and crystallize the concept which seemed to be blocked.

Third, I used memos to document the beginnings of a conceptualization which had emerged from the data, "tracking" its levels from the raw data (words used by the respondents) to my notes in the coding and finally, to the concept. As an example, I recall when I first heard one daughter describe how she gave her mother coffee with her ice cream. The treat was obviously more important to the daughter than to the mother. As I sat in her living room and listened to the ways in which "Nora" took pains to give her mother treats, I felt my eyes tear and the hair on my arms went up.

Later, reading the description of the coffee and ice cream, I kept asking myself why is this so important—other than being touching? For I felt sure that this was important and wrote a memo about what I had heard and then read. I found myself writing about everyday living, idiosyncrasies that make us unique to our loved ones. I thought of the words to the popular song "The way you hold your knife, the way you sip your tea." Here was a relationship between identity and temporality for as I went back in the data, I found that caregiving relatives used poignant rituals to "hang on to" the loved ones *as they were remembered.*

At this point, let me make note that the use of memos varied. At times, I would use them to unblock; other times, to crystallize a conceptualization. They did not get "better" as time went on; rather, they were used differently for what seemed to be most important at the moment: to unblock, integrate, crystallize, or to "blue sky."

Diagrams. I used diagrams in several ways. First, I used them *to show process.* Informed by the interactionist philosophy, my study was indeed of a process, that of identity loss. As such, I wanted to "see" the changes that occurred as they were apparent in the data. I also wanted to see the interactions between the players and to graphically document the process as it moved temporally and existentially. These diagrams noted the conditions, strategies, and consequences (or new conditions) of the dyadic relationship as identity of one partner began to slip. For example, it was by way of diagramming that my concept of "existential coordinate" emerged.

Second, I used diagrams *to depict lines of action* with social relations and finally, I used them *to integrate* the relationship between concepts. In this way, I was able to understand the relationship, for example, between the subjective and objective elements of time and how temporality as a dimension impacted the caregiving experience. In much the same way, it was a diagram which "showed" me how objective time and knowledge were related.

I believe diagrams are the least utilized tool in the analytical process yet can yield great understanding of the conceptualizations being developed. If the researcher is unable to graphically depict "what all is going on here," he or she is probably not genuinely clear of the process yet.

What I have tried to depict are several snap shots of one person's experience in the use of grounded theory as a qualitative approach to research.

Merely describing the techniques seems insufficient. Intertwined to the utilization of technique—any technique—is how the individual person interprets and makes use of them. In this regard, I have tried to describe, albeit briefly, how I myself used them, and how they fit my own basic style of working. Grounded theory provided the framework for taking observations, intuitions, and understandings to a conceptual level and provided the guidelines for the discovery and formulation of theory.

As I noted previously, four major "themes" or categories emerged from the data: social relations, reciprocity, moral obligation, and temporality. What follows now is a brief discussion of one dimension in the process of identity loss as perceived by the caregiving relative of an Alzheimer's person. More specifically, the following is my conceptualization of the temporally subjective aspects of the caregiving experience.

Each conceptualization is drawn from the empirical world in which a relative encounters the loss of a loved one as "once known" due to Alzheimer's disease. Typically, indicators of identity loss were temporally centered and apparent in activities of everyday living. Three concepts which focus on the temporal aspects of identity loss are: (1) existential coordinates, significant events which alter the person's perspective or world view; (2) paradoxical meaning in which meaning emerges in a field of mundane tasks of everyday living; and (3) memories of consequence, past experiences which have endured as influential ingredients in the identity maintenance of the respective members of the dyad.

Background

The social construction of one's identity is a continual, life-long process in which maintenance and transformation occur in daily interactions [15-20]. Many of these interactions take place between members of a family constellation. However, identity is vague, complex, evolving, and often volatile. Thus, a person is never fully "known." Even so, members of a dyad, for example, come to know aspects of one another through countless daily interactions [21]. Indeed, over time, there develop in such relationships myriad gestures, nuances, and idiosyncrasies of everyday living which tell me the other is who I perceive him/her to be, and which in turn, let me know he/she recognizes me. This pool of knowledge is usually accessible only to the two members of the dyad, and often, is not regarded as "knowledge" by either participant.

Although it is often taken for granted, identity can nevertheless be called into question by a crisis or problematic situation such as the physical and mental deterioration of a loved one who has Alzheimer's disease. Facing personality change, loss of cognition and memory, and physical disability, the person with Alzheimer's disease is typically cared for by a family member [5].

Accounts by family members of Alzheimer's disease patients indicate a common theme: The person with Alzheimer's disease undergoes tremendous change, often to the point of being unrecognizable as the person once known. Moreover, an underlying theme which inextricably informs the process of identity transformation is subjective temporality [22-29]. In the following discussion, I will describe three key ways in which the consequences of identity change are manifested in temporal dimensions.

Three assumptions in a dyadic relationship which are central to my discussion on identity are reciprocity, social structure, and temporality. First, each member *reciprocally* participates in the maintenance and transformation of the other's identity in social interactions. Further, each member, over time, develops an understanding of the boundaries of identity attributes. That is, negotiated boundaries emerge beyond which the person may not venture without the relationship becoming strained; newly formed boundaries are renegotiated. So long as each member continues to relate to the other *as expected,* he or she sustains and maintains the other's identity in taken-for-granted interactions. An understanding of perceived attributes is thus constructed.

Second, there is a *social structure* into which the dyad fits. This web of social relations constitutes the arena for the individual's multiple roles. At work, Jackie is a bus driver providing service to the public as well as a friend to her coworkers. At home, she is a mother, partner, and daughter. In each situation, her role and sense of who she is may be different. Whatever the case, in each situation, the social relations sustain or alter aspects of her identity in daily interactions. Thus, persons confront the conditions of Alzheimer's disease with more than one role as they move, over time, into the respective primary role of "Alzheimer's victim" and "caregiver."

Finally, the formation and maintenance of relationships includes a *temporal* dimension. Dyadic relationships occur in absolute, clock time, and can usually be located on a specific point on the calendar. Spouses recall their first meeting; parents remember the child's birth. From its beginning point, a history emerges indicating the passage of objective time. Of specific significance to caregivers of the early 1970s is their temporal locations within a historical framework of the disease. This historical location becomes, in itself, yet another temporal dimension. That is, the experience was directly influenced by a lack of knowledge of Alzheimer's disease, both among the lay populace and among health care practitioners at the time. In the terms of Znaniecki [30], a social circle of caregivers was emerging before the authority with expert knowledge had been defined.

However, if identity is formed and maintained in objective, clock time, its formation—and transformation—is experienced in subjective, "lived" time. Indeed, the social construction of reality cannot be "isolated" from time [31]. Participation in relationships is experienced existentially, that is, as experiences in which meaning is created. Memories, good and bad, are socially constructed in the context of the intersecting biographies.

In addition, events are anticipated in a potential future, many of which are taken-for-granted. In this taken-for-granted world, a person remains "as before," forever performing the little idiosyncrasies that come to make the person as he/she has come to be known. However, as seen in the case of Alzheimer's disease, the person does *not* remain "as before."

This preliminary study draws on in-depth interviews of 10 relatives who assumed the moral responsibility of providing care for a relative with Alzheimer's disease in the early to late 1970s. Open-ended interviews lasted from 2 to 4 hours each and with two exceptions were held in the homes of the caregivers. Interviewees ranged in age from 34 to 74 years and came from varied backgrounds and income groups. In addition, over the past year, data were gathered from weekly case conferences at the Memory Clinic associated with the University, and from participant-observations made at two separate Adult Day Health Care Centers over two 10-week periods. Data collection, coding and analysis proceeded in the tradition of grounded theory as outlined by Glaser, Strauss, and Schatzman [11-14] and is informed by the interactionist school of thought as well as by Whitehead's theory of time [32].

The Analysis

Early Indicators

Each respondent described incidents which were examples of his/her relative with Alzheimer's disease symptoms pushing against the negotiated boundaries of identity. That is, their actions in the world of everyday living were uncharacteristic though explainable for a while. Often, the behavior change was subtle and, *in itself,* would not appear problematic to others.

Karla, for example, reported that her husband was a devotee of classical music and proud of his collection of albums. Music was described as "a part of his life." There was not a day when he did not listen to music or record it. "Suddenly," she said, "he was not interested in music anymore. I knew something was wrong." The absence of an identity attribute (his love of music) became an indicator to her that something was amiss.

These type of indicators are often perceived as problematic only to those with intimate knowledge of what the boundaries are.[2] Yet, early signs, both blatant and subtle, were frequently misattributed by friend and relative alike. In the course of trying to normalize the situation, the caregiving relative sought a reason which fit the conditions at that time ("He's just having trouble adjusting to being retired"). In some cases, the relative accepted the reasons given by the person exhibiting the behavior—again because they seem to fit the situation at the time ("There's a lot going on at work").

These points are elaborated on because they form a critical temporal base of the caregiving trajectory.[3] At point "A" of the trajectory is what I call "irritating indicators": uncharacteristic behavior which caused initial uneasiness in the caregiving relative. The behavior was significant enough to cause attention and concern, but not so grave as to be anxiety-provoking. It is significant to note once again that little was known about Alzheimer's disease in the early 1970s. The "experts" had yet to emerge. The early signs did not portend of disaster to these particular relatives due in part, to a lack of knowledge of the disease.

Point "B" is the *reciprocal response* to the uncharacteristic behavior, indicated by the relative's attempt to normalize the situation. Thus, "misattributions" emerge in the form of a definition of the situation. Believing he/she had a "real" understanding of what is happening, the caregiving relative relinquished concern, albeit somewhat uneasily. Kate reconstructed the initial months of the disease when neighbors had asked, "What's wrong with Howard? He moves so slowly." She went on to tell me:

> So I said, "Well, he had a Plantar's wart on his foot and he has gone to a doctor and had surgery for it." After the surgery, it was almost every bit as painful. He couldn't exercise and this whole thing slowed him down and I thought that's what was bothering him, and all the overtime at work—because of the plant closing down.

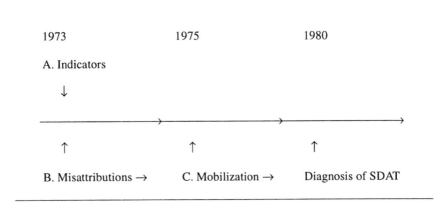

Figure 7.1. Beginning Trajectory of One Caregiver

However, there came a point when Kate—like the others—could no longer ignore, deny, or accept any of the prior "normalizing" explanations for the behavior. The person with Alzheimer's symptoms had gone beyond the negotiated boundaries of identity attributes. "I knew something was wrong" is the common theme running through accounts of this time period. Uncertainty prevailed as they "know" something is wrong—but what? To paraphrase Mead, by virtue of uncharacteristic behavior, the Alzheimer's person has ceased to be the person he/she once was [33].

It is at this juncture (Point C) that the relative mobilized to take action. In most cases, several years elapsed between Points A and B (irritating Indicators and Misattributions) and Point C (Mobilization) (see Figure 7.1).

Because experts were learning alongside the caregiving relative, the diagnostic process itself took considerable time for these caregivers and often involved several misdiagnoses. Consequently, entering the medical maze frequently added to the pain, uncertainty, and confusion of the caregiver. For example, one doctor responded to Sandra's description of her mother's behavior: "Sounds like syphilis to me" and began appropriate treatment based on that diagnosis.

However, at the point of diagnosis for dementia of the Alzheimer's type, several things happened: uncertainty was diminished and the behavior was legitimized through a name. More critically, *for these particular relatives—*

who had no previous knowledge of the disease—the diagnosis with all it implied became a catalyst for what I call an existential coordinate.

Existential Coordinates

> She was a wonderful driver. . . . As a matter of fact, that was the—that was the one thing when I think I noticed something was wrong. *I knew then and there.* ("Nora": Interview notes)

Existential coordinates are those events which stand out to the person, and *on reflection, reorder the individual's understanding of his/her past and future, and of his/her identity.* In essence, the individual retrospectively reconstructs his/her idea of the past and of the future in terms of current understandings (e.g., the diagnosis). As the person's extant worldview is shattered, what is called for is a different perspective and meaning to life's past events or beliefs as well as new parameters to identity.

These realizations are existential because they are given meaning by the individual and call forth personal values. They are coordinates because they locate the person's sense of identity vis à vis a breach in the taken-for-granted construction of a past and future and one moment in time—in this case, the diagnosis. For Nora (who is quoted previously), the moment of time was when she realized her mother could not pass a simple driver's test. Although she did not yet have a diagnosis, she realized the event of that day was fundamentally significant.

Similarly, on hearing the diagnosis, Karla's memories of her husband's neglect of his music, his uncharacteristic quiet moods—all took on new meaning. Her anticipated future (travel in retirement, spending time with grandchildren) was also altered. Moreover, she was faced with the question of who she was in the situation and how she would respond. Said Karla:

> You have to figure out what you're going to do with your life. . . . [When] my daughter asked how I was going to cope, I said, "I don't know. I may just have to turn things around and find some way I can work this out." You can't flounder. You have to do something positive. This was my decision.

The events, then, are more than "markers" in a person's life. They are also more than a specific memory, as for example, when we recall where we were when Kennedy was shot. Existential coordinates, then, reorder time and the parameters of identity through the reflection of a single event which crystallizes an ongoing process.

Paradoxical Meaning

> I used to do her nails all the time . . . but I'm lucky if I get to cut mine! I don't paint hers anymore. I just don't have the time. I'm just so overwhelmed that I get to bed so late—and then, it's time to get up! ("Jane": Interview notes)

Across the board, caregiving relatives spoke of how their views of time had changed. More than ever, time was experienced as a resource no longer to be taken-for-granted. In addition, time was also defined in terms of the caregivers' respective realities, that is, "time" became a social construction which emerged in the caregiving experience. One particular aspect which stands out in the social constructions is that of pardoxicality.

Whether it is a child being socialized to specific meal "times" or a tourist fitting into the pace of a different city, we each must respond to a linear time frame superimposed by the social structure. Indeed, in most societies, there is some visible indicator for the most mundane of daily activities, an obdurate reminder in the taken-for-granted world.

In the caregiving experience, relatives faced *paradoxical meaning,* a process in which taken-for-granted activities of everyday living were transformed from a mundane to meaningful level. This juxtaposition of the mundane to the meaningful was paradoxically brought into sharp focus by an ubiquitous element of modern society: the clock.

For the relative caring for an Alzheimer's person, then, the clock became more than an indicator of objective time. It was the symbolic representation of lived or experiential time. Indeed, the clock forced an awareness of the inextricability of lived life and the objective, calendar time.

First, management of taken-for-granted activities was redefined in terms of the clock. Simple tasks like eating and dressing became unremitting challenges. Mundane and routine aspects of day to day living were not only problematic for the caregiver, in fact, they came to dominate the day. Other activities, like gardening or reading, dropped away and with them, aspects of the caregiving relative's identity as the most ordinary of chores took more and more time to execute.

As an example, the act of dressing the Alzheimer's person was once a relatively easy task, taking but a few moments. However, dressing progressed to an experience in which each point in the sequence was like a stop frame of a moving film: "Lift this arm, (tapping it) hold it there, let me slip this on, put it down (tapping again). Now let's do the other; lift your arm, hold it there" until the sequence becomes a classic time and motion study. Though *subjectively experienced* as "relatively more" burdensome, in fact, activities of everyday living were also being objectively defined *by the clock* as "taking more time."

Thus the clock became a comparative measure, indicating a "before" and an "after" to activities of everyday living. Today, it took 60 minutes to feed the Alzheimer's person; last month, only 40 minutes. Before that, well, who can remember "before that"? The taken-for-granted aspects of everyday life were no longer experienced as such. When asked what changes had occurred in her life since her mother's illness, Nora sighed, "You know, you never get a whole night's sleep. I don't know what that's like anymore!"

Second, space was existentially redefined by the clock. Sandra, who was in her early forties when she cared for her mother, described how home had evolved into a "prison." For a while, she was able to work and hire a caretaker for her mother; however, the end of her work day had taken on a different meaning for her during the time her mother lived with her:

> So after 5:00, when I would come home, *there was no life after that.* I mean, it was hard for me to go to the store if we were out of milk. You know what I mean? (Interview notes; emphasis added)

However, if taken-for-granted activities became challenges, they were also transformed into "treats," valued for their scarcity in a redefined world. For example, Nora described the bliss of being able to get away for a "lunch where everything is hot and I get waited on for a change"; where the meal is eaten without interruption, a treat made possible by the services of adult day health care. Yet, even here the clock was her constant companion since her "free time" ended at the return of her mother from the day center, as she said,

> You miss being able to—Well, at the drop of a hat, you want to go somewhere. You can't. You always have to stop and think: Now wait a minute; can I go? But you know, you're always up against the time. You're always against the clock. You rearrange your life.

The paradox of the caregiving experience is that in the act of commitment, in the process of transcending the tragedy of loss, the individual comes up against the most mundane, banal, and obdurate fact of life: the clock. The ticking of the clock becomes the tune to which the dance is played. It is the one constant variable around which daily life is organized, and as conceptualized by George Herbert Mead [33], the clock converts a self with a Me and I—to one in which slowly the Me dominates. Spontaneity diminishes and all but disappears. The clock becomes another reminder of a shattered world.

Memories of Consequence

> Anyway, one of the skills which lasted to very near the end was his piano playing. And they found out at [the Adult Day Center]. And he gave a concert and got his picture in the paper . . . brought all this humor into it, like Victor Borge or something. I would love to have been there. I wasn't aware of it. I don't have any of that to remember. (Kate: Interview notes)

It is part of the human condition that identity is inextricably tied to kinship [20]. Like it or not, my name, appearance, and even reputation provide a biographical connectedness to others. One way that this connectedness is socially constructed is through the sharing of memories. However, *memory sharing* requires that I have the ability to be conscious of the temporal aspects of existence. I must have the ability to "recall" past experiences in reminiscing with another. Yet, as the disease progresses, it is this very ability which was being lost to the Alzheimer's person.

No longer able to share family memories—thus providing continuity to the relationship and to the person—relatives nevertheless developed various strategies to use memories in the identity maintenance of the Alzheimer's person.

The third temporal conceptualization, *memories of consequence,* involves the designation and utilization by the caregiving relative of those past experiences which endured as "influential ingredients" in the identity maintenance of the Alzheimer's person. These influential ingredients, in turn, also affected the caregiver's identity by virtue of the reciprocal relationship.

For example, caregiving relatives became aware that they were losing access to a biographical history as reciprocity faded. As the disease progressed, the Alzheimer's person could no longer bear witness to the caregiver.

The caregiver was losing a partner who once could validate his/her past existence. Sandra describes the moment her mother no longer recognized her:

> I knew I was losing her. . . . When she did not recognize me, that's what bothered me the most. I'm under the illusion—well, she birthed me. I know she knows me. I've been here, and I *know* she knows me! But she didn't know me. And that was very traumatic for me. (Interview notes)

In turn, the Alzheimer's person was irrevocably losing the opportunity to "render coherent" his/her long life through a shared review of life's memories [31]. Often, a shared life review can help the terminally ill give meaning to life's experiences as well as to provide continuity for those remaining. Yet, most caregiving relatives became painfully aware that this opportunity has been lost. As one wife described:

> However sad it is with cancer patients, it's just worse with Alzheimer's. With Alzheimer's physically they're well, but emotionally and mentally, *he's gone.* With a cancer person, he's still the same person: an Alzheimer's isn't. He has died a long time ago. (Interview notes, emphasis added)

Mitchell, who had decided to keep the truth of the disease from his wife, agonized over his decision long after her death:

> Later, this decision which we managed to keep from her caused me much agony. Too late, I realized I had robbed her of the opportunity to . . . share her emotions and to plan . . . how to use the time we had left to the best advantage.

Memories of consequence were used in a second way as memories of everyday living were recalled and reenacted by the caregiving relatives in order to maintain the symbolic form of social interactions as they once occurred. In the process of *memory keeping,* remnants of the "old" self seemed apparent once again. For example, one young woman told me of the things she did to "hang onto" her mother as she was remembered:

> I would take her out, you know, to movies. I would read to her . . . and she would keep coming in and out, in and out. . . . Oh, she'd kiss me and say, you're so nice—which wasn't different [from before]. She always used to do that. (Interview notes)

The caregiving relative did not assume that the Alzheimer's person understood the significance of the poignant ritual. Instead memory keeping appears to have significance for the relative as an acknowledgment of the person "as before." Said Nora:

> She used to love coffee. Can't stand it now. . . . I give it to her, and of course, I say, "Now it's awful hot." And she lets it get cold, and 'course, cold coffee is terrible. And hot coffee is too hot for her to drink, and she'll taste it and say, "Oh that's bitter. I don't like that." She used to be a great coffee drinker. So now, I spoon a little hot coffee—when we have it—over her ice cream . . . so she gets a little taste of coffee that way. [imitating her mother] "Ohhh, it tastes good."

These memory-keeping rituals were not moments of ostentatious ceremony, but rather, reenactments of activities of everyday living in which the situation was "normalized" yet simultaneously "made special."

There came a point, however, when even the most durable of memories, memories of the most significant consequence, were not enough. Finally, it became apparent to the caregivers that *even as life was being experienced at the time,* only one participant would have a "memory" of it. Threatened by lack of reciprocal validation, *memory making* became a lonely endeavor for the caregiver, no longer shareable with the Alzheimer's person.

Describing how she had turned her life around in the process of caring for her mother, Debbie sighed wistfully. She told me how unsettled her adolescent years had been and how she had dropped out of high school. She recalled that "toward the end," her mother did not know who or what Debbie had become and how she had changed. Her mother never knew that she had become a grandmother, and although there were "sparks" of recognition, there was no acknowledgment that Debbie had created a good life for her self and for her family:

> I felt sad that she didn't know my girls; she didn't see how I turned out, not that I think I turned out all so great, but I don't think she would have been too unhappy with how I did turn out. (Interview notes)

In the context of caregiving, memories emerged as indicators of events in everyday living that "identified" the Alzheimer's person. More than fleeting images, these enduring memories took on special significance. These memories of consequence endured precisely because they provided value to a number of past experiences which shaped the caregivers' current worldview.

Thus, once designated by the caregiving relative as being "of consequence," the memories were utilized in several ways:

1. Through *reenactment* to preserve the past experiences for continuity;
2. To aid in the *social interaction* with a person as "once known"; and finally,
3. To serve as the basis for *new memories* for another day.

Discussion

Caring for a loved one who suffered from dementia of the Alzheimer's type was a devastating experience in the early seventies when little was known of the disease or its trajectory. Indeed, until Alzheimer's disease became a public issue, the particular caregiving relatives in my study faced the situation alone in a world of "private troubles."

As the Alzheimer's persons changed to the point of being unrecognizable, the caregiving relatives lost remnants of their own identity as the impaired partners were no longer able to reciprocally participate in the relationship.

The caregiving relatives lived with countless daily reminders of the loss that was occurring, progressively apparent as the disease symptoms intensified. While one personal characteristic stood out as significantly lost, the loss was comprised of many subtle actions that were once taken for granted, may have even been endearing or irritating, and were fading.

However, loss of the person "as once known" did not occur without a struggle. These struggles took place in the arena of everyday living. Moreover, caregiving relatives fought to maintain vestiges of the person as known, even when it was not clear if the Alzheimer's person "knew" what was happening, as for example, when Nora gave her mother coffee.

In the accounts of caregiving relatives of Alzheimer's patients, patterns of identity loss emerge. Of special significance to this discussion, attempts at identity maintenance occurred in commonplace activities with little, if any, fanfare. Indeed, the caregiving relatives provided vivid vignettes of identity maintenance where the most profound of commitments is played out in the taken-for-granted world of everyday living. It is as if, once invested in a relationship, the caregiving relative worked to salvage remnants of the other, of their relationship and its history, and of parts of him/herself as well. As reciprocity was lost, the caregiving relative "worked" both sides of the relationship.

With the explosion of information via the popular media, many relatives who face the moment of diagnosis in the late 1980s have greater awareness of the disease and its social, physiological, and emotional consequences. With this understanding come opportunities that the early caregivers did not have, especially as the disease impacts on identity.

First, today's caregiving relatives have the opportunity, if they choose, to participate in the life review process with their loved one before the disease obliterates cognition and memory. This process addresses the issue of continuity vis à vis a *past*. In addition, both members of the relationship may face the *future* together while the ability still exists. For example, those with the disease may be adamant about certain aspects of their care (such as heroic measures) and its cost to the family. It is recognized here that Alzheimer's disease is not truly diagnosed as such except by autopsy. Nevertheless, even the remotest chance that such a condition exists may serve as a catalyst for serious dialogue of topics often undisclosed.

Second, those in the support and health services can provide an understanding and acknowledgment of the disease vis à vis its existential ramifications. Support must be forthcoming to aid in the loss that is being sustained: that of a person, a relationship, and of a self. If the chronically ill face a loss of self-image as Charmaz [15] suggests, so, too, do those who assume the moral responsibility for providing care.

Identity provides perspective to life's challenges, guides action and renders coherent a life of change and constancy. This examination of the caregiving experience, then, is presented as a "temporal slice" of a whole, a slice which demonstrates how some relatives faced identity loss and of the struggle which took place in the world of everyday living.

Acknowledgments

My thanks to Steve Wallace (University of St. Louis, Missouri) and Eric Juengst (Pennsylvania State University, Medical Center) for taking the time to edit and critique this paper. Special appreciation is also extended to Pat Fox and Barbara Hayes both of UC, San Francisco. Thanks also to Dr. Todd May for his help on memory and cognition. Portions of the data were collected as resident-in-training at the Alzheimer's and Memory Clinic, University of California, San Francisco.

Notes

1. Each team was comprised of one graduate student from the Schools of Dentistry, Medicine, Nursing, Pharmacy, and the Social Sciences.

2. At the other end are those cues which are immediately perceived as problematic by the observer regardless of relationship: erratic driving and the inability to handle simple money transactions, etc. Here, even a stranger would remark on the behavior. Interpretations on the cause of the behavior would vary, of course, and not necessarily be correct, as for example, when erratic driving is attributed to alcohol or drug use.

3. Used in conjunction with "illness trajectory," a term coined by Glaser and Strauss which "refers not only to the physiological unfolding of a patient's disease but to the total organization of work done over that course, plus the impact on those involved with that work and its organization" (Strauss A. et al. *Social Organization of Medical Work*, 1985).

References

1. Terry R. D. and Katzman R. Senile dementia of the Alzheimer type. *Ann. Neurol. 14*, 497-506, Nov. 1983.

2. Cohen G. Historical views and evolution concepts. In *Alzheimer's Disease: The Standard Reference* (Edited by Reisberg B.). Free Press, New York, 1983.

3. Boyd D. A contribution to the psychopathology of Alzheimer's disease. *Am. J. Psychiat.* 93, 155-175, 1936.

4. Reisberg B. (Ed.) An overview of current concepts of Alzheimer's disease, senile dementia and age-associated cognitive decline. In *Alzheimer's Disease: The Standard Reference*. Free Press, New York, 1983.

5. Brody E. M. and Schoonover C. B. Patterns of parent care when adult daughters work and when they do not. *The Gerontologist 25*, 373-381, 1986.

6. Brody E. M. Patient care as a normative family stress. *The Gerontologist 25*, 19-29, 1985.

7. Fontana A. and Smith R. W. The shrinking world: Caring for senile dementia patients. Paper presented at *Pacific Sociological Association Conference,* Eugene, Oregon, 1987.

8. Gilhooly M. L. M. *et al. The Dementias*. Prentice-Hall, Englewood Cliffs, NJ, 1986.

9. Johnson C. L. and Catalano D. J. A longitudinal study of family supports to impaired elderly. *The Gerontologist 23*, 612-619, 1983.

10. Zarit S. H. *et al.* Subjective burden of husbands and wives as caregivers: A longitudinal study. *The Gerontologist 26*, 260-266, 1986.

11. Glaser B. and Strauss A. *The Discovery of Grounded Theory.* Aldine, New York, 1967.

12. Glaser B. *Theoretical Sensitivity.* Sociology Press, Mill Valley, CA, 1978.

13. Schatzman L. and Strauss A. *Field Research.* Prentice-Hall, Englewood Cliffs, NJ, 1973.

14. Strauss A. *Qualitative Analysis for Social Scientists.* Cambridge University Press, New York, 1987.

15. Charmaz K. Loss of self: A fundamental form of suffering in the chronically ill. *Sociol. Hlth Illn. 5*, 169-195, July 1983.

16. Gubrium J. *Time, Roles, and Self in Old Age.* Human Sciences Press, New York, 1976.

17. Hazan H. Continuity and transformation among the aged: A study in the anthropology of time. *Curr. Anthrop. 25*, 567-578, 1984.

18. Kaufman S. *The Ageless Self: Sources of Meaning in Later Life*. University of Wisconsin Press, Madison, WI, 1986.

19. Myerhoff B. *Number Our Days*. Simon & Schuster, New York, 1978.

20. Strauss A. *Mirrors and Masks*. Sociology Press, Mill Valley, CA, 1969.

21. Simmel G. *The Sociology of Georg Simmel* (Edited by Wolff K. H.). Free Press, New York, 1950.

22. Mead G. H. *The Philosophy of the Present* (Edited by Murphy A. E.). University of Chicago Press, Chicago, IL, 1932.

23. Calkins K. Time: Perspectives, markings and styles of usage. *Soc. Probl. 17,* 487-501, 1969.

24. Denzin N. Under the influence of time: Reading the interactional text. *Sociol. Q. 28,* 327-341, 1987.

25. Flaherty M. Multiple realities and the experience of duration. *Sociol. Q. 28,* 313-326, 1987.

26. Lewis J. and Weigert A. The structures and meanings of social time. *Soc. Forces 60,* 432-462, 1981.

27. Maines D. *et al.* Sociological import of G. H. Mead's theory of the past. *Am. Sociol. Rev. 48,* 161-173, April 1987.

28. Glaser B. and Strauss A. Temporal aspects of dying as a nonscheduled status passage. *Am. J. Sociol. 71,* 48-59, 1965.

29. Maines D. The significance of temporality for the development of sociological theory. *Sociol. Q. 28,* 303-311, 1987.

30. Znaniecki F. *The Social Role of the Man of Knowledge*. Harper Row, New York, 1940.

31. Juengst E. Time and value in Whitehead's cosmology. Unpublished paper. Pennsylvania State University, School of Medicine, Hershey, PA, 1981.

32. Whitehead A. N. *Process and Reality*. Free Press, New York, 1929.

33. Mead G. H. *On Social Psychology* (Edited by Strauss A.). University of Chicago Press, Chicago, IL, 1956.

8

Of Lungs and Lungers

The Classified Story of Tuberculosis

SUSAN LEIGH STAR

GEOFFREY C. BOWKER

Commentary

This innovative chapter is by Susan Leigh Star (another former student of
Anselm Strauss), and her husband (a historian of technology and science),
Geoffrey C. Bowker. The chapter illustrates still other features of grounded
theory, besides the same second-nature internalization of the methodology
rather than its self-conscious choice and use in the research. Here the research
processes through which·the data are discovered and interpreted are not so
visible as in Clarke's deliberately direct narrative about them. But some of the

This chapter previously appeared in January 1997 as an article in *Mind, Culture, and Activity,* 4(1).
© Lawrence Erlbaum; reprinted with permission.

AUTHORS' NOTE: Correspondence regarding this chapter should be sent to Leigh Star or
Geoffrey C. Bowker, Graduate School of Library and Information Science, University of Illinois,
501 East Daniel, Champaign, IL 61820. E-mail: s-star1@uiuc.edu; bowker@alexia.lis.uiuc.edu.

grounded theory processes can be discerned or inferred. Among them are the following.

The sources of data are less common than the usual reliance on interviews or even field observation. Yet, one can sense the researchers' theoretically driven search for materials: the historical and contemporary materials by physicians and medical commissions, as Star and Bowker pursue the characteristics of tuberculosis, but also the characteristics of medical classifications of the disease, and the difficulties of making standard classifications that make empirical sense. Probably the authors already knew some of the literary history of this famous and previously much romanticized disease, but they take pains to document some of this romantic imagery. (They do not document the more terrifying historical imagery; that is not part of their analytic story.) The same is probably true of their knowledge of Mann's (1929/1992) famous book, *The Magic Mountain,* but with theoretical formulations now guiding their search, they carefully dimensionalize and in other ways analyze the substance of the novel's account. The same dimensions and analyses are made comparatively of Julius Roth's (1963) participant observations in his monograph. In Roth's case, Star (a sociologist) certainly knew this material from her graduate student days, but like the procedures used for examining *The Magic Mountain*, the rereading is now specific and analytically focused.

The authors' use of disciplinary literature is interesting. Their minor use of it is the drawing of occasional comparisons, usually of similarities; their major use is of theoretical frameworks available in the writings of Strauss/Corbin, Timmermans, and Charmaz. These they use when presenting a model for thinking about their main problem: In what ways and how are standard classifications affected by temporal considerations, biographical developments, and bureaucratic structures and actions? Our guess is that these theoretical frameworks and implicated concepts were already part of the authors' thinking, functioning at first as sensitizing concepts. Then, later, these made integrative sense when reasoning more generally about how to diagram and better understand their major problem and its answer. A thoroughly admirable feature of the chapter is that it relates their final model to earlier formulations of the concept/theory of trajectory, thus adding to its future research power.

Knowing the authors ourselves, we can also say their interest in the social and political implications of classificatory action (and struggle) led them to study the classifications of this particularly interesting disease while it also sensitized them to a wide ranging, but not pretermindedly dogmatic, investigation of the social and political implications of TB's classification history. The actual sequence and procedural detail of the study, however, is not spelled out in the chapter itself.

* * *

The experience of a long-term chronic illness weaves together problems in biography, the body, and the cultural and organizational meanings of the disease. Time meets infrastructure; experience meets classification. We present here a close reading of two studies of tuberculosis, Thomas Mann's (1929/1992) novel *The Magic Mountain* and Julius Roth's (1963) empirical work, *Timetables.* Drawing on research in medical sociology and information science, we show how the trajectories of disease, biography, and institution weave together. Mismatches in the trajectories produce distortions (or torques) in time and sense of self, accounting for the phantasmagoric imagery often associated with tuberculosis. We conclude with some general observations about how the concept of trajectory might be used in understanding the intersection of biography and organization.

Introduction

TB is a disease of time; it speeds up life, highlights it, spiritualizes it.

Sontag, 1977, p. 14

The further one stands away from the disease of tuberculosis, the more it seems like a single, uniform phenomenon. It is associated with one of the great philosophical breakthroughs in medicine—Koch developed his "postulates" for defining disease agency partly with TB in mind. Indeed, he could hardly avoid it because epidemiologists assure us that at the time he wrote them, 1881, *one seventh of all reported human deaths, and one third of deaths of "productive middle age"* groups were attributable to TB (Brock, 1988, pp. 117, 179-180, emphasis added). Yet this single disease, the holocaust of those in their prime, has historically proved an elusive thing to classify. The work of classification has involved at many levels a complex ecology between localization, standardization, and time.

TB also holds an important place in popular culture. For example, the gambler Doc Holliday was a legendary "gunslinger" and partner of Wyatt Earp and his brother, the famed American Wild West law enforcers. He suffered from TB, and a number of movies and books portray him with the disease. . .

Body-snatching and the failure to reach a final localized resting place permeate the history of tuberculosis. As we proceed with this story, the interweaving of myth, biography, science, medicine, and bureaucracy becomes thicker and thicker, eluding attempts at standardization and localization from every angle. Just for this reason, though, the story of TB holds some profound insights about how those threads intertwine, tense against each other, and form the texture of a landscape of time.

We bring a number of intellectual tools to the analysis of this landscape. Social studies of science have moved to crisscross nature, culture (including artifacts), and discourse in a seamless web (Latour, 1993); activity theory adds the concept of mediation for tools, cognition, and community. We emphasize as well the importance of ongoing hybrid arrangements, in the form of infrastructures of classification and bureaucracy (Bowker & Star, 1994; Star, 1995; Star & Ruhleder, 1996; Timmermans, Bowker, & Star, 1995). We draw as well on some concepts from medical sociology: notions of body-biography-trajectory (Corbin & Strauss, 1988, 1991) and the temporal lessons of chronic illness (Charmaz, 1991). We seek to recenter the ways in which time and infrastructure interact, to illuminate the texture of this web so crisscrossed with great divides in literature and popular myth; the whole borderland has taken on a phantasmagoric shape, unrecognizable to those undergoing the experience.

Part One: Classification

The question has often been posed in the social and cultural study of medicine: Whose body is it anyway that is getting analyzed? (Berg & Bowker, in press) This question is as old as the development of statistics (Hacking, 1990): Quetelet sought the "ideal type" in a statistical analysis of a regiment of Scottish soldiers. With tuberculosis, the body is constantly in motion, and the disease is constantly in motion. The disease may be localized or spread throughout the body; the state or general condition of the body and of the person's life enters into the treatment regime, which may take months and historically has taken years or a lifetime. Thus, any classification system should include both spatial and temporal dimensions, but standardized classifications tend to emphasize space alone. That is, classifications are rarely developmental, and are often presented as spatial demographic distributions. Even where stages of a disease may be categorized, these stages are abstracted away from biographical continuity and more subtle temporal issues. As the problems of time emerge in the lives of patients and the work of classifiers, those spatial compartments break down in interesting ways: A formal hierarchy of mutually exclusive categories becomes a set of overlapping contradictory classes. The formal thesis of this chapter is that when the work of classification abstracts away the flow of historical time, then the goal of standardization can only be achieved at the price of leakages in the classification system (cf. Hacking, 1995). Under certain conditions, the shifting terrain between standardized classification and the situated biography of the patient is twisted across an axis of negotiation, scientific work and instruments, suffering, and time.

The Disease Is Constantly in Motion

Tuberculosis is a moving target. It is often presented as the great epidemic disease with a cure—heralding the famous optimism (ironically, just as AIDS was developing and newly resistant strains of TB were on the rise) that epidemic disease could be eradicated from the planet. In September 1994 the World Health Organization made a worldwide press release predicting the eradication of polio from the planet by the year 2000 (http://www.who.ch/programmes/gpv/tEnglish/avail/polio.htm). A year earlier, sociologist Fred Davis, who suffered from polio in his youth and was one of the most eloquent analysts of uncertainty in illness (Davis, 1963), died of a stroke at the age of 65—was this stroke in part the legacy of his earlier illness? Many of those who had polio in the 1940s and 1950s are now beginning to lose their ability to walk because their overburdened spinal cells, designed for backup purposes, are wearing out after years of tough therapy and rehabilitation. Is the disease thus eradicated—or delayed? In the lives of these patients, the answer is not so clear. And they remain invisible to the original classifications.

As Barbara Bates has pointed out (Bates, 1992, pp. 320-321) many observers "now attribute the decline of tuberculosis chiefly to socioeconomic changes." A historically fully contingent rise in standard of living accompanied by less crowded conditions in cities may have worked the real miracle. Others, she points out, offer a more brutal, but still completely historical cause for the cure: They argue that it is a matter of natural selection; what has happened is simply that those humans most susceptible to the disease are now dead. This sort of convergence is a problem in much scientific and medical research, and increasingly so (Bowker, 1994; Latour, 1993; Timmermans &

Berg, in press). Here we have a "global truth"—the cure for TB—that may have been true because the "fitter ones survived" (the susceptible members died out), or because human environments changed (better living conditions), or because there is now an allopathic cure. It is impossible to decide between these three causes, because according to the first two, humanity before the "cure" (whichever one plumps for) is not the same thing as humanity after the cure—either the race will have changed biologically or the infrastructure that makes us know what we are will have altered.

The disease has its own history, a broken and contested path. In a series of works put out by the National Tuberculosis Association from 1950 to the present, TB often figures wryly as an actor in the text: much as Roy Porter (1990) has noted that "gout" in the 18th century had a character of its own. Thus, the 1961 edition of the *Diagnostic Standards and Classification of Tuberculosis* noted that:

> For our present purposes, therefore, tuberculosis is defined as that infectious disease caused by one of several closely related mycobacteria, including M. tuberculosis, M. bovis, and M. avium. It usually involves the lungs, but it also involves and sometimes produces gross lesions in other organs and tissues. The clinical and pathologic pictures may range from acute to chronic. (p. vi)

TB taken as an agent traverses history and human bodies, taking hold in some and leaving others in a contingent historical progression, reaffirming the uneven, hierarchical value given to different patient's lives (Glaser & Strauss, 1965). The disease hits at different points in the life cycle (Glaser & Strauss, 1965, p. 6); thus becomes a complex mirror composed of nature, culture, discourse, and infrastructure.

The Body Is Constantly in Motion

The development of x-rays was perhaps the most significant breakthrough in the detection and diagnosis of tuberculosis (Pasveer, 1989). Unfortunately, the body itself is constantly in motion and varies by individual: Therefore, the ideal measurement is always a projection from a moving picture onto a timeless chart:

> The perfect chest roentgenogram . . . is the aim of those who practice roentgenology. The very nature of the problem prevents the realization of this aim. The chest is a moving, dynamic part of the body and cannot be completely still. It varies from

person to person. In some it is thin and easy to penetrate. In others it is thick and heavy from fat or muscle and hard to penetrate. Some lungs are stiff and hard to inflate. Others are made full and voluminous without great effort. To register lungs satisfactorily with these variables is at all times difficult. (*Diagnostic Standards,* 1955, p. 71)

Furthermore, each body subject to TB is going through its own biographical and physiological, historical development—and as it develops TB changes. Thus: "the clinical picture of serious necrotic lesions of primary tuberculosis and widespread disseminations from them is observed more often in infancy than in later life and more frequently in non-white than in white persons" (*Diagnostic Standards,* 1955, p. 17). Thomas Mann describes one of the TB sanitarium patients in *The Magic Mountain* responding to another's new diagnosis of a "moist spot":

"You can't tell," Joachim said. "That is just what you never can tell. They said you had already had places, of which nobody took any notice and they healed of themselves, and left nothing but a few trifling dullnesses. It might have been the same way with the moist spot you are supposed to have now, if you hadn't come up here at all. One can never know. (Mann, 1929/1992, p. 192)

Not only the disease and the body, but also the patient's experience, moves constantly. Thus Bates points out that institutionalization in a sanitarium may well have worked because the relationships with nurses, doctors, and other patients, together with removal from bad home conditions, may have done the work. She summarizes: "Psychological factors have long been thought to alter the course of tuberculosis, but their actual impact on outcomes is not known." (Bates, 1992, p. 320).

Classification: A Still Life Constantly in Motion

With all these historical trajectories being inscribed into the course of tuberculosis at whatever unit of analysis one took (humanity, the disease, the body, or the experience of the patient) it will come as no surprise that the work of classifying tuberculosis has generally had very complex temporal ramifications; and these ramifications have often led to problems in classification. It has also led to a sense by those in sanatoria of TB as inhabiting a phantasmagoric landscape, a borderland filled with monstrous experiences and distortions of time and self (Mann, 1929/1992; Roth, 1963). The reasons for this are not simply the physical horrors of the disease, although those are terrible enough, but also the ways in which our strands play out against each other in imagination.

One wants to classify tuberculosis first and foremost to say yea or nay, whether a particular patient has the disease. This information can be used to suggest a treatment plan for the patient, and a map of action for officials in public health (Should we quarantine, isolate, educate, or give antibiotics?) This classification work is not easy. In the first place, the disease itself is multifaceted: "When faced with a difficult diagnosis, the clinician does well to keep tuberculosis in mind, for its mode of onset and course are protean. This needs to be urged all the more now that tuberculosis is becoming relatively less frequent." (*Diagnostic Standards,* 1955, p. 23)

Furthermore, it does not have a single cause: Most TB in humans, according to official accounts, is caused by mycobacterium tuberculosis, but one should not forget mycobacterium bovis and mycobacterium avium. It does not appear in a single place—generally the lungs are affected, but it could produce lesions in many other organs and tissues. Star (1989) notes that the disease's spread implicated it in all investigations of nervous and brain disease in the 19th century; whether a patient had a brain or spinal tumor or TB was often unclear; the disease may cause seizures, paralysis, lameness, or dementia. Thomas Mann poses of one of his characters "the question whether the disease would be arrested by a chalky petrifaction and heal by means of fibrosis, or whether it would extend the area, create still larger cavities, and destroy the organ" (Mann, 1929/1992, p. 447)

And indeed even pulmonary TB, its most common form and one of the greatest killers in the history of humanity, cannot be simply classified:

> The lesions of tuberculosis are highly diverse in appearance, and their manifestations are numerous. No single system of classification can give information which completely describes the lesions. Certain classifications and descriptions are needed, however, for records and for statistical purposes . . . the status of a patient's disease at the time of diagnosis, and at any time in the months and years thereafter. These basic classifications should be used for all cases. (*Diagnostic Standards,* 1961, p. 39)

And they recommend that this basic classification should tell a story, detailing extent of disease, status of clinical activity, bacteriologic status, therapeutic status, exercise status, and other "lifestyle" variables as they are called nowadays.

Medical classification work as based on the International Classification of Diseases (ICD), however, does not tell a story—it records a fact (one died of the disease or not). There is a complex narrative written into the death certificate that is the primary outcome of the ICD: Doctors and later health workers must sift multiple causes of death to determine proximate, contributing, and underlying causes (Fagot-Largeault, 1989). But this is an impoverished story, with only a small range of contributing causes. The ICD cannot contain a protean disease. It is oriented toward a cause-and-effect that resembles a set of slots or bins, or blanks on a form, even where it is multivalanced and multislotted; it is not, like disease and diagnosis, messy, leaky, liquid, and textured with time. Indeed, the problem of tuberculosis has been a long-standing problem for the ICD—leading to the convening of several special committees to produce a standard (Biraben, 1988).

Standard medical classifications, although they may leak at the edges and become configurationally complex, do not reflect the temporal complexity of the disease itself (Clarke & Casper, 1996). They do not represent its composite, amodern nature: culture, nature, discourse, and infrastructure. They posit a single answer to the question of whether this person has TB or not. As Desrosiàres (1993, p. 296) has pointed out with respect to all statistical work, however, this kind of difficulty leads to a contradiction between a logical, top-down approach that accounts for all traits, and a local, pragmatic one that registers the phenomenon as locally encountered. It is one of the purest forms of a deduction versus induction debate.

For most of the 19th century, and into the 20th century, TB was believed to be hereditary. What was classified was a tuberculoid kind of a person, a temperament: romantic, melancholy, given to emotional extremes, hot cheeked and so on.

Sontag (1977) notes that just before Koch discovered the tubercule bacillus, a standard medical text gave the cause of TB as "hereditary disposition, unfavorable climate, sedentary indoor life, defective ventilation, deficiency of light, and 'depressing emotions'" (p. 54). She also writes of the literary and popular cultural images of TB, noting that many writers have referred to TB as "ethereal," "chaste," and somehow pure and mental, not physical. "TB is celebrated as the disease of born victims, of sensitive, passive people who are not quite life-loving enough to survive" (p. 25). In some circles in the 19th century, this became a romantic image, especially for middle-class white women: "The recurrent figure of the tubercular courtesan indicates that TB was also thought to make the sufferer sexy" (p. 25). Eventually, this romance bled over into a more diffuse concept of style of life and crafting of self. Sontag even states: "The romanticizing of TB is the first widespread example of that distinctively modern activity, promoting the self as an image. The tubercular look had to be considered attractive once it came to be considered a mark of distinction, of breeding" (p. 29).

The mythic person with TB became a romantic exile, and the myth "supplied an important model of bohemian life, lived with or without the vocation of the artist. The TB sufferer was a dropout, a wanderer in endless search of the healthy place" (p. 33).

The work of finding a cure thus involved myriad classificatory activities inserted into a shifting ecology of metrologies and images about temperament and constitution (Star, 1995). Bates (1992, p. 28) notes that members of the Climatological Association in the 1920s compiled measures of altitude, humidity, temperature, sunlight, dampness of the soil, ozone in the air, and emanations from pine and balsam forests to uncover and classify the ideal placement for sanitarium situation. As she somewhat sardonically notes, though, a skeptic: "might notice that many of the otherwise disparate conclusions shared one characteristic: Physicians tended to discover health-giving attributes in their own locales" (p. 28).

It was (and is) also not clear when to stop classifying TB. As the following report on Bergey's manual of determinative bacteriology notes, apparently without irony, there is a need to bring order into the classification "unclassified" when talking about TB. The manual lists four subtypes of unclassified strains (*Diagnostic Standards,* 1961, p. 17) So one can have an "other" or residual category, but at some point even the garbage can will have to be ordered, when it becomes large enough.

Furthermore, the committee on the classification of tuberculosis was forced to recognize in general that: "All classifications are ephemeral" (*Diagnostic Standards,* 1955, p. 6, quoting the 1950 edition). They fully recognized the temporary, agreed-on nature of their classification work. In infrastructural work such as the development of classification systems, there is much greater sensitivity to such factors than appears in the published scientific papers: "Complete agreement . . . is impossible. . . . The classification presented represents a well-considered compromise of the views of outstanding clinicians" (*Diagnostic Standards,* 1955, p. 5, quoting the 1950 edition).

Indeed, the historiography presented by the texts of diagnostic handbooks was a mixture of pure Whiggish progress tinged with despair ("without roentgenology the fight against TB would be back where it was in the 19th century" (*Diagnostic Standards,* 1961, p. 67) and a cyclical view of history that Vico would not have been ashamed to espouse:

> Readers will note another of those shifts in emphasis which have characterized expositions of the pathogenesis of tuberculosis for 35 years. The concepts presented in the current edition are more closely allied to those of former years than to the views expressed in the last edition. (*Diagnostic Standards,* 1955, p. 7)

Or again, from the 1961 edition:

> The one item of change upon which all of our consultants agreed was the need for a classification to include the increasing number of cases which are neither truly "active" nor "inactive," and, chiefly, cases of the "open negative syndrome." In defining such a new class and seeking a suitable name for it, we have reached back 10 years and reinstated the once-retired term, "quiescent," which was previously applied to an intermediate class. (*Diagnostic Standards,* 1961, p. v)

This example moves us into the terrain of tuberculosis and activity, which we will consider in the next section. For our purposes here, though, it underscores the situation of the classification act in an historical flow, where the pure progress of natural science is transmogrified by time, biography, institutions, and myth.

Part Two: Freeze Frames— Snapshots of a Disease in Progress

TUBERCULOSIS TEST

A positive skin test does NOT mean that you have tuberculosis; rather, that you may have been exposed to the organisms at some time in the past. In this case, a chest x-ray must be obtained in order to be certain there is no active disease. Additionally, if the reaction is positive, we will want to review your history and talk to you about what you should do in the future.

SOURCE: Information given to students by the health center at the University of Illinois; © University of Illinois Board of Trustees.

Throughout the history of tuberculosis classification, one of the key problems has been how to convert a progressive, protean disease to a single mark on a sheet of paper. Many categories have been experimented with. One suggested hallmark was whether or not one tested positive to the tuberculin test. But as with HIV, it was decided that those who tested positive did not have the disease, they were: "considered to have tuberculous infection but not disease" (*Diagnostic Standard,* 1955, p. 25). Only those who could bring other evidence of disease to the table would be considered worthy of the classification of pulmonary and nonpulmonary tuberculosis.

Those who did have the disease could be lumped into the categories inactive/active/activity undetermined. If, however: A "provisional estimate of the probable clinical status is necessary for public health purposes, the terms (a) "Probably Active" or (b) "Probably Inactive" should be used. Every effort should be made to classify cases and to avoid this category" (*Diagnostic Standards,* 1955, p. 28). By 1961, it was agreed that a classification somewhere between active and inactive was needed: This would be the "open negative syndrome" and would, as we have just seen, have the word "quiescent" attached to it. "Inactive" would be redefined to include: "constant and definite healing." Ironically, and to underscore the attempt to separate disease from biography, "dead" was also recognized in this classification (p. 41)— presumably to stand as a cross between highly active and completely inactive!

Bubbling out of the freeze frame with these leakages are the struggles with a shifting infrastructure of classification and treatment. Turning now to other presentations and classifications of TB by a novelist and a sociologist, we will see the complex dialectic of irrevocably local biography and of standard classification.

Part Three: Moving Through Tuberculosis and Its Classification

The next sections rely on two detailed readings of classic studies of TB sanatoria and hospitals. The first is Thomas Mann's (1929/1992) *The Magic Mountain,* written in 1912, a 900+ page tome chronicling a Swiss hospital and the 7-year sojourn of a young German engineer there, Hans Castorp. The account was based on Mann's experience as a visitor to a similar institution during his wife's incarceration for lung disease. The second is Julius Roth's (1963) *Timetables,* a comparative ethnographic analysis of several American TB hospitals in the late 1950s. This volume, too, has a strong base in Roth's own experience as a TB patient while he was writing his doctoral dissertation.

The Texture of Time: Lost to the World

When Hans Castorp, the hero of Mann's (1929/1992) novel, arrives in the Alps as a visitor to his tubercular cousin, one of his first lessons in local culture is the way that values about time change for those "up here." Everything normal seems to change for him, and the whole place seems macabre and oddly funny. Later in the novel he will explain to another newcomer: "I have no contact with the flat-land, it has fallen away. We have a folk-song that says: 'I am lost to the world'—so it is with me" (p. 614). This lostness first takes on the form of time passing very slowly, and in chunks that seem unimaginable to the newcomer: "We up here are not acquainted with such an unit of time as the week—if I may be permitted to instruct you, my dear sir. Our smallest unit is the month. We reckon in the grand style—that is a privilege we shadows have" (p. 59).

Roth compares the commitment to a TB sanitarium with having an "indeterminate sentence" for one's first year of jail—not knowing how long one will be incarcerated, not having any milestones or turning points that make sense, also makes time seem endless, and distorted with respect to known landscapes, both inner and outer. "Where uniformity rules; and where motion is no more motion, time is no longer time." (Mann, 1929/1992, p. 566)

The patients in both Mann's and Roth's hospitals begin to speculate on the meaning of this lost time, this "time out." Is time real, objective, something that can be measured externally—or subjective, illusory? Hans originally opts for a relativist explanation: "After all, time isn't 'actual.' When it seems long to you, then it is long; when it seems short, why, then it is short. But how long, or how short, it actually is, that nobody knows" (Mann, 1929/1992, p. 66). His cousin Joachim, a rather hard-nosed soldier who wants only to get off of the mountain and back to his regiment, disagrees, and says "We have watches and calendars for the purpose; and when a month is up, why then up it is, for you, and for me, and for all of us" (p. 66). Hans proceeds to demonstrate how slowly seven minutes can go by while taking one's temperature, and we indeed feel the seconds creep by in Mann's precise language. What is "the same?" he asks. "The schoolmen of the Middle Ages would have it that time is an illusion; that its flow in sequence and causality is only the result of a sensory device, and their real existence of things in an abiding present" (p. 566).

As time goes on, up on the magic mountain and in each of the hospitals studied by Roth, people inside begin to develop a sense of how to fragment, break up this unbroken monolith. "We are aware that the intercalation of periods of change and novelty is the only means by which we can refresh our sense of time, strengthen, retard, and rejuvenate it, and therewith renew our perception of life itself" (Mann, 1929/1992, p. 107). In one of his many meditations on the nature of time, Mann argues that time and action and space are not separable—nothing "fills up" time in a platonic-container sense, but that these facets are only knowable with respect to each other:

> What is time? A mystery, a figment—and all powerful. It conditions the exterior world, it is motion married to and mingled with the existence of bodies in space, and with the motion of these. Would there then be no time if there were no motion? No motion if no time? We fondly ask. Is time a function of space? Or space of time? Or are they identical? Echo answers. Time is functional, it can be referred to as action; we say a thing is "brought about" by time. What sort of thing? Change? (Mann, 1929/1992, p. 356)

At the core of this theory of action is the development of what Roth calls "timetables," and what is alluded to in more symbolic terms by Mann. Timetables are breaks in space-time that give meaning to action. They are constructed mediational tools that help order and control mismatches between institution and individual. When will I get out? What will become of me? How will I survive the boredom and the uncertainty of incarceration? Such questions are asked against the specter of unbroken time or eternity, or as Roth's patients and doctors put it for the hopeless cases: "a rather horrifying tubercular Siberia—a seemingly endless waster (of time) without any signposts along the way." (Roth, 1963, p. 21) or in Mann's words: "Only in time was there progress; in eternity there was none, nor any politics or eloquence either" (1929/1992, p. 479).

Gradually a sense that there is in fact no such thing as unbroken time comes about for the patients:

> Can one tell—that is to say, narrate—time, time itself, as such, for its own sake? That would surely be an absurd undertaking. A story which read: "time passed, it ran on, the time flowed onward" and so forth—no one in his senses could consider that a narrative. . . For narration resembles music in this, that it fills up the time. It "fills it in" and "breaks it up," so that "there's something to it," "something going on." (Mann, 1929/1992, p. 560)

The patients begin to fill their days with measurement. On the magic mountain, people walk around with thermometers in their mouths, measuring their temperatures several times a day; in both books, patients are conversant with the details of diagnosis and measurement, the myriad of ways in which the monolithic diagnosis may be broken up and measured. As Roth says: "Everyone is frantically trying to find out how long he is in for. The new patient questions the doctors, nurses, and other hospital personnel in an effort to discover how many years, months, and days it will take him to be cured" (1963, p. xvi).

Metrology

The importance of mediational tools appears in struggles with measurement. One woman has been a patient on the magic mountain for the better part of her life. Eventually, she is cured of the disease and told to go home. But she knows no other life, and panics at the thought of leaving. She sabotages her release: runs out in the snow, jumps in the lake, and sticks her thermometer into her tea to make her appear feverish. When she is discovered by the staff, they make her use a thermometer without any marks on it. The device can only be read by a doctor with a measuring stick. The patient thus cannot calibrate her faking illness. The patients come to call this unmarked instrument "the silent sister," and it becomes the symbol for the ways in which the world of the asylum acquires its own bizarre culture of metrication and control.

Roth notes that patients are quite systematic in creating measurements for the blocks of time they will spend in the asylum. They begin to construct timetables for themselves (I will get out in 6 months; I will have surgery in 2 weeks, and so on). "After they have been in the hospital for some time, they find that 'mild' and 'bad' are not very meaningful categories," and much more detailed matching categories develop (Roth, 1963, p. 19). Patients begin observing how other patients are treated. There is an elaborate system of privileges in TB hospitals, based ostensibly on how healthy one is. If one is making good progress, for example, one is allowed out on brief shopping trips, and so forth. "He divides the patient group into categories, according to his predictions about the course of their treatment. He can then attach himself to one of these categories and thus have a more precise notion of what is likely to happen to him than he could from simply following the more general norms" (Roth, 1963, pp. 16-17).

Roth goes on to describe an equally elaborate system of observations and comparisons made by all the patients with respect to their own bodies, the length of time "served," the predilections of the individual doctors, and the technical diagnostic material such as x-rays. Not surprisingly, much of the information available is partial or misleading:

> Reference points may be more or less clear-cut and stable. If they are prescribed in detail and rigidly adhered to, as in the career of pupils in a school system, one's movement through the timetable is almost completely predictable. As the reference points become less rigid and less clear-cut, they must be discovered and interpreted through observation and through interaction with others of one's career group. The more unclear the reference points are, the harder it is for members of a career group to know where they stand in relation to others and the more likely it is that they will attend to inappropriate clues and thus make grossly inaccurate predictions concerning future progress. The degree of stability is related in part to the changes in timetables through time. (Roth, 1963, pp. 99-100)

Managing this instability increases the intensity of comparison and a sense, often, of bewilderment, unfairness, or even madness. Hans Castorp says to his cousin:

> I cannot comprehend why, with a harmless fever—assuming for the moment, that there is such a thing—one must keep to one's bed, while with one that is not harmless you needn't. And secondly, I tell you the fever has not made me hotter than I was before. My position is that 99.6° is 99.6°. If you can run about with it, so can I. (Mann, 1929/1992, p. 176)

Give me a standard, give me something to hold on to, something clear—in the face of uncertainty, patients become positivists. Mann describes the rebellion of Hans' cousin against the system of metrication in the hospital, the "Gaffky score." This is a composite score for each patient's progress based on a number of measures:

> Yes, the good, the patient, the upright Joachim, so affected to discipline and the service, had been attacked by fits of rebellion, he even questioned the authority of the "Gaffky scale." Whether only a few isolated bacilli, or a whole host of them, were found in the sputum analyzed, determined his "Gaffky number," upon which everything depended. It infallibly reflected the chances of recovery with which the patient had to reckon; the number of months or years he must still remain could with ease be deduced from it. (Mann, 1929/1992, p. 357)

This questioning of authority appears inevitable in a landscape so filled with uncertainty. One character, a business person, attempts to quantify health care costs and the tradeoffs:

"The expense," he whispered, "was fixed at a thousand francs, including the anesthesia of the spinal cord; practically the whole thoracic cavity was involved, six or eight ribs, and the question was whether it would pay . . . he was not at all clear that he would not do better just to die in peace, with his ribs intact." (Mann, 1929/1992, p. 315)

In the absence of metrics such as this, however, the relationships between doctors and patients come under considerable strain as patients strive to assign themselves to the proper categories, and then to see whether the doctors agree with them (Berg, 1992). In *The Magic Mountain,* the inmate Settembrini, a slightly satanic character, whispers constantly to Hans about how subjective the reading of the objective measures such as x-rays really is:

You know too that those spots and shadows there are very largely of physiological origin. I have seen a hundred such pictures, looking very like this of yours; the decision as to whether they offered definite proof or not was left more or less to the discretion of the person looking at them. (Mann, 1929/1992, p. 250)

Both physicians and patients struggle to find a standard and to localize it, in the face of a constantly shifting interpretive frame. As Roth (1963) notes:

The physician finds it difficult to carry out the medical ideal of an individual prescription for each case when at the same time he recognizes the fact that his timing of a given treatment event for a given patient is to a large extent a highly uncertain judgment on his part. If you are going to guess, you might as well make the process more efficient by guessing about the same way each time, especially if you are in a situation where your clients are likely to think that you do not know what you are doing if you change your guess from one time to another. (p. 24)

This uncertainty leads to the struggles and negotiations that are at the heart of Roth's analysis. Whose timetable will prevail?

Classification Struggles: Putting in Time

"The TB patient conceives of his treatment largely in terms of putting in time rather than in terms of the changes that occur in his lungs" (Roth, 1963, p. xv). The length of time one has been inside, combined with patients' observations about where they belong in the general scheme of things, acquires a moral character over time:

A classification system contains within it a series of restrictions and privileges. When no rigid classification system exists, these privileges themselves become part of the timetable. . . . How long is it before he is allowed 2 hours a day "up time" [out of bed]? . . . these privileges are desired not only in themselves, but for their symbolic value. They are signs that the treatment is progressing, that the patient is getting closer to discharge. (Roth, 1963, p. 4)

Timetable norms differ from hospital to hospital and from patient to patient. Trust, often in the form of moral condemnation or approval, may play a big part in structuring the timetable negotiations between doctor and patient. For example, alcoholic patients are often refused outside passes, or sometimes a patient with a "recalcitrant attitude" is refused a pass simply to convince them that he or she really is very ill. These moralizing attitudes, well documented within medical sociology, add another texture to the landscape we are examining here, twisting it a little away from a simple formal-situated or realist-relativist axis.

Doctors as well as patients may hold the "deserving" attitude toward someone who has "served their time." Roth (1963) notes that in treatment conferences, how long the patient has been confined is always taken into account in deciding the timetable, "this in itself is given considerable weight entirely aside from the bacteriological and x-ray data" (p. 27). Even those who seem to be getting better much faster according to these tests are kept in longer because, "TB just isn't cured that fast" (p. 27).

Patients know almost to the day when which privileges will arrive: "This relative precision of the timetable results from the emphasis placed upon the classification system by the staff, the consistency in the decisions of the physician in charge, and the physician explicitness in telling the patients what they can expect in the future" (Roth, 1963, p. 7). There can be a "failure to be promoted" in severe cases, and the reaction to this "varies greatly among TB patients, just as among engineers some of the failures are emotionally disorganized when they do not make the grade whereas others accept their inferior position with relative equanimity. Some patients regard a few days' delay as a tragedy" (Roth, 1963, p. 15). Bargains are made: "Patients are sometimes given regular and frequent passes to induce them to remain in the hospital" (p. 53).

Uncertainty plays a big role in negotiations about classification in the hospital. When a patient tries to guess their classification, and the physician disagrees, "In effect, the physician tries to get Jones to change his criteria for grouping patients so that his categories will be closer to those of the physician" (Roth, 1963, p. 39). The doctor will provide the patient with examples of others like him or her, and relates details about other similar cases. But the physician too is caught in a double bind: Ethically he or she is not allowed to give too many details about others' cases. The doctor is thus reduced to vague generalizations like "No two cases are alike" (p. 39). For the patient, this contributes to the house-of-mirrors effect:

> Most physicians . . . vary their approach from one patient to another according to their own judgment of what the patient can take . . . the physicians do not know with any precision how long it will take the patient to reach a given level of control over his disease. To allow themselves a freer hand in deciding what the best time is for the patient to leave the hospital, the doctors try to avoid being pinned down to any precise estimates by the patients. (Roth, 1963, p. 45)

This twisting effect of these silences is especially clear where the norms about timetables are also shifting, either due to changes in medical practice, technology, staff, or organizational change. One patient in these circumstance said: "You never seem to get anywhere because people here don't pay too much attention to the classifications. I've been here now since November and I'm still in Group 1. My husband comes to visit me and looks at this tag and thinks I'm never going to get promoted. He wonders what's going on. Then when you do get promoted to Group 2, you don't know what it means, anyway. You have no idea what additional privileges you have. . . . *It's like an ungraded school room"* (Roth, 1963, p. 10).

The ungraded schoolroom, combined with uncertainties, shifts in bureaucracy, and changes in the person's biography, begin to form the tapestry of a monstrous existence.

Part Four: Borderlands and Monsters— Time's Torquing of Standards and Experience

> Greta Garbo as Camille drifts across the screen in a cloud of white organza. She is alternately cruel and flirtatious, vulnerable and powerful. She plays with the affections of her lovers, a baron and a struggling young diplomat, from her position as a farm girl who came to Paris. Early in the movie, we understand that she has been ill; from time to time she discreetly covers her mouth with a handkerchief, or seems to swoon (always artistically). At times she recovers, and in a rhythm

complexly played out against her wardrobe, she moves from white to black in dress, from sick to well, from powerful to powerless, from country to city. As the movie progresses she becomes more and more ill, and more and more "pure"—thinner, whiter, more in love with the worthy poor man and less with the nefarious rich Baron. During the whole course of the movie, no one speaks the name of her illness, any prognosis or diagnosis, nor do we see any blood, sputum, feces, or other despoiling of the purified background. Of course, she has tuberculosis—and she is the ideal type, the shadow puppet against which both the medical story and the rich cultural criticisms of TB have been played out.

> There were those who wanted to make him "healthy," to make him "go back to nature," when, the truth was, he had never been "natural." (Mann, 1929/1992, p. 482)

On the magic mountain, or in any of the hospitals analyzed by Roth, the sense of unreality, of being outside of "normal" time and of making up an idiosyncratic timing is very strong. Furthermore, the very insides and outsides of people become mixed up in an almost monstrous way; Hans carries around his love Claudia's x-ray in his breast pocket so that he may really know her. External time drops away as does one's biography:

> (The inhabitants) accorded to the anniversary of arrival no other attention than that of a profound silence. . . . They set store by a proper articulation of the time, they gave heed to the calendar, observed the turning-points of the year, its recurrent limits. But to measure one's own private time, that time which for the individual in these parts was so closely bound up with space—that was held to be an occupation only fit for new arrivals and short-termers. The settled citizens preferred the unmeasured, the eternal, the day that was for ever the same. (Mann, 1929/1992, p. 427)

This sense of time begins to blur important distinctions between life and death, time and space: "But is not this affirmation of the eternal and the infinite the logical—mathematical destruction of every and any limit in time or space, and the reduction of them, more or less, to zero? is it possible, in eternity, to conceive of a sequence of events, or in the infinite of a succession of space-occupying bodies?" (Mann, 1929/1992, p. 356). As we approach the zero point in the story, Mann notes in an afterword that time-space relations are shifted so that "the story practices a hermetical magic, a temporal distortion of perspective reminding one of certain abnormal and transcendental experiences in actual life" (p. 561). In the following section we offer a model for how such a monstrous borderland terrain is constructed.

Trajectories and Twists: The Texture of Action

> No one can ever know for certain just when tuberculosis become active or when it becomes inactive. For that matter, one can never be certain that the disease is inactive, and a patient could logically be kept in the hospital for the rest of his life on the assumption that some slight undetectable changes might be occurring in his lungs. (Roth, 1963, p. 30)

> The same train brought them as had Hans Castorp, when years ago, years that had been neither long nor short, but timeless, very eventful yet "the sum of nothing," he had first come to this place. (Mann, 1929/1992, p. 520)

The model developed below has three parts (note that these are not stages). The original work of Corbin and Strauss was elaborated by Timmermans, and in this chapter, we add to both of them. They are thus parts of an ongoing conversation between all these authors. (For simplicity of representation, time in the diagrams below appears to be a linear unfolding along the x-axis. Clearly, we are arguing against this simple "unfolding" temporal structure; our own limits on drawing prevent a more complex representation, which would probably resemble a weaving-in-motion in at least 4 dimensions!)

Body-Biography Trajectory: Corbin and Strauss

A model developed by Juliet Corbin and Anselm Strauss (1988, 1991) describes what happens in the course of a chronic illness. They posit that bodies and biographies unfold along two intertwined trajectories (the "body-biography chain"), nestled in a matrix of other structural and interactional conditions (Strauss, 1993). For example, a heart attack may temporarily interrupt work, home life, creativity, dragging "down" the trajectory of biography; of course, this in turn is contingent on a number of other circumstances such as having access to health care, living in a war zone, having another illness, which makes recovery longer. The chain can be viewed geometrically, as a topography emerging from the interplays of these factors. Many illnesses do not have such an acute nature; during a long chronic illness there is a back-and-forth "tugging" across the trajectory of the disease/body and of the person's biography, within the conditional matrix. The title of Kathy Charmaz's (1991) *Good Days, Bad Days: Time and Self in Chronic Illness* throws this relation into relief. A long, slow downswing may only very gradually affect biography; a brief acute phase, experienced over and over, may be compensated for by the person's and family's resources, so that the overall trajectory of the biography remains fairly smooth. Many possible shapes are envisioned: a looping shape in the case of a "comeback" after a serious, debilitating illness; a very, very gradual progress of the disease, which slowly erodes the biographical trajectory.

This model (Figure 8.1) does not seek a Cartesian "mind-body" dualism, but rather to find a language for the ways in which two (or more) different processes become inextricably intertwined into one thick chain or braid. It makes more complex the sick-well, able-disabled dichotomies, and brings in people's active conversations with and work with their ill bodies as a central concern.

The body's trajectory and the self's are bound together, but not completely tightly coupled. Careers, plans, work, and relationships may continue in spite of, around, and through illness; or, a sudden illness may interrupt plans and biography and reshape the topography. The background "landscape" is a nested set of contingent possibilities and structural features that in turn act on the shape of the trajectory. Here, the solid line represents the trajectory of the body, as it follows up and down the course of a disease and recovery.

The dotted line represents the person's biography, which is "pulled" and "pushed" metaphorically by the body, but is not necessarily wholly determined by it (Corbin & Strauss, 1988, 1991).

Multiple Identities Along a Body-
Biography Trajectory in Sudden Illness or Death

Timmermans (in press, 1995), in a dialogue with the Corbin/Strauss BBC model, suggests emphasizing multiple identities rather than a single biographical identity. He studied more than 100 cases of attempted resuscitations (CPR) with victims of cardiac arrest, in the emergency rooms of hospitals. He attempted to use the trajectory model to explain the sequence and flow of events as people were brought in by the ambulance crews, "worked on" by staff, and either declared dead or saved. (The vast majority of people die.) In this extreme case of the interaction between body and biography, he observed

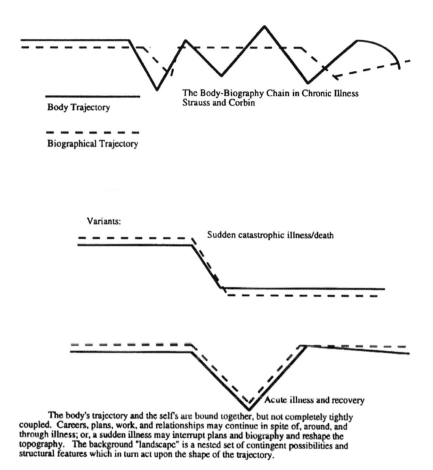

The body's trajectory and the self's are bound together, but not completely tightly coupled. Careers, plans, work, and relationships may continue in spite of, around, and through illness; or, a sudden illness may interrupt plans and biography and reshape the topography. The background "landscape" is a nested set of contingent possibilities and structural features which in turn act upon the shape of the trajectory.

Figure 8.1. The Strauss-Corbin Model of Body-Biography Trajectory

an interested elaboration of the relationship by focusing on the multiple biographies all people do have.

Many have noted that no individual is unitary; we are all multiple selves (Star, 1991). Timmermans notes, along these lines, that each patient who undergoes CPR has multiple intertwining identities outside that of "heart attack victim," each with its own trajectory. A single patient is at once father, farmer, church member, student, and president of the Rotary Club. Each of

Timmermans' Modifications to Trajectory in Acute, Severe Illness (Cardiac Failure)

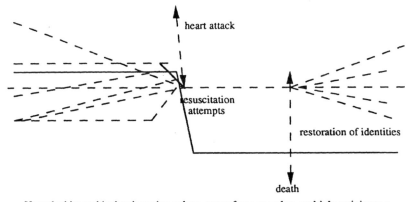

Here the biographical trajectories, selves, move from complex, multiple activity to a single focus: life-saving. At death, the identities are restored. If the patient survives, they are the same-but different: an *isomorphic transformation* (Timmermans, in press).

Figure 8.2. Multiple Identity Trajectories Along the Body-Biography Trajectory

those selves has its own trajectory, which although intertwined, are also historically independent. During the moments of resuscitation attempt, these multiple selves collapse into a single identity: that of the body/machine (Timmermans, in press). That is, the nurses and doctors and technicians focus down, relating only to the body aspect of the person, and collapsing all of the potential selves and identities of the person into one (Figure 8.2).

After resuscitation (whether or not this is successful) the multiple identities restart. The body is again accompanied by the other selves, and the father, farmer, and so on, returns. On return, each identity will have been differentially altered by the experience; perhaps the farmer can no longer farm, yet the person is the same person. In Timmermans' terms, there has been an isomorphic transformation.

Timmermans' modifications to the trajectory model in acute, severe illness (cardiac failure) are pictured here. Here the biographical trajectories, selves, move from complex, multiple activity to a single focus: life-saving. At death, the identities are restored. If the patient survives, they are the same, but different: an isomorphic transformation (Timmermans, in press).

The Twisted Landscape:
Adding Texture to Multiplicity and Standardization

In this chapter, we have added a third trajectory dimension to play off against the interacting trajectories of bodies and multiple identities: the trajectory of classification systems (as part of infrastructure). In looking at an extreme case temporally, in which the "time" of the body and of the multiple identities cannot be aligned with the "time" of the classification system, we have suggested that the latter gets twisted by the former. In the case of TB, a variety of monstrous classification schemes bubble through the rift in space/time. There are mismatches between lived experience and the rigidities of institutionalized classifications; there are struggles and negotiations between doctor and patient that are situated and that may seem erratic. For the patients, they have a chronic illness that necessitates withdrawal for a prolonged period from "normal life," sequestering with others with the disease, in an uncertain time frame that is partly dependent on the ways classification schemes are perceived, negotiated, and used by health personnel. As with the models of Corbin, Strauss, and Timmermans, our model (Figure 8.3) draws on a matrix of possibilities for the basis for these negotiations. These are culturally and historically specific, and include such factors as how medical knowledge is represented by public health agencies, how classifications are modified during the hospital stay, and includes images from literature, film, and popular science about "what people with tuberculosis are like." The rich topography of body and biography intercalates with a bureaucratic/infrastructural typology (classification scheme).

The twisted landscape of multiple identities and classifications is pictured here. In the torqued model, the thick solid line represents the institutionalized classification schemes; these get modified and "broken" more slowly than the timeline of the patients' bodies or biographies. There is still a body trajectory, indicated by the thinner solid line, which classically moves up and down over time, during the long course of the disease. Finally, after Timmermans, we have multiple biographical trajectories—patients are struck with the disease as they are progressing in studies, family raising, love affairs, careers, and so on. Unlike the Timmermans model, the long years passed "out of time" may

Tensions between Bodies, Biographies and Classification

Figure Three: The Twistd Landscape of Multiple Identities and Classifications
Figure 3: Typology and Topology. The topology created by the body-biography trajectory is pulled against the idealized, standardized typology of the global classification of tuberculosis -- itself a broken and moving target

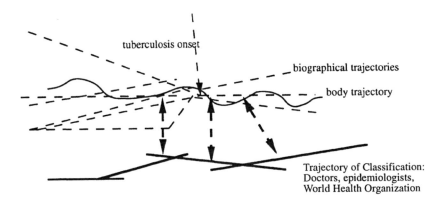

When standard classifications are added to the scheme, patients try to fit their experiences along both body and biographical trajectories to a standard picture or metric.

Changing definitions, local arrangements, and complex relations of all three trajectories contribute to "torquing" the typology/topography via the dotted lines which represent negotiations.

Figure 8.3. The Topology-Typography Twist

fracture these identities and transform them beyond familiarity, another echo of a "monstrous" or distorted sense of the disease.

The topology created by the body-biography trajectory is pulled against the idealized, standardized typology of the global classification of tuberculosis, itself a broken and moving target. When standard classifications are added to the scheme, patients try to fit their experiences along both body and biographical trajectories to a standard picture or metric. Changing definitions, local arrangements, and complex relations of all three trajectories contribute to "torquing"; this may be amplified by unsuccessful negotiations.

Conclusion

Twists and Textures: Classification and Lived Experience

Time morality is not cut and dried. (Condon & Schweingruber, 1994, p. 63)

The information infrastructure that deals with tuberculosis, as with other diseases, operationalizes a classification system that does not cope well with the subtleties of biographical time, experience, or negotiations about reality. It often uses spatial coordinates: The disease as localized in this body or not; in this region of the body and no other; it is present among this population but not that one; the cure can be found in this place but not that, and so forth. The closest that one gets to the flow of time is the description active or passive, latent or virulent; occasionally, in links with rough life stages such as geriatric or pediatric. But this describes an information infrastructure dealing with medical knowledge, a knowledge that defines itself as being true "for all time" about its subject and so able to abstract contingent historical and biographical flow to uncover the underlying reality.

There is not just one kind of classification in the world, however: Classification work is always multiple. As we get further from medical knowledge and closer to the suffering patient, time seeps into the classification systems that get used: How long does Group 1 stay here? (Roth); How may I get reclassified so that I can pass more (or less) time on the magic mountain? (Mann). Camille's morality tale unfolds in time in binary oppositions of good/bad, fit/ill, black/white; promotion or demotion from class to class in a continually downward career trajectory. Tuberculosis is the archetypal disease of time: chronic, recurrent, progressive.

So what happens when the disease of time meets the classification of space? As we have shown, the formal, spatial classification twists. "Other" categories run rampant, each seeking a way of expressing the elusive, forbidden flow of time (words like "quiescent" and "nonactive" abound). A macabre landscape is born. And the historiography of the classification system twists back on itself: In stunning contrast to most medical scientific texts, tuberculosis classifiers speak of a cyclical flow to their own historical time (not linear progress). From the other point of view, that of the patient, orthogonal classifications are developed that do not even interact with medical categories ("I have put in my time here, and I am a good person, so I deserve to be better and to leave.") The individual's disease is given a temporal texture at the price of becoming purely local; abstracted away from the standardized language it becomes once again temporally textured and immediate.

This way of framing the problem introduces the idea of texture as an important one in the representations-work-body-biography literature emerging from both social studies of science and cultural/historical psychology. Lynch's (1995) work on topical contextures implies a similar direction, we think: the look and feel of being in a place and using a genre of representations. Kari Thoresen (personal communication, Jan. 20, 1996), a former geologist, is developing a model and vocabulary for different aspects of texture in organizations and technological networks, examining layers and strata, crystallization processes (a term also used by Strauss and Timmermans), and other metaphors to examine how wires, people, and bits are put together by a large organization.

Why should social scientists be interested in such twists? We have suggested that we can move on from exploring the seamless web of science and society, of nature and knowledge to an analysis of the information infrastructure that acts as matrix for the web. The web itself is textured in interesting ways by the available modes of information storage and transfer. Medical classification work, typified by the ICD, deals in primarily spatial compartments; these compartments cannot hold when biography and duration are a necessary part of the story. In general, the information infrastructure holds certain kinds of knowledge and supports certain varieties of network; we believe that it is a task of some urgency for our field to analyze which kinds of knowledge and network. We have also heard echoes throughout this research of the ways it is for those living with and researching AIDS (Epstein, 1995), and hope to add to the rich analysis of AIDS, experience, activism, and research currently taking shape in our field. As well, the notion of activity theoretic spaces with development proceeding dialectically between individual, community, and the mediations of material artifacts may be augmented by these notions of texture (cf. Engestrom, 1987). The zone of proximal development, and the contradictions posed by mismatches between individual experience and institutional mores, may have some of the textural qualities we discuss here. Under some conditions (of silence, of denial of experiential validity, of delayed answers or justice), the sense of torquing could be quite an important quality. We need ways to understand experience that seems monstrous, or out of place, or "queer" (in the negative sense). We are reminded here of Michel Serres' (1980) invocation of the passage between the natural and humanistic sciences as indeterminate, twisted, and full of ice floes; of the images of cyborg and monster pervading feminist theory about technology (Casper, 1994a, 1994b, 1995; Haraway, 1992).

Much of our previous work (Bowker & Star, 1991; 1994; Star, 1991) has concerned itself with the relationship (which we first conceptualized as a kind of gap) between formal systems of knowledge representation and informal, experiential, empirical, and situated experience. Berg (in press) has shown convincingly that it is never the case of "the map OR the territory," but always, using the example of medical protocols, "the map IN the territory." This is a modest attempt to look at one kind of map in a territory marked by severe biographical interruptions, solitude, and aspects of total institutions, and in dialogue with a compelling infrastructure (both informatic and managerial). We see the map-actant in this case as a warping factor, not in the sense of deviating from any putative norm, but in the sense of reshaping and constraining other kinds of experience.

Acknowledgments

Robert Dale Parker suggested several helpful references on the literary background of women and disease in the 19th century; Marc Berg, Kirk Johnson, Helen Verran, and an anonymous referee gave us very useful comments. Our colleagues in the Illinois Research Group on Classification, University of Illinois at Urbana-Champaign, have been helpful in forming the basis for a social analysis of classification (Niranjan Karnik, Randi Markussen, Laura Neumann, Karen Ruhleder, Stefan Timmermans). We also thank the Advanced Information Technologies Group, University of Illinois, for project support. Conversations with Kari Thoresen about the notion of texture in organizations were very helpful, as were ongoing conversations with Anselm Strauss about trajectory. The work of Mark Casey Condon on the nature of time morality in a men's homeless shelter was helpful in thinking through issues in the concluding section.

References

Bates, B. (1992). *Bargaining for life: A social history of tuberculosis, 1876-1938.* Philadelphia: University of Pennsylvania.

Berg, M. (1992). The construction of medical disposals: Medical sociology and medical problem solving in clinical practice. *Sociology of Health and Illness, 14,* 151-180.

Berg, M. (in press). *Rationalizing medical work: Decision support techniques and medical practices.* Cambridge: MIT Press.

Berg, M., & Bowker, G. (in press). The multiple bodies of the medical record. *Sociological Quarterly.*

Biraben, J.-N. (1988). La tuberculose et la dissimulation des causes de deces. In J.-P. Bardet, P. Bourdelais, P. Guillaume, F. Leburn, & C. Quetel (Eds.), *Peurs et terreurs face la contagion* (pp. 184-198). Paris: Fayard.

Bowker, G. (1994). *Science on the run: Information management and industrial geophysics at Schlumberger, 1920-1940.* Cambridge: MIT Press.

Bowker, G., & Star, S. L. (1991). Situations vs. standards in long-term, wide-scale decision-making: The case of the international classification of diseases. In *Proceedings of the 24th Hawaiian International Conference on Systems Sciences: Vol. IV* (pp. 73-81). Washington, DC: IEEE Computer Society.

Bowker, G., & Star, S. L. (1994). Knowledge and infrastructure in international information management: Problems of classification and coding. In L. Bud (Ed.), *Information acumen: The understanding and use of knowledge in modern business* (pp. 187-213). London: Routledge.

Brock, T. D. (1988). *Robert Koch: A life in medicine and bacteriology.* Berlin: Springer-Verlag.

Casper, M. (1994a). At the margins of humanity: Fetal positions in science and medicine. *Science, Technology, & Human Values, 19,* 307-323.

Casper, M. (1994b). Reframing and grounding nonhuman agency: What makes a fetus an agent. *American Behavioral Scientist, 37,* 839-856.

Casper, M. (1995). Fetal cyborgs and technomoms on the reproductive frontier, or which way to the carnival? In C. H. Gray, H. Figueroa-Sarriera, & S. Mentor (Eds.), *The cyborg handbook* (pp. 183-202). New York: Routledge.

Charmaz, K. (1991). *Good days, bad days: The self in chronic illness and time.* New Brunswick, NJ: Rutgers University Press.

Clarke, A., & Casper, M. (1996). From simple technology to complex arena: Classification of pap smears, 1917-1990. *Medical Anthropology Quarterly, 10,* 450-475.

Condon, M. C., & Schweingruber, D. (1994). *The morality of time and the organization of a men's emergency shelter.* Unpublished manuscript, University of Illinois, Urbana-Champaign, Department of Sociology.

Corbin, J., & Strauss, A. (1988). *Unending work and care: Managing chronic illness at home.* San Francisco: Jossey-Bass.

Corbin, J., & Strauss, A. (1991). Comeback: The process of overcoming disability. In G. Albrecht & J. Levy (Eds.), *Advances in medical sociology* (Vol. 2, pp. 137-158). Greenwich, CT: JAI.

Davis, F. (Ed.). (1963). *Passage through crisis: Polio victims and their families.* Indianapolis, IN: Bobbs-Merrill.

Desrosiàres, A. (1993). *La raison statistique.* Paris: Découverte.

Diagnostic standards and classification of tuberculosis. (1955). New York: National Tuberculosis Association.

Diagnostic standards and classification of tuberculosis. (1961). New York: National Tuberculosis Association.

Engestrom, Y. (1987). *Learning by expanding: An activity-theoretical approach to developmental research*. Helsinki: Orienta-Konsultit Oy.

Epstein, S. (1995). The construction of lay expertise: AIDS activism and the forging of credibility in the reform of clinical trials. *Science, Technology, & Human Values, 20*, 408-437.

Fagot-Largeault, A. (1989). *Causes de la mort: Histoire naturelle et facteurs de risque*. Paris: Librairie Philosophique J. Vrin.

Glaser, B., & Strauss, A. (1965). *Time for dying*. Chicago: Aldine.

Hacking, I. (1990). *The taming of chance*. Cambridge: Cambridge University Press.

Hacking, I. (1995). *Rewriting the soul: Multiple personality and the sciences of memory*. Princeton, NJ: Princeton University Press.

Haraway, D. (1992). The promises of monsters: A regenerative politics for inappropriate/d others. In L. Grossberg, C. Nelson, & P. Treichler (Eds.), *Cultural studies now and in the future* (pp. 295-337). London: Routledge.

Latour, B. (1993). *We have never been modern*. (Trans. Catherine Porter.) Cambridge, MA: Harvard University Press.

Lynch, M. (1995). Laboratory space and the technological complex: An investigation of topical contextures. In S. L. Star (Ed.), *Ecologies of knowledge: Work and politics in science and technology* (pp. 226-256). Albany: SUNY Press.

Mann, T. (1992). *The magic mountain*. (Trans. H.-T. Lowe-Porter.) New York: Modern Library. (Original work published 1929)

Pasveer, B. (1989). Knowledge of shadows: The introduction of x-ray images in medicine. *Sociology of Health and Illness, 11*, 360-383.

Porter, R. (1990). *English society in the 18th century*. London: Penguin.

Roth, J. A. (1963). *Timetables: Structuring the passage of time in hospital treatment and other careers*. Indianapolis, IN: Bobbs Merrill.

Serres, M. (1980). *Le passage du nord-ouest*. Paris: Éditions de Minuit.

Sontag, S. (1977). *Illness as metaphor*. New York: Farrar, Straus, & Giroux.

Star, S. L. (1989). *Regions of the mind: Brain research and the quest for scientific certainty*. Stanford, CA: Stanford University Press.

Star, S. L. (1991). Power, technologies, and the phenomenology of standards: On being allergic to onions [Monograph]. *Sociological Review, 38*, 27-57.

Star, S. L. (Ed.). (1995). *Ecologies of knowledge: Work and politics in science and technology*. Albany: SUNY Press.

Star, S. L., & Ruhleder, K. (1996). Steps toward an ecology of infrastructure: Problems of design and access in large-scale information systems. *Information Systems Research, 7*, 111-134.

Strauss, A. (1993). *Continual permutations of action*. New York: Aldine de Gruyter.

Timmermans, S. (1995). *Saving lives? A historical and ethnographic study of resuscitation techniques*. Unpublished doctoral dissertation, University of Illinois, Urbana-Champaign.

Timmermans, S. (in press). Saving lives or identities? The double dynamic of technoscientific scripts. *Social Studies of Science*.

Timmermans, S., & Berg, M. (in press). Standardization in action: Achieving universalism and localization in medical protocols. *Social Studies of Science*.

Timmermans, S., Bowker, G., & Star, S. L. (1995). Infrastructure and organizational transformation: Classifying nurses' work. In W. Orlikowski, G. Walsham, M. Jones, & J. DeGross (Eds.), *Information technology and changes in organizational work. Proceedings IFIP WG8.2 Conference* (pp. 344-370). London: Chapman and Hall.

9

Trajectories, Biographies, and the Evolving Medical Technology Scene

*Labor and Delivery and
the Intensive Care Nursery*

CAROLYN WIENER

ANSELM STRAUSS

SHIZUKO FAGERHAUGH

BARBARA SUCZEK

Commentary

The theoretical framework of this chapter has its origin in a team project involving three sociologists and a sociologically trained nurse researcher, all associated with the Department of Social and Behavioral Sciences, University

An earlier version of this chapter appeared in *Sociology of Health & Illness, 1*(3), 261-283, © 1979 Routledge & Kegan Paul, reprinted by permission.

of California, San Francisco. Carolyn Wiener, one of the sociologists, collected most of the specific data bearing on the delivery and infant care units, and wrote the chapter for which she did most of the immediate analysis.

What must immediately strike a reader is the chapter's explicit conceptualization, integrated around three central concepts (trajectory, biography, and work); but, a reader also is bound to note the tremendous complexity of substantive detail that called in turn for conspicuously complex analysis. Thus, also required was a great amount of ethnographic *and* conceptual detail (i.e., the "density" of descriptive and conceptual connections).

In this extended and detailed analysis, it was especially important for Carolyn Wiener to specify and give some sense of salience to a great many sets of conditions "located" at various levels—that is, of varied scope, historical depth, and degree of specificity and generality. The same can be said for a large number of significant consequences, described, specified, and conceptualized. In short, we see the conditional-consequential matrix used with complexity and subtlety.

Especially arresting also is the explicit focus on temporal matters, including the historical, evolutionary, and the future—proximate, immediate, and probable distant future. Despite the intricate interweaving of substantive events and enormous diversity of types of actors and interactions, this chapter is well integrated around the interrelated core categories mentioned earlier. Quite possibly, however, readers could have been aided in grasping the chapter's integration of dense materials by systematic italicization of key phrases and sentences.

*   *   *

Introduction

An essential feature of medical-nursing work is that it is work on and with humans. Staff focus is on doing something about the course of illness, but in so doing, staff have to deal with the patient as a human being who responds, has a life/biography, a family, etc. Bearing on the work are various structural conditions: Staff have their own personal and work *biographies,* and in a real sense so does the hospital, the medical-specialization, the ward itself, the machines within that ward—all of these elements have histories and futures. Also affecting staff work are external conditions: the medical-machinery industry, consumer movements, etc.

In addition, the work on illness implies courses of illness, varying from relatively anticipatable to quite unpredictable. In shaping the illness course, to bring it to a successful-as-possible conclusion, work is prescribed, tasks are parcelled out or required, work needs to be articulated. We call this, to distinguish from the physiological course of illness, the *trajectory*. The trajectory requires "management," to use the medical-nursing terminology. It can end when the patient leaves the hospital, although for patients who have a chronic illness, and for infants who have been in the ICN, it can continue on with trajectory work in clinics, repeated visits to the hospital and physicians' offices.

Relationships between a trajectory and attendant biographies can be very complex. The staff work pertains to both. But there are issues of when and under what circumstances and with what consequences either the trajectory or a biography is primarily in focus. There is also interaction between biographies, which can affect both the trajectory work and the biographical work. Ordinarily, staff's primary concern is in shaping the trajectory, and their biographical work is in furtherance of that. But patients (here parents) are concerned primarily with their own biographies and that of their infant. All of these aspects of trajectory and biography will be developed below, as we trace the conditions and consequences of trajectory and biography relationships.

Thus this chapter presents one analytic approach to understanding many of the events on hospital wards, much of the work there, the division of labor, the patterns of actions, the impact of technology, and the larger issues such as the ethical ones. Substantively, the intention is to illuminate the evolving nature of labor and delivery wards and intensive care nurseries and their work, as well as consequences for families, staffs, hospitals, and "society."

Our use of the terms, "trajectory," and "biography" may render them more static than these categories are in actual practice. It should be noted that these are merely analytic concepts and that focus on one or the other is constantly moving in and out, shifting from day to day, sometimes moment to moment. Also, in what follows, readers may think we lose sight of the many infants who leave the hospital for home to lead healthy lives. The issue of what proportion do that, and what constitutes "doing well," is hotly debated within this arena. Our own emphases may tend to highlight the more problematic, dangerous aspects of birth. We ask readers to make the necessary correction, reminding themselves that infants' lives are saved and that there is tremendous variation regarding where each parent and each infant fit within the scheme we present.

We shall first examine the biographies which are interwoven in the birth trajectory: ward, machine, medical specialty, hospital, staff, parent, infant. Next, we look at the conditions for a central focus on biographical work: patient competition as related to social value; the intrusion of a machine biography; and the emergence of ethical and ideological issues. We then turn to the complex calculus of intertwined biographies within the birth trajectory by closely examining this interplay around a specific machine, the fetal heart monitor. Next, we analyze the consequences of an extended birth trajectory: new and expanded career lines, a changed hospital biography, and altered personal biographies. Finally, we examine the reverse effect of this interaction: the biographical impact on the further shaping of the birth trajectory.

This chapter is based on a fairly extensive study of a labor and delivery ward and an intensive care nursery in a hospital located in a metropolitan area, conducted through observational techniques and nonstructured interviews over a five-month period, and a rather less intensive observation at a comparable hospital. It is part of a larger study on "Nursing Care of Patients on Medical Machinery."

The Interweaving of Trajectory and Attendant Biographies

Interwoven in the birth trajectory, giving it shape, are multiple biographies: ward, machine, medical specialty, hospital, staff, parents, and, of course, that of the infant itself. These biographies are also linked in complex ways with each other.

1. Ward Biography. Labor and delivery wards are moving from what was considered the practice of an "art" (abetted by analgesic intervention) to heightened application of technology ("we are now more clinically definitive"). With the explosion of new knowledge and new medical technology in the last decade, a quasi-fatalistic attitude in obstetrics has been replaced by aggressive intervention, in order to maximize the possibility of conception and to maintain formerly hopeless pregnancies. At the same time, goaded by a consumer movement that labeled hospital births too impersonal and technological, and by the competition of a midwife and home-birth movement, hospitals have opened alternative birth centers (called ABCs) which offer no technology and no drug intervention. . . .

Alternative birth centers in most cases represent a philosophy rather than actually constitute a separate center: ABC rooms within the conventional hospital have been furnished in a home-like decor, complete with plants, stereo, and a double bed to serve for labor, delivery, and after-rest. Nurses, who are no longer identifiable by uniforms, remain with the mother the entire time, as may fathers, siblings, and others of the mother's choosing.

Well-baby nurseries have also undergone a change, being sparsely populated since babies now spend more time in their mothers' rooms. But adjacent to a near-empty nursery, there is a beehive of activity in the highly machined and highly staffed intensive care nursery, where radical survival techniques are being performed.

2. Machine Biographies. Machines—to a large extent responsible for the changing shape of the birth trajectory, especially for those infants who go to the ICN—also have unique biographies. Each vital machine (fetal heart monitor, cardiac pulmonary monitor, ultrasonograph, brain scanner) has its variety of specialists (biochemists, biophysicists, physiologists, biomedical engineers, physicians) who converge at different stages of its research and development. Physicians, nurses, and technicians become involved in assessing machines on the wards and this leads ultimately to their further refinement. As machines move to industrial production, types, models and complexity increases, as do competitive sales—requiring greater sophistication on the part of the purchasers. (Machine biography may become interwoven with ward biography, as when the design problems of $10,000 monitors only become apparent after six months' use, or the manufacturer declares bankruptcy, cutting off access to parts and creating maintenance problems.)

To take a closer look at a specific example of machine biography: Continuous fetal monitoring, the simultaneous electronic recording of fetal heart rate and uterine contractions during labor, developed out of the desire to more accurately assess fetal and/or maternal distress. Used during pregnancy by applying external electrodes or, if necessary, adding an intravenous administration of oxytocin, this machine has been found to be a useful tool to gauge fetal capability of withstanding the stress of labor, thereby guiding the best timing and mode of delivery. For indicated cases (such as diabetes, hypertensive disease of pregnancy, intrauterine growth retardation, Rh sensitization, previous stillbirth or premature birth, low esterol excretions) a periodic oxytocin challenge test (OCT), or "non-stress test" as it is sometimes called, can be used to determine whether the respiratory function of the placenta is adequate. The goal is to keep the pregnancy going long enough to give the baby the best start, without endangering either mother or baby. This test is often used in conjunction with drugs and/or other techniques, such as ultrasonography.

The popularity of this machine peaked as its use became more widespread during the actual labor. . . .

What started as a useful tool for "high-risk" labor became, in many hospitals, routine—now evoking attack. Critics point to a sharp rise in caesarean births (a riskier and costlier procedure than vaginal delivery) which they attribute to panic readings of the fetal monitor. Defendants maintain that the problem is merely one of interpretation and skill. . . .

Thus, this machine's biography has gone through research, development and refinement, to controversy.

3. Medical Specialty Biography. As machines are assessed on the units—and this information is converted into improvements by industry—specialization and associated work and procedures become more sophisticated. Hence, technological innovation and medical specialization proceed in a parallel and interactive manner. What were the formerly relatively static and low-status specialties of obstetrics and pediatrics are being sliced smaller and smaller to correspond with the technology of controlling the correspondingly smaller slices of the birth trajectory itself. Thus there emerges both perinatology and neonatology. The first is the specialty defined as pertaining to before, during and after the time of birth, time designation arbitrary. Neonatology relates to the period immediately succeeding birth, and continuing, roughly, through the first month of life. Each of these medical specialties has spawned attendant clinical nurse specialists, and a growing cadre of pediatric specialties in associated services like cardiology and neurology. Staff nursing, too, has become more specialized, requiring special ABC nurses, experienced nurses to accompany and care for high-risk mothers and babies on transports from outlying hospitals. Entwined with the growth of medical machinery has been the expanded knowledge of biochemistry and microchemistry, through which results can be obtained from an ever smaller amount of blood. In addition to juggling the tasks required of all nurses, the intensive care nurse must be an alchemist, striving to achieve and maintain a delicate balance of body chemistry based on sophisticated reading of blood gas studies, an ear ever-attuned to the beeping of the heart and respiratory monitor—a far cry from the nurse who rotated from labor and delivery to post-partum to the nursery.

4. Hospital Biography. Each hospital has its own complex biography, as specialties wax and wane in importance. Yesterday's challenge becomes routine work in time (for instance, hemodialysis). Or developments from outside a specialty may eclipse a popular therapeutic approach. For example, during the 1950s one frontier of medicine was stereotaxic surgery, a form of surgery employing tools and frames to guide passage of electrical currents to the brain. Although controversial at the time, this procedure (to correct symptoms of dystonia, Parkinson's disease, epilepsy) attracted huge research grants which, coupled with the increased patient load and a serious publicity campaign, justified the purchase of expensive and massive equipment. Neurosurgeons, physiologists, electronic engineers, anesthesiologists applied computer technology to their team skills, building neurosurgery departments which, in turn, redounded to the benefit of hospitals in which they were housed. Some years later, development of a new drug, El Dopa, for Parkinson's Disease, presented another option and resulted in the declining popularity of this technique. The machinery lies dormant—a Stonehenge for future generations to ponder—as the hospital moves on to other investments, other divisions of labor, and so on.

Wards may also vary within the hospital structure in relationship to the aggressiveness of their Chiefs of Medical Services. A dynamic Chief, bent on building a department, will attract personnel and grants accordingly. What is more, an intensive care nursery that generates income by virtue of its laboratory and x-ray needs, is in a position to actively affect the decisions that mold the future biography of the hospital.

Other conditions impact on a hospital. For example, the drive for regionalization of services, in the interest of cost control and better utilization of skills, has divided hospitals into three classifications for the newborn: primary care (small hospitals with no support services for distressed babies); secondary care (minimal support, like oxygen, intravenous assistance); tertiary care (acute services). An Infant Medical dispatch Center can direct the transport of at-risk babies to the appropriate hospital. These transports allow information to fan out from the medical center to the outlying districts. Since they are vital to the information flow, *and* to the economic structure and prestige of the receiving hospital, staff are ever mindful of the public relations aspect of their work. Greater skill, knowledge, and experience are seeds for judgments of mismanaged labor and/or delivery "out there"; being received as the saviors from the Big City (sometimes augmented by press coverage) adds nourishment to these seeds. The transport staff must be reminded constantly that an irritated and angry local hospital staff is not likely to remain a source of referrals, and that effective teaching under these conditions must be tactfully presented in order to be effective.

5. Staff Biographies. Staff biographies are both social (a history of encounters with kinsmen, friends, acquaintances, colleagues, etc.) and experiential (the dimension of biography stemming from life and work experiences). Obviously, each member of the staff brings a host of individual attitudes, impressions, conceptions, mood changes, to the work—based on personal biography. In addition, a nurse or doctor may or may not have had her/his own birthing experience, or may have had the special experience of a caesarean birth or a premature baby. Similarly, each will have a different degree of therapeutic experience. These experiences may or may not have been shared. Such physician experiences, and the nurse's perception of those experiences, are part of the biography to which we refer.

6. Parent Biography. That parents have biographies based on who and what they are, and that these are brought into relationship with the birth trajectory, is self-evident. But crucial to the experience are the expectations they bring to the birth. For all parents, the birth of a child represents a radically changed biography, which may or may not jibe with their expectations. Add to this the delivery of a distressed baby, immediately subjected to a barrage of diagnostic and monitoring equipment, and the effect on parents is intense. Feeding into the parental identity change are the anxieties and attitudes of grandparents, friends, and the common wisdom regarding "premies" and/or handicapped children. (Impact on parental biographies will be discussed further, later.)

7. Infant Biography. Last, only by virtue of its being least researchable by interview techniques, is the infant's emergent biography. Logic, and the plethora of child development theories which mark the last thirty years, suggest that the infant's biography is being affected by all the above biographies. Although differences exist regarding *time* (pre- or post-natal) and *degree* of this impact, few would argue that the infant's individuation process is a slowly unfolding one and that extending the hospitalization period adds to the problematic nature of child development. Nurses speak of each baby having "a distinct personality" and worry about their difficulty in remembering to make the affectionate gestures while under the pressures of giving critical care. Mobiles, toys, and pictures (for instance, a wedding snapshot) which decorate the infant's isolette, are testament to the understanding that a new biography is emerging.

Biographical Work in Focus

For most birth trajectories biographical work is brief—confined to making judgments about the parent's character, psychology, or lifestyle in relation to the extent of intervention necessary during labor. There is not only a snapshot quality to this biographical work, but the pictures are "candid" shots: The mother is quite often unaware that a biographical mosaic is being hastily pieced together by the staff.

For the mother who presents prematurely, biographical work intensifies. Although the protocol remains the same, there are subtle differences in attitude toward a fifteen-year-old single mother ("the Pepsi-potato chip crowd") whose 28-week baby stands a chance of not only physical but socioeconomic impairment, as against a thirty-year-old mother whose reproductive abnormalities have resulted in three miscarriages, and for whom all technology has been brought to bear in maintaining a precarious pregnancy. In addition, if these women deliver in the same hospital that has followed their pregnancies, the former, being more teenager than mother, may have covered her fear with surliness and hostility toward staff, while the latter was building the dedication of a team. These examples of two extremes illustrate the problem potential in the crossing of mother and staff biographies. (This phenomenon has been called *social value,* denoting the criteria—age, education, social class, race, etc.—by which staff establish priorities when patients are competing for immediate care.)

There are times when biographical work crowds in. Sometimes it can be work in relation to the machine's biography. New machines are often a mixed blessing, as when the advantage of a digital readout on a new respirator is offset by a collection of fluid that requires hand pumping. In such a case, the nurse is aiding the machine biography by providing evaluation that will be fed back to the manufacturer, but her trajectory work is increased.

More often personal biography crowds in, for example, when ethical or ideological issues arise. When work along the trajectory is being questioned for *ethical* reasons, it is because future biography is at risk. . . . Obviously, hospitals vary greatly in their ability to respond to a crisis birth, and major centers (tertiary hospitals) have learned to resuscitate first and then look:

> That's why we push transports. We've had our share of babies whose parents were told they were dead. One hour later they are kicking and are brought to the intensive care nursery, but they've already suffered oxygen deprivation. . . .

Since delivery allows little or no time for quality-of-life decisions, such decisions move from the delivery room to the intensive care nursery. If the infant has a congenital defect, parents may decide they want no corrective procedures. Staff must then continue maintenance care, knowing the baby will not survive. The prolonged agony of such cases is a tremendous strain on parent and staff, and great effort is made to ease the effect on the infant.

With premature births, the staff watches closely during the first six to eight hours. If the baby is judged to be a 25- to 27-weeker, on 80% oxygen with oxygen support going higher and higher, the family is told that the outcome is highly questionable, and asked if life-sustaining care should be continued. The following is a composite quote about this situation from one ward:

> The response can be everything from the father who says "Where are the autopsy papers?" to the one who says, "I don't care if he's blind and retarded, save him." . . . In most instances, the family will say, "Withdraw support." If we can't read the family, or if the family says they want the baby to survive, we will go great guns.

Decisions which follow in rapid succession must be made on the basis of various assumptions. The base of knowledge is recent, rapidly changing, and largely unpredictive. For example, it has only been two years that knowledge about intercranial bleeding has become more conclusive. Now that a brain scan is part of the routine workup, bleeds have been found in 50% of the babies who are less than 1200 grams (usually the babies who have been transported). Occasionally the bleed is massive, or shows that major motor function has been affected. More often the results are ambiguous. In addition, it is not unusual for the baby to be too distressed to be subjected to a scan until considerable time has elapsed. Furthermore, a scan which indicates no bleed does not rule out oxygen damage.

If the infant needs the aid of a respirator to ventilate, the delicate balancing begins: close monitoring of the respirator pressure to minimize lung damage/insertion of tubes to drain air/insertion of an umbilical line to monitor oxygen level through blood gas tests/anticoagulant drugs to correct clogging in the line/drugs to repress the normal breathing that would compete with the respirator/drugs to aid lung development/ transfusions to replace blood taken for tests/periodic brain scans and x-rays/insertion of a line to feed through the jugular vein (hyperalimentation)/antibiotics to ward off infection. The succession is totally open ended, as are the complications that can further snowball. Such babies may spend as many as six to nine months in the intensive care nursery, during which time staff members *and* parents may be asking *at any point,* "What are we doing?."

Faced with a parent who wants "everything done," staff is often unsure if that parent hears or understands what is meant by "brain damage." During this period there may be vast differences of opinion and judgment among staff, and they attend to different indications of improvement. When a physician focuses on trajectory and says, "She's doing well—she's off the respirator," the nurse may still be agonizing over biography, to wit: "What is her life going to be?"

Intensive care nurseries which place utmost importance on quality of life, although encouraging family involvement in life-sustaining decisions, know that the family does not have the criteria to make such decisions. And they know their own criteria are weak. What sustains the staff is the understanding that as their knowledge base increases, it becomes possible to decrease the implicated assumptions. A baby who survives precarious months as described above (including a succession of some 40 insertions of chest tubes) and goes home breathing room air, showing no intercranial bleed, with eye problems that are correctable, becomes the rationale, despite ethical questions, for continuing treatment on future babies. Bulletin boards covered with snapshots of successes, and a Christmas party for graduates serve this same purpose.

Biographical work also becomes paramount when there are strongly held *ideologies.* Many childbearing couples who question the hospital system do so on the instruction of theorists like Frederick Leboyer, Fernand Lamaze, and Robert A. Bradley, who teach that birth is a normal process and that with attention to prenatal preparation and an appropriate atmosphere, parents and child can avoid the stress associated with the conventional hospital delivery. For some of these couples ideological stakes ensue. Having reached this final moment of truth, this long-awaited delivery, they place accentuated and negative symbolic significance on each dimension of hospital intervention: enema, prep, drugs, forceps, episiotomies, silver-nitrate for the infant's eyes. Any of the above, if deemed necessary by the hospital staff, are potential points of contention. Conversely, staff too may have ideological stakes in the normal childbirth controversy—may be critical of doctors who believe in responding to the patient's pleas, "Do something!" with, "We'll take care of it, honey,"—but may not have a choice in their assignment to specific women in labor. And while some prospective mothers have made a conscious choice regarding the camp in which they wished to be placed—some take a defensive posture ("I'm no pioneer") while others are enthusiastic believers in the alternative birth center—many are not aware that in selecting a physician they may have placed themselves in one ideological camp or another. Most important, they are not likely to be aware of staff ideological stakes. Frequently, the situation will become clear in retrospect. . . .

The course of each labor is totally unpredictive. As with ethical issues, the absence of clearcut answers merely increases the rivalry of ideological positions. For every staff member who feels that drug intervention during labor impedes labor, leads to learning or motor disabilities, detracts from a normal process, another can be found asserting that despite a reassuring physician, partner, and nurse, a significant number of women are going to remain anxious and are going to need intervention. Furthermore, the tone of many of the books *about* the Leboyer-Lamaze-Bradley methods has contributed to public competition and peer pressure. (Nora Ephron, writing of her own experience with Lamaze reflects perhaps a growing reaction: "The trouble is that it has the capability of being every bit as fanatical and narrow-minded as the system it has replaced.")

Another ideology which has had popular impact concerns parent attachment, labeled "bonding." This term—based on research spanning the last three decades, but accelerated in most recent years—signifies the whole range of nurturing stimulation (stroking, swaddling, cuddling) felt to be necessary for the infant's emotional development. Marshall Klaus, whose research led to guidance on how the hospital can fulfill these needs, even in an acute care setting, recently stressed the "fantastic adaptability" of infants and warned against the danger of assuming that bonding must occur immediately at birth. Nevertheless, as with all such theories, popularization brings a certain degree of fanaticism. To quote one nurse recalling a "rough case":

> She was a 35-weeker, who wanted an ABC delivery and bonding, and was so freaked out by ending up in labor and delivery with a baby headed for the intensive care nursery. She had already been worn down, and accepted stirrups, draping. I had to convince her that doing an APGAR on the baby during the first five minutes was more important than bonding.

Belief in the bonding ideology also complicates the imparting of information to parents of sick infants:

> You don't want to scare them, and you don't want to affect their ability to bond, so you tell them enough to be concerned and not enough to divorce their feelings. It's hard to know what they understand.

The ward ideology also figures prominently. An intensive care nursery which believes in bonding, is mindful of quality of life, and encourages parent participation, is opening up the possibilities of confrontations with parents. Access to the infant's chart may result in a deteriorating relationship between staff and parent, as the following case illustrates. An unfortunate characterization of the mother noted in the chart by her obstetrician both fed into the composite mother-biography that staff was building, and antagonized *her* to the extent that her behavior became increasingly withdrawn. A confrontation finally occurred when staff, fearful that the baby was not getting sufficient nutrition, encouraged supplemental bottle feeding. The mother, imbued with the necessity for breast feeding which is part of bonding ideology, refused. This had been preceded by her accusations of negligence against a midwife and a premature delivery which thwarted plans for delivery in the alternative birth center. A downward spiral was created which culminated in a mutually agreed on, but earlier than warranted, discharge of the infant. Staff and parent shared concern for the future biography of the infant. They differed on managing the course of the trajectory. Such confrontations arise when an ideology like bonding remains central for parents but, due to other considerations, recedes from staff focus. The emotional blow of an expected ABC delivery that has turned into the nightmare of a sick baby is apparent, and staff are mindful of this trauma. However, ABC parents are quite often assertive— questioning, and sometimes refusing, procedures. As one nurse put it, "Just like we would be in the same position!"

Such behavior is often "understood" in retrospect, but viewed as "hostile" when it adds to the strain of "work." Staff is being called on to do biographical work with the parent, when "pure" trajectory work would be preferred.

The Complex Calculus and Impacting External Conditions

This multiple interplay of biographies in relation to the birth trajectory can become a complex calculus upon which external conditions can impinge. For instance, a high infant mortality rate gave additional impetus for greater acceptance of the continuous fetal monitoring, because of an effort to lower that rate. Moreover, current theory held that mental retardation and cerebral palsy were closely tied to oxygen deprivation during the time immediately before and after birth. Smaller family size, coupled with generous resources for frontier medicine, heightened the value placed on saving each baby. Intensive care nurseries, which started out focusing on babies, soon saw the advantage of monitoring the mother, preferably during pregnancy, but at least predelivery, leading to the expansion from baby-transport to mother-transport.

These external conditions which furthered the fetal monitor then affect the trajectory-biographical relationships. Machinery purchased to aid such high-risk cases takes on a life of its own. As stated above, unknowns abound in labor: A woman can evince optimal pelvic physiological construction, and still not progress, just as the opposite can occur; labor can be slow for hours, and suddenly speed up, requiring quick and pressured decisions. Not only do staff experiential biographies differ (varying degrees of interpretation-competence can lead to confrontations between nurses and physicians), but variability comes into play. Questioned about the routine use of the fetal monitor on low-risk laboring women, nurses answered that it *is* easier for themselves, that is, the nurse can leave the room, since presumably *someone* is watching the monitor at the central nurses' station (called the "slave monitor" by one nurse). Additionally, there is the ever-present fear of malpractice suits. The machine's printout is part of the record and, to quote one physician, "If you've done the right thing, it will support you in court; if you've done the wrong thing, it will damn you." Malpractice notwithstanding, the tyranny of this machine is that a compulsion has been set up to take all possible precautions against missing the signs of fetal and/or maternal distress: "You get afraid after a couple of bad experiences." The fetal monitor has become an *evidence machine,* by which staff make accusations of negligence, defend action or inaction. As expressed by a nurse, "The old philosophy was everything is normal until proven otherwise; now it's everything is abnormal until proven otherwise." In teaching hospitals especially, this monitor becomes part of the convincing process. . . .

The monitor can also be reassuring. . . .

> We had a woman in the ABC who was having a hard time, and was getting panicky. We brought her back, attached the monitor and in ten minutes the baby's head had turned around and she was ready to deliver. I talked to her afterwards, and she agreed that in here she felt like someone had a handle on things.

While some women's trajectories clearly benefit from use of continuous fetal monitoring, others get caught in the interplay of machine and staff biographies. A woman in normal labor may look on the monitor as a nice gadget for gauging her contractions and listening to the baby's heartbeat—may, in fact, have heard of it and want it used. She is not likely to know that her positioning in bed may be prolonging the length of her labor. Nor is she likely to know that inconclusive readings or any ambiguities in the course of her labor will lead to internal electrodes being applied to the baby's head. The social/psychological consequences are frequently not discussed, particularly if no complications ensue and attention is focused on a normal baby. But the consequences are there, nevertheless, insofar as they affect the future biography of the mother.

Consequences of an Extended Birth Trajectory

For those infants who require the special attention of the ICN there is a stretching out of the birth trajectory. The effects of an extended birth trajectory are evidenced in (1) new and expanded career lines; (2) a changed hospital biography; (3) altered individual biographies.

1. New and Expanded Career Lines. As already noted, the explosion in perinatology and neonatology has meant that new specialists have evolved and are involved with the increasingly smaller phases of the birth trajectory. Perinatologists are reliant during various phases on technical experts in specialties like ultrasonography and amniocentesis; neonatologists on specialists in radiology, opthalmology, cardiology, neurology. In order to qualify as a regional center, the labor and delivery unit must have a fulltime obstetrical anesthesiologist who, as patient load increases, calls for increased staff and equipment. Respiratory therapists are employed to help assess respiratory needs of infants, plan and execute this aspect of care, and upgrade physicians' and nurses' knowledge of respiratory function. Physical therapists are needed for babies who have had a prolonged stay in the ICN. These particular specialists help assess the infant's development—exercise the baby, look at muscle tone, and watch for suspected signs of cerebral palsy. Specialists in neonatal medical and nursing staff have evolved; they must be experienced, finely skilled and attuned to every nuance in the given trajectory phase, since they are dealing with delicate bodies, and reversibility can be quick, unpredictable, and damaging.

Expanded services have led to a splintering of the role of the head nurse. Her new title, Nursing Care Coordinator (NCC), is fitting since the major part of her work has to do with coordinating the many services that feed into the unit (for instance, in the nursery: laundry, x-ray, clinical laboratory, pharmacy, and central services for the massive amount of supplies). New middle-level administrative classifications, such as "staff development nurse," have been created to take over some of the former head nurse tasks, like the hiring and orientation of new nurses, and their instruction on new equipment. In the labor and delivery ward a liaison nurse handles the administration of the alternative birth center and family follow-up; a master's-degreed perinatal clinical nurse specialist serves as resource person for transports and other high-risk patients, and spreads new obstetrical knowledge to staff nurses and to outlying feeder hospitals.

The ICN has added a liaison nurse whose work also reflects the outward stretch of the trajectory. Families with babies who have spent long months in the nursery need support after discharge. Often these babies have immature nervous systems and are hyper-irritable after months of continuous twenty-four hour stimulation. Emotional adjustment places a huge strain on families:

> It's the isolation that gets to them. They are feeling trapped; they are afraid that the babies will get sick and be back in the hospital and they get to resent their responsibility. These were often first babies—the parents were active, young, vibrant people. . .

The liaison nurse, and the baby's primary nurse, look for ways to make the parents' lives easier, and contact continues long after hospital discharge. The liaison nurse also reflects the changed organizational structure brought on by regionalization of services. A large part of her job has to do with furthering the network of in-feeding hospitals, and tactfully teaching staff nurses in these hospitals. Hers is a dual goal: to decrease mismanaged deliveries while maintaining good public relations in the service of an expanded referral pattern.

A social worker also assists in the support of families and, in conjunction with the above administrative nurses, in sensing and responding to the staff tension which mounts whenever ethical, quality-of-life issues arise. Because of the close interweaving of staff and family biographies, periodic "stress meetings" are held: One hospital's social worker holds weekly social service rounds, while another employs an ethicist, who hold monthly ethics rounds—an open acknowledgement of the need for biographical work. Addition of a behavioral pediatrician to record and study infant behavior with computerized recording of a number of variables like sleep/awake state, motor activity, color, is another example of this felt need.

Further support is given to babies who are judged to require long-term evaluation, by providing a follow-up clinic which is offered to all babies who fall within the following categories: under 1250 grams; those with central nervous system bleeds; those who while on the respirator were given drugs to paralyze the musculoskeletal system; those who were given drugs to speed lung development; those who had cytomegalo virus, a respiratory infection which runs about 30% in premature babies; any other special conditions indicating a need for follow up. This service is staffed by a nurse practitioner, a pediatrician, and a psychologist.

2. Changed Hospital Biography. Since it is no longer economically feasible for every hospital to offer every service, in one of the hospitals being studied the decision was made to focus on geriatric and newborn services. This was in keeping with two considerations. The hospital had a long tradition of support for family services, which could be continued by extending geriatric care and by encouraging family involvement in newborn care through open access to the nursery, inclusion of siblings, rooms for parents when babies are hospitalized. The second consideration was economically realistic: Reimbursement from the government is greater for critical care (including intensive care for the newborn) than for other services.

Intensive care nursery charges are high. In this hospital, beds are $472 for the most critical level; $333 for semi-intensive care; $234 for recovery care. These charges cover physician's and nurse's costs. The major impact on hospital biography lies in the generation of additional income. Every time a blood gas study is done, which can be as frequently as every 10 to 30 minutes, the charge is $35. Respirators cost $150 a day; a brain scan, $300; an x-ray, $75. One of the new machines, the transcutaneous oxygen monitor, is charged at $50 for 4 hours, plus $25 every time the electrodes are shifted—every two hours. Chest tubes are $150 an insertion; suction catheters and gloves used, approximately $25 a day; hyperalimentation, $100. "You can figure a baby on a respirator costs $1000 to $1200 a day, and that doesn't count extra procedures." Nursery charges represent a major part of the budget for x-ray and clinical laboratory services. What is more, the nursery provides enough income to cover other hospital losers: labor and delivery, the alternative birth center, post-partum, well-baby nursery, and pediatrics. The interdependency of these particular services may appear one-directional economically, but the needs are reciprocal. A skilled labor and delivery unit will funnel babies into the ICN through its management of high-risk mothers; in order to obtain residents to serve as house staff in the nursery, a full residency in pediatrics must be offered. Of course, knowing that one is being "carried by Big Brother" financially does not make for felicitous feelings: "We have a lot of pull in the hospital; there's resentment that we get a lot, like expensive equipment, which we do."

Other feelings are generated by this interdependency of services. Accusations of mismanaged deliveries—often not explicitly stated—are most often directed toward outlying hospitals, as already discussed. However, the accusations can be interhospital as well. Or, disagreements may arise between obstetrical (perinatal) and pediatric (neonatal) staffs over subjecting a woman with a 24-week fetus to a caesarean birth—the former staff focused on what it will do to the mother, the latter on giving every child every chance. When the nursery census is low, wry comments are made about labor and delivery treating premature pregnancies with drugs, and forestalling delivery. Conversely, transported mothers may be greeted happily by a labor and delivery unit that is experiencing a low census of patients, and anticipated with groans by a nursery staff already under stress because of a high census.

The effect on hospital biography of the consumer movement—in the form of alternative birth centers—has already been noted. Perhaps more radical is the extension of hospital privileges to midwives. By offering perinatal backup for women whose desired home birth takes a troubled turn, or for those who decide close to term that they would prefer an ABC to a home delivery, the hospital has both coopted a segment of competition and increased its own base of financial support.

3. Altered Personal Biographies. A third general consequence of the stretched-out birth trajectory lies in the shaping of various implicated personal biographies. These include the infant's biography: Through the ICN's technology the infant has been given increased biographical time; but it is, in a sense, gestational time. The finished product is still unfinished—the nursery is, in effect, an institutionalized womb. Parents can get their child back *at any time in any shape.* Logically, parents can say "I don't like what you're doing," but structurally they are fatefully locked in. Nurses who remain in contact with these families are learning that the deep anxiety being experienced by parents, as well as any displeasure over staff management, is often suppressed until the baby has been at home for quite awhile. Parental dependency is felt too keenly to risk disturbing the staff.

For parents of a premature or sick child the birth trajectory is of heightened relevance, forcing a new definition of *their own* biographies and what happened to them—a realignment of expectations. The financial strain on them is substantial, sometimes causing bankruptcy. Only the very poor (for example, a four-member family making $10,000 to 12,000) qualify for state support. The rest incur liability proportionate to income before government funding takes over. Financial and emotional costs are interwoven:

Some of these families are in turmoil. Their financial status takes a tailspin—they're having to live on a shoestring

Some babies are covered by private insurance, but obviously such coverage is not limitless. It is possible, as happened recently, for a baby born at 27 weeks to be in the nursery for six months, coming close to a lifetime insurance limit of $250,000. In order to qualify for reinsurance, this particular baby cannot be readmitted to the hospital for two years, which places a tremendous, and probably impossible, burden on the family to keep her well.

The emotional investment of a mother or father who has visited the nursery daily for three to six months, becoming a mini-nurse—asking about laboratory values, picking up the jargon, assessing, "He looks a little dehydrated today"—is incalculable. In a moving account of her own experience one mother reports that her child's small size conjured up feelings of weakness, deficiency, guilt:

It left us with the sense that we wanted to make up for it. It was like a scale: The child was lighter, therefore we stepped down harder. We overreacted.

Overreaction, as this parent reports, may take the form of overfeeding; responding nervously to every hint of danger; treating the baby as "superchild," by letting him rule the family; or as "supertarget," by blaming everything on his prematurity. Clearly, to weigh these costs against the benefits would require separate calculating for each case.

Staff biographies, too, are being shaped by the extended birth trajectory. When the nursery census is high, the unit is physically hot, and noisy with the beeping of machines. The work requires close attention. There is also a complication: Since parents are both giving their child over, and are not giving it over to the staff, problems arise because of staff expectations and assessments of parents—judgments about parental qualifications for taking on this child, this artifact that the staff have sustained and nurtured by their skills and technologies. As hospital discharge approaches, further discordances of biography appear. When parents have not conformed to staff values (frequency of visits, visible signs of bonding), staff will be much concerned over the social conditions of the child's future.

Today's birth-trajectory nurses are young and energetic, becoming bored when their learning begins to level off. They place high demands on themselves—how they should function, how much they should accomplish. Faced with the emotional strain and the intensity of the work on such a unit, these nurses are candidates for that technologically related work hazard, "burnout." Here, too, as for parents, the benefits and satisfactions of this work are incalculable, and individual, and as it is with parents, the staff response is complex. One obstetrical nurse expressed her mixed feelings regarding transport cases:

> It's scary. The women may be sick and are terrified. Delivery of a premature or sick baby is emotionally traumatic. The nursing care is all technological—two ambulance sirens going. I, personally, get a kick out of it. It is exciting, intellectually stimulating to see these strange cases.

Yet the reverse shaping—that of biography on the stretched-out birth trajectory—is the very force that is keeping that trajectory going.

Biographical Impact on Trajectory

Expansion of perinatal and neonatal knowledge, skills, technology, and the ICN itself has made it possible to save babies who formerly were lost, with a paradoxical consequence. It is possible to move infant biographies farther and farther back, thus saving *younger* babies, who are *more at risk* by virtue of their *being younger* and having a less developed physiology. "We used to get excited at saving a 28-weeker, now it's 26 weeks." "Small" has moved from 1500 grams, to 1200, to 1000. This push-back is not infinite; prior to 26 weeks there are no lungs and the eyes are sealed. However, there is some ambiguity even here, since each organism progresses at a different rate. Just as the neonatologists feel they have a partial predictive grasp about these babies, along comes a 25 to 26 weeker, 600 grams, who defies the odds and goes home in five weeks, gaining weight and breathing room air.

This stretching out of the birth trajectory has so far been continuous, for developments have been rapid and revolutionary. As already mentioned, brain scans have provided a tremendous breakthrough in predicting the infant's future. Another fundamental change has come about through the combined efforts of biochemical research and the development of a new technique, Continuous Positive Airway Pressure (CPAP). The discovery that surfactant, a detergent-like substance, is essential for normal lung function has led to the administration of hormones to speed the infant's production of this natural substance. CPAP is the application of continuous air pressure; tubes through the mouth keep the infant's lungs inflated between breaths, and can be used continually until the body begins to produce its own surfactant, and the lungs mature. For babies who are not so small and so sick as to need the aid of a respirator, CPAP has been a tremendous boon in radically decreasing the incidence of respiratory disease syndrome, formerly called hyaline membrane disease, and formerly the leading cause of newborn death. . . .

. . . . Accidental discoveries are sustaining to staff—as when waterbeds, employed as a method of preventing depressed heads, surprisingly were found to decrease the problem of decelerated heart rate. On the other hand, many procedures remain controversial. For example, the administration of hormones to speed lung development is not used in some hospitals for fear of long-term effects. Some parents and staff are wary of subjecting these infants to a substance whose iatrogenic consequences, like DES, may not show up for years. But to those working within this arena there is the constant challenge of new discoveries around the bend, new information which will enlarge the possibilities of saving more infants with hopes of better biographies. . . .

Conclusion

Although the medical technology scene is complex, patterns which explain the complexity can be discerned. This chapter has focused on the labor and delivery ward and the intensive care nursery as an instance, employing the concept of trajectory and attendant biographies to illuminate these patterns. Conditions which bear on hospital work were discussed: the biographies of the wards, machines, medical specialties, the hospital, staff, parents, infants; external influences, such as the medical machinery industry, consumer movements, midwife and home birth movements. Also examined were the conditions under which biographical work becomes central: patient competition as related to social value, the intrusion of a machine biography, and the emergence of ethical and ideological issues in relation to the birth trajectory. Finally, we turned to the interactive consequences of this complex scene: the effect of an extended birth trajectory on new and expanded career lines, a changed hospital biography, altered personal biographies and, circularly, the effect of attendant biographies on the continually expanding shape of the birth trajectory.

The "overuse" of continuous fetal monitoring is becoming a public issue—questions heretofore raised only within the ranks of perinatology are gradually being reflected in the news media and in the public consciousness. However, the larger implications of technology as related to this arena have yet to reach the public. Since the huge leaps in perinatal and neonatal knowledge and skills are very recent it is too soon to assess what the expanded birth trajectory means in relation to the growth of specialties outside the hospital in the post ICN period. Presumably, there will be an enlarged need for specialized attention to those ICN graduates who have respiratory, eye, heart, and/or developmental problems. Thus the birth trajectory ties in to the major national health problem of chronic illness. The expansion in medical technology is directly related to the changed character of contemporary disease. As infectious and parasitic diseases have come under control, as life has been extended, a proportionate rise in the incidence of chronic illness has occurred. Physicians increasingly rely on advanced technological methods and devices in an effort to help their patients "live with" these chronic illnesses. This, then, is the major implication of whether the ICN is producing a generation of partially, temporarily, or permanently chronically ill Americans, suffering from a variety of illnesses and disabilities. Answering this question is not within the purview of this chapter. We can only surmise that some of the parents of ICN graduates face some measure of dependency on the hospital, the clinic and the physician's office for remedial aid or chronic care of their children—with an impact on the biographies of all of these institutions and on the medical technology industry which serves them. It will be another decade before the collective biographies of ICN graduates shed light on this larger public issue of where the extended birth trajectory is leading us.

10

On Some Characteristics of Contemporary Japanese Society

SETSUO MIZUNO

Commentary

Part of this chapter, although it was later published in an English version, was given as a talk to a Japanese audience. Setsuo Mizuno, whose major research and writing are in the areas of biography and the analysis of qualitative data, is a social scientist at Hosei University in Tokyo. We have chosen, however, to reprint this chapter, which we find fascinating both in content and form, because it illustrates several points likely to be instructive for our readers. We will address those shortly.

Professor Mizuno was the principal translator (with two other people) of the Japanese version of *Discovery of Grounded Theory* (1996). He had already begun this task when visiting the United States several years ago, where he became increasingly intrigued with grounded theory methodology and some of its procedures. Since then, he has given seminars on grounded theory, and has also developed a version of it suitable to his own research interests.

An earlier version of this chapter appeared in *Society and Labour, 37,* 143-175, used by permission.

What we find especially interesting about this chapter about features of Japanese society is that although Professor Mizuno did not explicitly employ our conditional-consequential matrix (he did not actually know of it yet), nevertheless his analysis turns around systematically linking (a) macro conditions ("themes in Japanese ideology, both pre and post WWII) with (b) collective identity. He traces, in fair detail, many probable connections between the two. But, note that his interest is more than this. He is concerned centrally with the *changes* of ideology and identity, as each has affected the other, but also in concert with emerging events and trends (demographic, political, economic, and so forth). Note also how he has implicit conditional arrows running reciprocally between identity changes and ideological changes: the former influencing the latter, but *also* vice versa. If this were a monograph rather than a chapter, presumably his tracing of connections would be more detailed, additionally specific, and presented with more evidence. Overall, the chapter orders a great number of large-scale societal impacts and changes, and moves skillfully between macro sociological and social psychological emphases.

The chapter should also be interesting to you because its data are, aside from personal observations and experiences, drawn from commentaries and analyses of other Japanese scholars; and, too, because its author uses extensively various economic data, including tables, taken from technical literature and government sources. (We have omitted almost all of those data because they refer to well-known features of Japanese economic life in the last decades.)

One especially striking feature of the chapter is how Setsuo Mizuno presents his very complicated analysis—of great masses of data, and about features of entire society. Primarily he orders these through sets of analytic points, in a type of analysis that is a version of what, in our book, we have called "conceptual ordering." He gives order to the data, partly by his systematic treatment of sets of data, but also because of the equally careful conceptualization of these materials.

Reference

Goto, T., Ohode, H., & Mizuno, S., trans. 1996. *Deetataiwagata riron no hakken*. Tokyo: Shinyousha.

*   *   *

1. Introduction

The purpose of this chapter is to elucidate some of what I think are major characteristics of contemporary Japanese society. Here I'd like to approach this problem by making use of the twin notions of backgrounding and foregrounding. Backgrounding here refers to putting something in place as a background perspective in order to understand the foreground in question. The foreground in our case is . . . contemporary Japanese society. Foregrounding means the thematization of the foreground itself on condition that the task(s) of backgrounding is (are) finished.

I have prepared three background perspectives for deciphering contemporary Japanese society. They are (1) the identification of several mentalities which had supported, or had been affiliated with, Japanese modernization since the Meiji Restoration, (2) the examination of the consequences of Japan's defeat in the War, and (3) the description of characteristics of Japanese society in the era following its defeat until its emergence as an "economic power."

From the first perspective an attempt is made to thematize some of the mentalities which the Japanese people tended to internalize in the process of Japanese modernization following the Meiji Restoration, or which fitted well with Japanese modernization. The second perspective raises two questions. First, what did the defeat mean to the Japanese people? Second, what was the plausible impact of the defeat upon the prewar mentalities? That is, as a result of the defeat, what kind of mental transformations did the Japanese people have to undergo? My assumption is that these transformed mentalities must have set the stage for the basic orientations of the Japanese people after the War. The third perspective is a historical one. Focusing on the periods since Japan's defeat in World War II until now, I divide the postwar years into two major eras: one is the era before 1980 and the other that after 1980 (incidentally, when I talk about contemporary Japanese society, I am referring to Japanese society in the era after 1980). So the third perspective's focus is on the era before 1980, which I subdivide into three periods and touch briefly on some features of each period. These are what I regard as the works of backgrounding.

Finally, using the above information as three interrelated backgrounds, I will discuss some of the features of Japanese society after 1980.

2. Several Mentalities Which Had Supported, or Had Been Affiliated With, Japanese Modernization Following the Meiji Restoration

Here I'd like to point out the following eight mentalities which I suspect had been dominant among the Japanese people of the prewar era.

First, the mentality of "Fukoku-kyouhei" (enrich the country, strengthen the military). This mentality could be said to be the basic economic and military strategy which the Japanese leaders of the Meiji era found it necessary to adopt in order to survive and, if possible, rise in the severe world situation where it was the rule that the stronger preyed upon the weaker.

Second, the mentality of "Datsua-nyuuou" (out of Asia, into the West). Although Japan could have identified with Asia, what the Meiji Japan actually did was the mental division of the world into Asia and the West, and the assimilation of, and the identification with, the "superior" and strong West. This way of thinking might have had a very good fit with the basic strategy of "Fukoku-kyouhei," but it was a very unfortunate and unfair mental choice, the legacy of which can still be found even today in some Japanese's way of getting along with the outside world.

Third, the mentality of "Wakon-yousai" (Japanese spirit, Western techniques). The Meiji Japan, like every newly modernizing country, had to face the basic tension between the way of thinking which embodied its traditional values and the way of thinking required for the acquisition of technology. They needed some idea to resolve this tension and found their answer in the phrase "Wakon-yousai," obviously a kind of compromise formation.

Fourth, the mentality of "Risshin-Shusse" (make one's way in the world). This idea is said to have "derived, somewhat inaccurately, from Herbert Spencer and Samuel Smiles" (Beasley, 1990:129). This career-oriented advice was a basic command to the promising young Japanese to commit themselves to their work and move up the social ladder.

Fifth, the mentality of "Messhi-houkou" (suppress the private self and serve the public). This phrase could also be translated as "self-annihilation for the sake of one's country" or "sacrificing one's personal interest to the public good." This mentality, together with the last one, helped to channel the energy of the Japanese people into the work in the public sphere even at the sacrifice of private or personal interest.

Sixth, the mentality of the emperor as the spiritual core of the Japanese. This notion is closely related to the problem of national identity. By putting the emperor at the very center of Kokutai (national essence), the Meiji leaders attempted and successfully accomplished a high degree of national integration.

Seventh, the mentality of "Otoko-wa-shigoto, Onna-wa-katei" (the man's place is outside [work] and the woman's place is inside [home]). Each society has its own traditional stance toward gender relations. At least ideologically speaking, this was the typical stance found in the Meiji Japan concerning the sexual division of labour.

Eighth, the mentality of "Danson-johi" (respect the men, despise the women). This deep-rooted prejudice must have something to do with a very strong patriarchal character of the Meiji Japan.

Why these eight mentalities, and not others, you might ask. We could have chosen different ones (in that sense, I admit there's some arbitrariness about the selection) but, given my perception about the present-day Japan, these eight seem to have some relevance to the task of grasping contemporary Japanese society. In terms of the familiarity of the phrasing, except for the sixth formulation concerning the emperor, most Japanese can easily recognize the catchwords I have chosen and, even if they might add something else, they must at least agree that the importance of these mentalities for the majority of the Japanese people of the prewar era cannot be denied.

3. Consequences of Japan's Defeat in the War

1. What the Defeat Meant to the Japanese People

As far as the Japanese people's perception of the defeat in World War II is concerned, there seem to have been two major points. One is the fact that the defeat in the War generated economic and psychological catastrophes. The other is that the Japanese people perceived the defeat, naturally enough, as a traumatic experience.

Here I'd like to focus on some of the consequences which I believe were generated on a wide scale among the Japanese people by such perception. First, there emerged an overwhelmingly real feeling of "we-don't-want-to-go-into-the-war-again." This feeling, which was based upon the war-related experiences, such as the ordeals they had to endure because of the misery of the war itself and the economic catastrophe generated by the defeat, became the basis of a strong desire of the Japanese people to seek the peace of the nation and of the world, and this is still alive in today's Japanese people's consciousness.

Second, the Japanese people preferred (and adopted) the wording of "Shuusen" (the end of the War) to that of "Haisen" (the defeat in the War). This is, I believe, partly related to their perception of the defeat as traumatic experience. When we use the expression "the defeat in the War," then we expose ourselves, logically speaking, to the situation in which we could raise questions, such as "Who was defeated by whom?" "Who is responsible for the defeat?" etc. If we use the wording "the end of the War," however, there's no need to raise such questions, especially those concerned with the responsibility of the War. My impression is that to give an elusive or ambiguous wording to the situation in which the identification of the agent of responsibility is called for might be a typical Japanese way of response. Let me cite two recent examples. The first one is a gap in wording between the Japanese version and the American version of what is called "Japanese-American Structural Impediment Initiative Talk," which started in July 1989 between both governments to come to grips with trade frictions between the two countries. The Japanese version of this talk is "Nichibei Kouzoukyougi," which, if literally translated into English, means "Japanese-American Structural Consultation." The second example is from the way of apology made by Showa Emperor (i.e., Emperor Hirohito) concerning the period between 1910 and 1945, when Japan invaded and occupied Korea, to the then-South Korean President who visited Japan in 1984: "It is indeed regrettable that *there was an unfortunate past between our two nations for a period in this century,* and I believe that it must not be repeated" ("Japan Should Make Apology," 1990; emphasis mine).

Third, there occurred the virtual demolition and "denial" of what had been taken for granted in the prewar value system. This is, of course, a necessary consequence of psychological catastrophe brought about by the defeat.

2. Impact of the Defeat Upon the Prewar Mentalities

What could we say about the plausible impact of the defeat upon the prewar mentalities we examined in Section 2?

First, the mentality of "Fukoku-kyouhei" (enrich the country, strengthen the military) comes to be transformed into the mentalities of "Fuyuuka" (toward becoming rich) or "Fukokuka" (toward becoming a rich nation) and pacifism. The defeat in the War forced the Japanese people into the situation of near starvation. So it was quite natural that they did their best to get out of this poverty-stricken state, with the goal of becoming rich themselves (individually) or becoming a rich nation (collectively). As for the "Kyouhei" part of the prewar mentality, because it was quite obvious that the militarism had ruined the country, this orientation was totally denied and its opposite, pacifism, came to take root deeply in the minds of the Japanese people. There's a passage that says that "the Japanese people forever renounce war as a sovereign right of the nation" in the ninth clause of the Japanese Constitution, which was established under the leadership of the Supreme Commander for the Allied Powers (SCAP) (cf. Beasley, 1990:220). The content of this passage, regardless of the intention of SCAP, seems to have resonated with the dominant feeling of the majority of the Japanese people at that time.

Second, during the War, to legitimate the invasion of other countries, Japan advocated the ideology of "Greater East Asia Coprosperity," which was a kind of reaction formation against the mentality of "Datsua-nyuuou" (out of Asia, into the West). So the defeat meant the denial of this formal ideology, leading to the substantial reinforcement of the mentality of "Datsua-nyuuou."

Third, as for the mentality of "Wakon-yausai" (Japanese spirit, Western techniques), the defeat naturally brought about the suppression of Wakon (Japanese spirit) and the reconfirmation and positive evaluation of the superiority of Yousai (Western techniques).

Fourth, the mentality of "Risshin-shusse" (make one's way in the world), although the phrase itself was dropped because of its antiquated connotation, became what might be called the "Joushou-shikou" (upward orientation), or the orientation toward upward mobility.

Fifth, taking into account the mentalities of Fukokuka (becoming a rich nation) and Datsua-nyuuou (out of Asia, into the West) as well as the upward orientation, plus the positive evaluation of Yousai (Western techniques), it is little wonder that there emerged the mentality of "catching up" in the sense of catching up and, if possible, surpassing the economic and technological levels of the U. S.

Sixth, the mentality of "Messhi-houkou" (suppress the private self and serve the public) was denied by the defeat, bringing about a temporal reversal of the power relation between the public and the private. That is, instead of "Messhi-houkou," the mentality of "Mekkou-houshi" (suppress the public and serve the private self), or what is called the "desire naturalism" prevailed during the chaotic period after the War. This "desire naturalism" itself was to be transformed again, during the period of rapid economic growth, into what might be called the mentality of "Messhi-housha" (suppress the private self and serve the company), producing a great mass of "Kaisha-ningen" (company men). Incidentally, the three mentalities—the mentality of "catching up," the "upward orientation," and "desire naturalism"—became a big psychological reservoir to guarantee that tremendous subjective energy necessary for the postwar economic reconstruction and the following "economic miracle."

The mentality of the emperor as the spiritual core of the Japanese also had to undergo a drastic transformation. First, the divinity of the emperor was negated by the declaration of the emperor as a human being, which greatly damaged the emperor system. Second, the symbolic emperor system was newly established as a product of compromise between the interest of the then dominant strata in Japan, who were deeply committed to maintaining the emperor system at any cost on the one hand, and the interest of the occupation army, which judged that the existence of the emperor was vital for the successful occupation of postwar Japan on the other hand.

What happened to the mentality of "Otoko-wa-shigoto, Onna-wa-katei" (the man's place is outside [work] and the woman's place is inside [home])? In the chaotic situation after the defeat, no one could afford to talk such nonsense. It is highly probable that this mentality disappeared during this chaotic period, but that this situation was regarded as only temporary. At any rate, at least the mentality itself seems to have remained intact as an undercurrent.

In the social atmosphere of the "denial" of prewar values, it is quite probable that the mentality of "Danson-johi" (respect the men, despise the women) began to come apart. The chaotic situation and the abolition of Ie (family) system in particular must have contributed to the partial demise of this mentality, providing the psychological base for the idea of "sexual equality," which was to be introduced afterwards under the influence of the occupation army.

4. Characteristics of Japanese Society in the Era Following Its Defeat Until Its Emergence as an "Economic Power"

1. The Period of Postwar Reconstruction (from 1945 to 1954)

This was the period when the Japanese people as a whole had to live on a subsistence level, which can be inferred from economic indicators. These clearly show that the level of economic performance during this period is below that of 1944. In addition to this devastated economic situation, one can cite three features of this period: (a) de-militarization and democratization of Japan by SCAP, (b) proliferation of the idea of "peace and democracy" as dominant values of the newly born Japan, and (c) beginnings of favourable acceptance and imitation of things American.

When we think of the institutional nature of the postwar Japanese society, the feature (a) was a crucial one, because it meant drastic changes to the prewar system. Major changes included: the establishment of a new Constitution with the sovereignty of the people (not of emperor), the so-called "peace clause," and the symbolic emperor system: economic reforms such as the attempt at the dissolution of "zaibatu (financial combines)," the introduction of an antimonopoly law, and land reform: the establishment of a new legal system including the revision of the Civil Code, the labour laws, and the strengthening of local governments; and educational reform (cf. Beasley, 1990:213-226).

As a consequence of the feature (a), the feature (b) came into being on the plane of societal consciousness.

One might regard the feature (c) as rather surprising, but it was, in a way, a reflection of an overall evaluation by the Japanese people of the occupation practice, if not its policy conducted by SCAP.

2. The Period of Rapid Economic Growth (from 1955 to 1973)

This period, commonly known as "koudo-keizaiseichou-ki" (the period of rapid economic growth) in Japan, could be symbolized by the expression "economic miracle." . . .

3. The Period of the Transition Toward
Becoming an "Economic Power" (from 1974 to 1980)

As is well known, the first oil shock was triggered in October 1973 by the strategy of Arab countries to quadruple the crude oil prices and to cut back on the supply of the petroleum during the fourth war in the Middle East. This had an enormous influence upon the economies of the oil-consuming countries with Japan being no exception. The first feature of this period is the first oil shock being a symbolic turning point between the period of rapid economic growth and the following transitional period and its consequences. . . .

The repercussion could also be felt on the plane of societal consciousness. This is the phenomenon of what Mr. Kato Tetsuro calls "the drastic transformations in the Japanese people's national consciousness in the mid-1970s" (Kato, 1988:38). Among the transformations were three conspicuous trends. First, the political consciousness of the Japanese people became more conservative. This trend is revealed in the turnaround of the support ratio of the ruling Liberal Democratic Party. The LDP support ratio had been dwindling for some time, but after 1974 this trend was reversed and it came to increase (38% of the people supported the LDP in 1960, 25% in 1974, 33% in 1980), while the support ratio of the major opposition party, the Japan Socialist Party, continued to decline (21% in 1960, 13% in 1974, and 9% in 1981) (Kato, 1988: 40). The same tendency can be detected in the issue of the choice of societal system. Although before 1974 there was a rather strong voice to support a reformed system or even a socialist system, there was a turnaround in 1974 and after this year more and more people came to express the support for the maintenance of the current system.

Second, the Japanese people's perception of the U.S. became more favourable. . . .

The third trend is, that the evaluation of the Japanese people of themselves and of Japan itself became more favourable. . . .

Japan's relatively low and stable unemployment rates during this period. . . . Japan's rather successful accommodation to the difficult economic situation triggered by the first oil crisis. The stabilization of the Japanese economy was carried out in great measure by Japanese companies' efforts to export goods to other countries, leading to the trade conflicts exemplified by the continuing trade friction between Japan and the U.S. This export offensive as a survival strategy of Japanese companies could be seen as the second feature of this period.

The third feature of this period is the beginning of the transformation of the Japanese style of management. This is, in a way, a cumulative result of the streamlining efforts of Japanese companies mentioned above. From among the three main components in the Japanese style of management (lifetime employment, seniority system, and the company-based labour union), two of them, lifetime employment and seniority system, began to partially deteriorate during this period—a tendency which is becoming more prevalent these days, as we can see from a newspaper article titled "Recruiters Gain as Lifelong Jobs Wane" (1990).

5. An Attempt to Understand Contemporary Japanese Society—Focusing on the Periods After 1980

It's always difficult to grasp the contemporary situation, especially when you live within it. So what follows is an attempt to understand what I think are some of the major characteristics of contemporary Japanese society.

First, a demarcation of the era after 1980 is in order. We seem to have three periods so far; the first period (from 1980 to 1985) is Japan's first phase as an "economic power"; the second period (from 1985 to 1990) is Japan's second phase as an "economic power"; the third period started with Iraq's invasion of Kuwait in August 1990. Here the analysis is largely limited to the first two periods.

I'd like to point out four features of contemporary Japanese society: (1) emergence of Japan as an "economic power" and widening economic disparities among the Japanese people, (2) the coming of a full-fledged "internationalized" society and neo-nationalistic repercussions, (3) the increase in social participation by women and the development of a consumer-oriented society, and (4) the continued development of an information-oriented society.

1. Emergence of Japan as an "Economic Power" and Widening Economic Disparities Among the Japanese People

Let me start with what I regard as two turning points for the Japanese economy, which are related to the first part of the feature (1), that is, the emergence of Japan as an "economic power." The second oil crisis happened in December 1978, when civil war broke out in Iran and the oil supply was cut back, resulting in soaring oil prices. Although it is difficult to determine exactly when it happened, it became obvious that the Japanese economy successfully overcame the second oil crisis around 1980. This perception marks the first turning point, which ended the period of Japan's transition toward becoming an "economic power" and ushered in Japan's first phase as an "economic power." Because of this perception, Japanese economic leaders and opinion leaders became quite confident about both the resilience of the Japanese economy and Japanese economic capabilities.

The second turning point was the G5 Plaza Accord in September 1985. On September 22, 1985, finance ministers and the governors of central banks of five industrialized countries (the U.S., West Germany, the U.K., France, and Japan) got together secretly at New York Plaza Hotel to discuss, and tried to regulate, the current international financial situation. As a result of this Plaza Accord, the high-yen era was brought about in Japan, marking Japan's second phase as an economic power.

. . .

Two other characteristics of this second phase are (a) the emergence of Japan as the world's largest creditor nation, which incidentally came into being at the same time that the U.S. fell into the position of the world's largest debtor nation, and (b) the soaring prices of land and stocks. . . .

As we have seen, in the 1980s Japan gradually became an "economic power," but this very process brought about growing economic disparities among the Japanese people. . . .

2. The Coming of a Full-Fledged "Internationalized" Society and Neo-Nationalistic Repercussions

When we say "internationalization," we are referring, first of all, to the progress of economic globalization itself. But it also means the related phenomena, such as the inflow as well as the outflow of people, goods, and information. Internationalization itself, of course, could already be observed at the beginning of the 1970s or even before that period, but this trend is becoming more and more conspicuous recently. Some of the recent phenomena of internationalization include the inflow of the foreign workers into Japan, the Japanese language boom, the resurgence of interest in learning English conversation, and the reverse culture shock experienced by Japanese returning from life abroad.

What we are interested in here when we talk about the coming of an "internationalized" society is its domestic consequences, especially those consequences on the Japanese people's behaviour and way of thinking generated by the inflow and outflow of people, goods, and information. In this connection, I'd like to refer to the dual possibilities being opened to the Japanese people as they come to be exposed to what might be called "the encounter with the international." They are the evolution of *de*nationalization and the thematization of the problem of national identity.

Denationalization here refers to the inclination to go beyond the national boundary, that is, those behaviours and ways of thinking, including those of a cosmopolitan or a global citizen, which have the tendency to contradict and break through the logic of nationalism rather than to remain constrained by it. An example of denationalization is the economic activities of a multinational enterprise which chooses to act solely in the interest of the company. Another example can be found in the following passage: "A recent survey in Japan by the Nihon Keizai Shinbun, . . . indicated that many Japanese support the American demands (meaning the demands made in the Structural Impediment Initiative [SII] talk) for changes in the Japanese economy" (Doi, 1990).

The thematization of the problem of national identity refers to the fact that "the encounter with the international" has created a collective mental situation in which the Japanese people are obliged to think about and deliberate upon such interrelated questions as "What is Japan?" "What does it mean to be a Japanese?" "What is, and should be, Japan's position in the world?" "How should Japan be in the international community?" This thematizing tendency itself is quite natural and will continue to progress. What is worthy of attention in this context is the following: As a consequence of this kind of thematization, we seem to be witnessing the early phase of the revival of neo-nationalism as an ideology, which, because of its contribution to the disastrous involvement in the "Pacific War," had been very unpopular among the Japanese public until recently. Here neo-nationalism refers to such arguments which present rather provocatively, or sometimes even fanatically, positive evaluations of Japan and things Japanese. Mr. Ishihara's argument in his controversial book titled *Japan That Can Say "No"* (Morita and Ishihara, 1989) is a good example.

The thematization of national identity, however, is not the only circumstance which gives rise to the appearance of neo-nationalism as an ideology. Another circumstance is the historical situation in which a psychological mechanism of what might be called "the return of the suppressed" (if we make a pun on Freud's famous expression) tends to work. The suppressed here means the prewar values exemplified by the expression "the Japanese soul or spirit," which had to be suppressed after the defeat in the War. So when I talk about "the return of the suppressed," I am referring to the fact that these prewar values, which were once strongly "denied," are being reevaluated more positively lately among some Japanese (fortunately not many yet).

Three factors seem to have contributed to this "return." The first is the impact of the aforementioned growing self-confidence in Japan as an "economic power" upon the mentality of the Japanese people. The second is the fact that more than one generation has passed since the defeat in the War. It seems that this time period is long enough to let some of the people think twice about their previous value judgments. These are the people who now think that they had been forced to discard whatever they had held as positive because of the defeat in the War. My impression is that, being helped by the first factor, they begin to think again that the prewar values, at least some of them, might not have been that bad after all. The third factor is the illness of Emperor Showa in 1988 and his subsequent death in 1989. This was itself an accidental event, but it has made it necessary as well as compelling for the Japanese people to thematize the very topic concerning the emperor and the emperor system, which had been a major taboo even during the postwar years.

3. The Increase in Social Participation by Women and the Development of a Consumer-Oriented Society

As for the increase in social participation by women, three simultaneous developments are occurring: (a) the participation in the field of wage labour in the form of entering the workplace and becoming part-time workers and dispatched workers (incidentally, the law of the equalization of employment opportunity between men and women became effective in April 1986), (b) the participation in a variety of social movements and cooperative movements, and (c) the participation in the field of education and learning exemplified by the phenomenon of the increase in women's learning at so-called "culture centers."

Making use of the public image of women as being scandal-free and promising politicians (which was and still remains persuasive in comparison with the image of those incorrigible male politicians implicated in the Recruit scandal), quite a number of women candidates took part and actually won in the House of Councilors elections held in July 1989. This was the success of the so-called "Madonna" strategy, behind which seem to lie the cumulative experiences of women's steady efforts and everyday activities in social movements. Today we might be witnessing the second chance (the first chance came right after the War, when we had 39 female Diet representatives in the first postwar elections for the House of Representatives) to test the capabilities of women as a new political force to change the mechanism of male-dominated Japanese society.

Those women who attend classes at so-called "culture centers," which are similar to adult educational centers in the U.S., tend to have higher educational backgrounds, the eagerness to learn more as well as plenty of time for leisure, a reflection of economic affluence.

This affluence is also shown in the development of a consumer-oriented society, reinforced by various messages coming from mass media. This progress seems to be giving a very interesting twist to the meaning of the sexual division of labour. The traditional sexual division of labour in Japan has been, as mentioned in Section 2, a circumstance where "the man's place is outside (work) and the woman's place is inside (home)." This is still working for some couples, but it is taking on an intriguing additional meaning for those social sectors, where the husband can afford to let his wife attend classes at the "culture center": "You (meaning the man) make the money and I (meaning the woman) spend it."

Another indication of the progress of a consumer-oriented society is the emergency of the young people as Shinjinrui (a new breed). Their behaviour as consumer is quite different from that of the older generation: their thinking determined more by feeling than by logic, they are more careful about their appearances, much more sensitive to the new trends in clothing, music, food, etc., and very eager to acquire, at least, information about high-quality goods, if not high-quality goods themselves.

4. The Continued Development of an Information-Oriented Society

Concerning the feature (4), let me refer only to the contemporaneity being generated by the satellite broadcasting and its consequence. In Japan, NHK (Nihon Housou Kyoukai) or the Japanese Broadcasting Corporation has been the agent of the satellite broadcasting so far. NHK started its experimental broadcasting in 1984, shifting to the regular broadcasting in June 1989, and began to charge in August 1989. One consequence of the start of the satellite broadcasting for the Japanese audience is that they come to share with the people in the rest of the world the access to the news of the contemporaneous events almost simultaneously, as is evident from instantaneous spread to the whole world of such news as the Tiananmen incident in June 1989, the progress of Eastern Europe's prodemocracy movement in the same year and after, Iraq's invasion of Kuwait in August 1990. One implication of this development is that an event in some country or in some area is not going to be just a small event in that country or in that particular area, but, according to circumstances, could transform itself into a major world event. In terms of information, we are already global citizens, meaning that it's becoming almost impossible for the sender to intentionally limit or compartmentalize the potential audience. This fact has given rise to quite an interesting situation for the Japanese people, who have a traditional mentality to sharply distinguish Uchi (in, inside) from Soto (out, outside). In this connection, although it was not itself the event caused by the satellite broadcasting, repercussions against Mr. Ishihara's statement in *Japan That Can Say "No,"* (Morita and Ishihara,

1989) including the uproar and infuriation found among some American politicians, could be a good example of a consequence of contemporaneity. It is said that his statement was originally made to a very limited domestic group. In other words, he didn't seem to expect to have his text translated and his messages spread outside the country so quickly and to face such a strong backlash by publishing such a small book.

6. Epilogue

Let me wind up my discussion by referring to two points. In this chapter I tried to focus on those aspects of Japanese society, including several mentalities having to do with Japanese modernization, which seem to have contributed to the emergence of Japan as an "economic power." In other words, such important topics as the impact of the bombing of Hiroshima and Nagasaki upon the mentality of the Japanese public, the issues of discrimination and antidiscrimination involving ethnic or other kinds of minorities (Korean and Chinese residents, the Ainu, Burakumin, Okinawans, etc.), were left out, reflecting a limited scope of this chapter. These topics should have been discussed if more philosophical or existential meanings of contemporary Japanese society were to have been the focus.

One point I didn't point out explicitly above, but which deserves some comment, is the significance of the period of rapid economic growth to contemporary Japanese society. Whereas the institutional framework of the postwar Japanese society was established during the period of postwar reconstruction, the fact that the Japanese people underwent the transformative period of rapid economic growth seems to have been crucial for the formation of the basic mental framework of the postwar Japanese society.

References

Beasley, W. G., *The rise of modern Japan,* Charles E. Tuttle, 1990.
Doi, A., SII talks—New hope for the skeptical, *The Japan Times,* 8 April 1990, p. 17.
Japan should make apology clearer, advisor to Roh says, *The Japan Times,* 16 May 1990, p. 3.
Kato, T., *Japamerika No Jidaini (In the age of Japamerica),* Kadensha, 1988.
Morita, A., and Ishihara, S., *"No" to Ieru Nippon (Japan that can say "No"),* Koubunsha, 1989.
Tergesen, A., Recruiters gain as lifelong jobs wane, *The Japan Times,* 6 April 1990, p. 3.

Index

About the Authors

Isabelle Baszanger (Ph.D.) is a sociologist and Director of Research at the National Center of Scientific Research (CNRS) in Paris, France. She is currently working at the Center for Medical Research, Illness, and Social Science (CERMES) in Paris. She is the author of a book called *Douleur et Médecine, La fin d'un oubli*, Edition du Seuil (1995), analyzing the development of pain clinics and the world of pain patients and the physicians who treat them. She has translated into French parts of Anselm Strauss's works.

Geoffrey C. Bowker is Associate Professor of Library and Information Science, University of Illinois at Urbana-Champaign. He is the author of *Science on the Run: Information Management and Geophysics Research at Schlumberger, 1920-1940* and coeditor of *Social Science and Technical Systems: Beyond the Great Divide*. His current research is on the history and sociology of organizational memory and classification systems.

Kathy Charmaz is Professor of Sociology at Sonoma State University, where she has also recently served as faculty writing coordinator. Her book, *Good Days, Bad Days: The Self in Chronic Illness and Time,* received the Charles Horton Cooley Award from the Pacific Sociological Association. Her current projects include didactic works on conducting and writing qualitative research, edited volumes on medical sociology and death, and a study of bodily experience in health and illness.

276

Adele E. Clarke is Associate Professor of Sociology and of History of Health Sciences at the University of California, San Francisco. Her work centers on cultural studies of science, technology, and medicine with special emphasis on medical technologies affecting women's health such as contraception, the Pap smear, and RU486. Her book on the formation of American reproductive sciences in biology, medicine, and agriculture c1910-1963, *Disciplining Reproduction: Modernity, the American Life Sciences and the "Problems of Sex,"* is due out from the University of California Press in 1997. She regularly teaches a year-long sequence of courses on qualitative research and her current project is a book on *New Directions in Grounded Theory,* emphasizing postpositivist cartographic and positional approaches, including social worlds and discursive construct analyses.

Juliet Corbin (M.S. in Nursing, D.N.Sc. in Nursing) is a lecturer in the Department of Nursing, San Jose State University. She is coauthor with Anselm Strauss of *Basics of Qualitative Research* (1990), *Unending Work and Care* (1988), and *Shaping a New Health Care System* (1988). Her main research interests and publications have been in the areas of qualitative methodology issues and problems, health and illness, and in the sociology of work and the professions.

Shizuko Fagerhaugh (B.S. Hanline University, M.A. San Francisco State University, D.N.S. University of California-San Francisco) is affiliated with the University of California-San Francisco School of Nursing, Department of Social and Behavioral Science as a research nurse and lecturer. Her research interests include issues involving chronic illness such as pain, death, quality of life, and humanizing care and medical technology. She is coauthor of *Politics of Pain Management* (1977; with A. Strauss, B. Suczek, and C. Wiener), *Chronic Illness and the Quality of Life* (1986; A. Strauss, J. Corbin, B. Glaser, D. Maines, B. Suczek, & C. Wiener), *Social Organization of Medical Work* (1985; with A. Strauss), and *Hazards of Hospital Care* (1987; with A. Strauss, B. Suczek, & C. Wiener).

Joan H. Fujimura is Associate Professor of Anthropology and Henry R. Luce Professor in Biotechnology and Society at Stanford University. She is also a member of the interdisciplinary program in history and philosophy of science.

She received her Ph.D. in sociology from the University of California, Berkeley; taught at Harvard University; and joined the Stanford faculty in 1993. Her primary work is in anthropology, sociology, history, cultural studies, and feminist studies of science, medicine, and technology. Her current book project is on genetics, the human genome, and genome diversity projects, and bio-informatic technologies in the United States and Japan. She is also writing articles on the search for sex/gender genes, the use of the concept of culture in biology, and bodies in cyberspace. Her publications include *Crafting Science: A Socio-History of the Quest for the Genetics of Cancer* (1996) and a coedited volume (with Adele Clarke) on *The Right Tools for the Job* (1992). She is currently coediting (with Lucy Suchman) a volume on *Vital Signs: Cultural Perspectives on Coding Life and Vitalizing Code.*

Krzysztof Konecki (M.A. in Sociology of Culture, Lodz University; Ph.D. in Sociology of Organizations, Warsaw University) is Assistant Professor, Institute of Sociology, University of Lodz, Poland. His major research interests include organizational culture, sociology of human resources (especially the recruitment and selection process), symbolic interactionist theory of work and organization, and Japanese management and culture in sociological perspective. He has published more than 30 articles and 4 books, conducted field research in Poland, in Japanese industrial enterprises, and in executive search companies in the United States.

Lora Bex Lempert is Assistant Professor of Sociology at the University of Michigan—Dearborn. She learned grounded theory methodology in seminars with Anselm Strauss. She writes on issues of family, gender, and intimate violence against women. She is currently conducting research on African American grandparents who are raising their adolescent grandchildren.

Setsuo Mizuno is Professor of Social Psychology at Hosei University, Japan. Among his research interests are the clarification and specification of the procedures of qualitative analyses; analytical-interpretative work on human documents, such as S. Freud's letters and works, B. Malinowski's diary and Alice James' diary; comparative studies of social and cultural trends in Fin de Siècle Europe, the United States, and Japan. He is coauthor of *Historical Developments of Sociology* (1986), and *A Sociology of Life History* (1995). His translations in Japanese include those of P. Berger's *Invitation to Sociology* (1963-1979) and B. G. Glaser and A. Strauss's *The Discovery of Grounded*

Theory (1967-1996). He is developing a case mediated approach to personology, whose products so far include "Three-Step Analyses of a Book Called *The Teens of Showa Era Through the Eyes of a Junior High School Student,*" "A Reinterpretation of S. Freud's Case of Elisabeth von R.," and "A Life Trajectory in the Case of *Yuki's Diary.*"

Celia J. Orona received her degree from the University of California at San Francisco, where she focused on the caregiving experience of relatives who had a loved one with Alzheimer's disease. Anselm Strauss chaired her dissertation committee. *Identity Loss, Moral Commitment, and Alzheimer's Disease: An Interactionist Perspective* is the title of her doctoral study. She coproduced a documentary based on her research, *Alzheimer's: A Multicultural Perspective,* now in national circulation. She is currently Associate Professor of Sociology at San Jose State University, where she teaches courses on medical sociology, aging and society, and the family, as well as a course on qualitative research methods. Her current research interests include sociological aspects of genetics, ethics, and physician assisted suicide, and DNA used for identification purposes.

Susan Leigh Star is Associate Professor of Library and Information Science, University of Illinois at Urbana-Champaign. She also holds appointments in women's studies, sociology, critical theory, and computer science. She studied grounded theory at University of California, San Francisco with Anselm Strauss and Barney Glaser, and has used the approach in research on scientific work, the design and use of information technology, and to organize collaborative work with computer scientists. She is the author of *Regions of the Mind: Brain Research and the Quest for Scientific Certainty,* and the editor of *The Cultures of Computing* and *Ecologies of Knowledge: Work and Politics in Science and Technology.* Her current research is in the design and use of large-scale information technologies, including digital libraries and medical classification. This work can be found at http://alexia.lis.uiuc.edu/star/irgchome.html.

Anselm Strauss (Dec. 18, 1916 - Sept. 5, 1996) was Professor Emeritus, Department of Social and Behavioral Sciences, University of California, San Francisco. His main research activities were in the sociology of health and illness and in the sociology of work/professions. His research methods were principally a combination of field observation and interviews, with historical materials occasionally used as primary data. His (and coauthors') books on method include the following: *Awareness of Dying* (1965), *The Discovery of Grounded Theory* (1967), *The Social Organization of Medical Work* (1985), *Unending Work and Care* (1988), and *Continual Permutations of Action* (1993). He was a visiting professor at the universities of Cambridge, Paris, Manchester, Constance, Hagen, and Adelaide. At the time of his death, he was working on studies concerned with the flow of work in hospitals and the role of the body in action.

Barbara Suczek (Ph.D., Sociology, University of California, San Francisco; M.S., Counseling, San Francisco State University) was a lecturer in sociology at San Francisco State University for 14 years and has taught several classes in sociology in the School of Nursing, UCSF. She was for several years a research sociologist at UCSF on a research team headed by Anselm Strauss that also included Shizuko Fagerhaugh and Carolyn Wiener. Currently, and for the past 7 years, she has been a counselor/mediator for Family Court Services, Alameda County Superior Court, California.

Carolyn Wiener is Associate Research Sociologist in the Department of Social and Behavioral Sciences and the Department of Physiological Nursing, School of Nursing, University of California, San Francisco. She has published extensively on the social/psychological impact of chronic illness, sociological and organizational behavior as it relates to health care, and the policy implications of these dynamics. She was trained in grounded theory methodology by both Anselm Strauss and Barney Glaser and has lectured and held workshops, nationally and internationally, on this method. She has collaborated with Dr. Strauss on numerous research projects and has coauthored publications with him regarding social worlds and social arenas, the concept of "illness trajectory," and the impact of medical technology on health care. Her current research focuses on the process of hospital reorganization and the effect of reorganization efforts on hospital work and the quality of care.